BREAKING THE SOCIAL MEDIA PRISM

BREAKING THE SOCIAL MEDIA PRISM

How to Make Our Platforms Less Polarizing

Chris Bail

Riverhead Free Library
330 Court Street
Riverhead NY 11901

PRINCETON UNIVERSITY PRESS

PRINCETON & OXFORD

Copyright © 2021 by Chris Bail

Princeton University Press is committed to the protection of copyright and the intellectual property our authors entrust to us. Copyright promotes the progress and integrity of knowledge. Thank you for supporting free speech and the global exchange of ideas by purchasing an authorized edition of this book. If you wish to reproduce or distribute any part of it in any form, please obtain permission.

Requests for permission to reproduce material from this work should be sent to permissions@press.princeton.edu

Published by Princeton University Press
41 William Street, Princeton, New Jersey 08540
6 Oxford Street, Woodstock, Oxfordshire OX20 1TR

press.princeton.edu

All Rights Reserved

Library of Congress Control Number: 2020948001
ISBN 9780691203423
ISBN (e-book) 9780691216508

British Library Cataloging-in-Publication Data is available

Editorial: Meagan Levinson, Jacqueline Delaney
Production Editorial: Elizabeth Byrd
Jacket Design: Karl Spurzem
Production: Erin Suydam
Publicity: Maria Whelan, Kathryn Stevens

Jacket art and design by Karl Spurzem

This book has been composed in ITC Stone Serif Std

Printed on acid-free paper. ∞

Printed in the United States of America

10 9 8 7 6 5 4 3 2 1

For Richard Bail (1943–2019)

CONTENTS

1

The Legend of the Echo Chamber

I T IS 4:30 P.M. Dave Kelly has just finished his workday at an advertising firm in early September, 2018, and pops a CD into the stereo of his aging car. He is preparing to do battle with a formidable enemy: the New Jersey Turnpike at the beginning of a holiday weekend. When Dave finally reaches the exit for his hometown more than one hour later, he stops to perform a weekly ritual. Each Friday night, Dave checks out half a dozen books from his local library, cracks a can of overpriced craft beer, and settles in to read for at least an hour. This week he has chosen a mix of well-thumbed paperback novels, a book about the latest advances in cancer research, and a thick tome on human nature by an evolutionary anthropologist.[1]

Though he might not fit the stereotype of Donald Trump supporters, Dave voted for the former real estate magnate in 2016. Raised in a family of moderate Democrats, Dave veered toward the right in the 1980s because he was so impressed by the leadership of Ronald Reagan. But Dave is not a card-carrying member of the Republican Party. He cast two ballots for Bill Clinton in the 1990s, and takes liberal positions on most civil rights issues. "I'm perfectly happy with gay marriage," Dave says. "I don't understand why you would want to make an issue out of that." But on economic matters, Dave is more libertarian. When he learned that New York City officials were considering a new law that would require businesses with more than five employees to

CHAPTER 1

provide two weeks of paid vacation, Dave warned, "There's gonna be a lot of companies that fire people to get away from that. There's gonna be companies that just can't do it and are gonna go out of business."

Living outside liberal Philadelphia—and working in a profession dominated by Democrats—Dave normally hides his conservative views. "I have friends I won't discuss this stuff with," he says, "because I'm not going to change my mind and they're not going to change theirs—so what's the point?" The few times he tried to start such conversations, he explains, things quickly became heated—and the only thing Dave hates more than New Jersey traffic is heated arguments about politics. Because he feels like an unwelcome minority in his day-to-day life, Dave describes social media as a kind of refuge. He originally joined Facebook and Twitter to escape politics and follow updates about his favorite television shows. But he kept finding himself getting "sucked into political discussions."

Over the past few years, Dave—who does not use his real name on social media—has spent many late nights arguing with Democrats on Twitter. Remembering one of these conflicts, Dave said, "Don't judge me . . . I had a couple of beers." A local radio station, he explained, had reported a group of White supremacists were planning to march on the campus of a nearby university. "Turns out they're not," he says. "The whole thing is a hoax." After reading more about the story, Dave learned that one of the groups that raised the alarm was the progressive Southern Poverty Law Center. "They pretty much claim anyone who's to the right of Karl Marx is a hate group," he says. When he dismissed the incident on Twitter, another user quickly fired back, calling him a racist. "I called her an idiot," he says. She didn't know what she was talking about, he decided, because she was only getting one side of the story.

But so is Dave. Though he prides himself on being informed, Dave gets his news from a conservative talk radio station, the right-leaning website *Daily Caller*, and Twitter. Of the several hundred accounts that he follows on Twitter, only *New York Times* columnist Bret Stephens could be described as "centrist." Dave has consumed a steady diet of conservative views on social media for years. Each day, his feed gets filled with content from Fox News, posts by Trump and other prominent Republicans, and dozens of memes bemoaning liberal hypocrisy. Dave has even retweeted a few messages from Russian trolls masquerading as American conservatives along the way. And that drunken Twitter argument about the White supremacist march at a local university? It turns out that Dave used more colorful language than "idiot" to describe his liberal opponent that night.

The Echo Chamber about Echo Chambers

You might think you already know what's going on here: Dave is stuck in an echo chamber.[2] Social media sites allow people to choose what types of information about politics they want to expose themselves to—or learn what Justin Bieber ate for dinner last night. The problem is that most people seek out information that reinforces their preexisting views. We connect with newspapers, pundits, or bloggers who share our worldview. If you're a conservative like Dave, you might follow Tucker Carlson, the Fox News host, since you appreciate what he has to say about government spending or illegal immigration. And if you're a progressive liberal, you might follow CNN's Don Lemon because you appreciate his frequent posts about the issues you care about—racial inequality, perhaps, or climate change.[3]

The problem, the story goes, is that our ability to choose what we want to see traps us inside echo chambers that create a kind of myopia. The more we are exposed to information from our side, the more we think our system of beliefs is just, rational, and truthful. As we get pulled deeper into networks that include only like-minded people, we begin to lose perspective. We fail to recognize that there are two sides to every story, or we begin listening to different stories altogether. Echo chambers have their most pernicious effect, common wisdom suggests, when people like Dave are unaware of them: when people think that they are doing research about an issue, but they are actually just listening to what they want to hear. When we encounter people from the other side, their views can therefore seem irrational, self-serving, or—perhaps most troubling—untrue. If we could only step outside our echo chambers, many people argue, political polarization would plummet.

The concept of the echo chamber existed long before social media did.[4] Political scientist V. O. Key introduced the concept in the 1960s to describe how repeated exposure to a single media source shapes how people vote.[5] The concept gained major traction, however, with the rise of 24/7 cable news stations in more recent decades. Social scientists quickly realized that such stations were allowing Democrats and Republicans to perceive starkly different versions of reality.[6] A popular example of the echo chamber effect is the 2002 U.S. invasion of Iraq. During this period, Fox News repeatedly claimed that Saddam Hussein, the Iraqi dictator, was collaborating with Al Qaeda, the terrorist organization responsible for the September 11 attacks. It was later discovered that such claims were false. But an influential study found that Fox News viewers were two times more likely to believe that such links existed than those who got their news from other sources.[7] If you are a Democrat, don't pat yourself on the back too quickly. A recent study showed more Democrats are trapped inside echo chambers than Republicans.[8]

Concerns about echo chambers gained added urgency with the rise of the internet and social media. In his influential 2001 book, *Republic.com*, legal scholar Cass Sunstein warned that partisan websites and blogs would allow people to avoid opposing views even more efficiently than cable news.[9] The internet activist Eli Pariser pushed this argument even further in his 2012 book, *The Filter Bubble*.[10] He argued that algorithms employed by large technology companies made the echo chamber effect even worse. Facebook, Google, and other giant corporations exacerbate our built-in tendency to seek information that is aligned with our worldview via algorithms that recommend even more of such content to us. The most dangerous part of these algorithms, Pariser argued, is that social media users are not aware of them. Filter bubbles can preclude the very possibility of bipartisan interaction, Pariser warned, allowing our deeply biased views to go unchallenged.

Meanwhile, social scientists began to uncover substantial evidence of social media echo chambers as well. A 2015 study by data scientists at Facebook estimated only one-quarter of the content that Republicans post on Facebook is ever seen by Democrats, and vice versa.[11] A study of Twitter reached similar conclusions. More than three-quarters of the people who retweet—or share—a message, the study concluded, belong to the same party as the message's author.[12] These findings were particularly concerning since social media was rapidly becoming one of the most popular ways for Americans to get their news. Between 2016 and 2018, the number of people who got their news from social media surpassed those who learn about current events from print newspapers. By 2018, social media had become the most popular news source for people ages 18–29.[13]

It should come as no surprise, then, that a growing chorus of technology leaders, pundits, and policy makers now warn of a grim future in which any discussion of politics on social media will quickly devolve into tribalism. We hear calls for social media platforms to break our echo chambers—or at least revise the algorithms that reinforce their walls. And if social media companies won't relent, then social media users should begin stepping outside of their echo chambers themselves. Only then, many people believe, can we begin the difficult conversations needed to beat back polarization on our platforms.

It's a compelling story—especially when the people who tell it are those who helped build social media platforms and now regret their actions. But I believe the common wisdom about social media, echo chambers, and political polarization may not only be wrong, but also counterproductive.

A New Lens on Polarization

Common wisdom often becomes unassailable because it is very difficult to verify.[14] Social scientists have wondered whether echo chambers shape our political beliefs for decades, but studying this process is very challenging.[15] We can analyze people like Dave Kelly—the craft-beer-drinking Trump voter described above—but are his experiences typical? Echo chambers result from the coordinated behavior of millions of people across sprawling social networks that evolve in complex patterns over time. Even if we had the time and resources to identify thousands of Dave Kellys—and see that people like him develop increasingly partisan views over time—how could we be sure that people's echo chambers shape their political beliefs, and not the other way around? If our political beliefs guide how we try to understand the world, would we really give them up so easily? Would Dave Kelly begin to moderate his views if we suddenly began exposing him to social media posts from progressive groups like the Southern Poverty Law Center?

Regardless of what you think about echo chambers, Facebook, Twitter, and other social media platforms have produced exciting new opportunities to study them. The social sciences were once considered "data poor" compared to other fields of study. But some platforms now allow us to collect information about millions of people in seconds. Even more importantly, we can now conduct an epidemiology of ideas, tracing how beliefs about the world spread across large social networks over time. The age of computational social science—the study of human behavior using large digital data sets—also provides new opportunities for experimentation. By embedding randomized controlled trials within social media platforms, computational social scientists have been able to increase voter turnout, organ donation, and a host of other positive human behaviors.[16] These types of experiments also hold enormous power to provide insights into social media echo chambers, as we will see.

But there is also a dark side to computational social science. In 2013, the psychologist Michal Kosinski launched a study to determine whether patterns in social media data—such as information about the things we "like," or the accounts we follow—could be used to predict our ethnicity, sexual orientation, or even our intelligence.[17] Kosinski and his team produced an app that allowed Facebook users to perform a personality test on themselves via the data generated within their accounts. But the now-infamous political consulting firm Cambridge Analytica allegedly created a similar app to collect data for a nonacademic purpose: creating microtargeting campaigns to sway political elections.[18] Though many social scientists question whether such ads were effective, the story highlights a dangerous precedent: the tools of computational social science can be repurposed to violate privacy and potentially manipulate the behavior of people who did not consent to be studied.[19]

Computational social science has another problem too: the digital footprints we leave behind on social media platforms provide a very incomplete record of human behavior.[20] As a thought experiment, let's put Dave Kelly's data into the type of app created by Cambridge Analytica. We could easily conclude that Dave is a Republican by analyzing the news organizations and pundits he "likes" or "follows." A political campaign might even be able to identify which television shows Dave watches and buy commercials to reach people like him. But we would also misunderstand some of the most important things about Dave. Though his Twitter feed makes him seem like an angry "Make America

Great Again" warrior, the app would not reveal that Dave is actually worried about climate change and disappointed by his party's treatment of gay people. You'd never know that Dave thinks Trump is a bully, or worries about racial discrimination in policing. You would not learn that Dave was skeptical about whether White supremacists were really marching at a nearby university during the incident I described at the beginning of this book because he believes media organizations are stoking ethnic tensions for financial gain. Most important, you would not learn that this issue is particularly important to Dave because he is part Puerto Rican and suffered terrible discrimination as a child. I mention these details not only to show how many things are left out of the digital record of our lives. On the contrary, I believe the rapidly growing gap between social media and real life is one of the most powerful sources of political polarization in our era.

How did I come to this conclusion? I am a computational social scientist who has spent his entire career studying how social media shapes political polarization. Several years ago, I became so concerned about political tribalism that I founded the Polarization Lab—a team of social scientists, statisticians, and computer scientists at Duke University, where I am a professor. Our team diagnoses the problems with our platforms using scientific research and builds new technology to reverse the course. Together, my colleagues and I have collected hundreds of millions of data points that describe the behavior of thousands of social media users over multiple years. We've run new kinds of experiments with automated social media accounts, conducted some of the first studies of how foreign misinformation campaigns influence people, and ventured deep inside social media companies to help them fight polarization. We've even created our own social media platform for academic research—allowing us to turn on and off different features of platforms to identify better ways of connecting people.

This work has led me to question the conventional wisdom about social media echo chambers, but it has also inspired me to ask much deeper questions. Why does everyone seem so extreme on social media? Why do people like Dave Kelly spend hours arguing with strangers, even when they don't think it will change anyone's mind? Is using social media a temporary addiction that we can shake—like smoking—or is it fundamentally reshaping who we are and what we think of each other? No amount of data science wizardry can answer these questions. Instead, I wanted to see social media through the eyes of the people who use it each day. This is why our lab spent hundreds of hours interviewing people like Dave Kelly and carefully reconstructing their daily lives on- and off-line. And it's why I'm going to tell you the story of a recently bereaved extremist who lives in a motel where he wakes up and falls asleep watching Fox News—and a moderate Democrat who is terrified about school shootings but worries that posting his views on social media might cost him his job. These stories not only help me paint a more complete picture of how political polarization unfolds on social media; they also inspired me and my colleagues to run new types of large-scale experiments in turn.

Studying social media from the perspective of the people who use it is also important because they are conspicuously absent from public debates about social media and political tribalism. Instead, our current conversation is dominated by a handful of tech entrepreneurs and software engineers who helped build our platforms. These Silicon Valley apostates now claim the technology they created wields unprecedented influence over human psychology—technology that not only traps us within echo chambers, but also influences what we buy, think, or even feel. Facebook, Twitter, and other platforms were either asleep at the wheel when malicious foreign actors launched campaigns to influence social media users—these apostates claim—or willfully ignored them because they increased user engagement (and therefore their bottom line). This narrative is very seductive for anyone searching for a scapegoat for our current situation, but is it really true? Though social media companies are by no means blameless for our current situation, the evidence that people are simple dupes of political microtargeting, foreign influence campaigns, or content recommendation algorithms is surprisingly thin.

Instead, I will argue that our focus upon Silicon Valley obscures a much more unsettling truth: the root source of political tribalism on social media lies deep inside ourselves. We think of platforms like Facebook and Twitter as places where we can seek information or entertain ourselves for a few minutes. But in an era of growing social isolation, social media platforms have become one of the most important tools we use to understand ourselves—and each other. We are addicted to social media not because it provides us with flashy eye candy or endless distractions, but because it helps us do something we humans are hardwired to do: present different versions of ourselves, observe what other people think of them, and revise our identities accordingly. But instead of a giant mirror that we can use to see our entire society, social media is more like a prism that refracts our identities—leaving us with a distorted understanding of each other, and ourselves. The social media prism fuels status-seeking extremists, mutes moderates who think there is little to be gained by discussing politics on social media, and leaves most of us with profound misgivings about those on the other side, and even the scope of polarization itself.

If social media platforms are so deleterious to democracy, why not delete our accounts? After all, I might enjoy using carrier pigeons to communicate my latest musings on Justin Bieber. But deleting our accounts is just not realistic. Social media has become so woven into the fabric of our lives—and particularly those of young people—that it is here to stay. The good news is this: if we social media users are the main source of political polarization, this means we also have the power to push back against it. In the chapters that follow, I'll describe how you can learn to see the social media prism and understand how it distorts the political landscape. I'll explain how we can begin to break the prism by changing our behavior and introduce you to new tools that my colleagues and I created in the Polarization Lab to help you do it. In addition to these "bottom-up" solutions, I offer a new path from the top down. I'll explain how social media platforms could be redesigned to bring us together, instead of pushing us apart. But first, I need to explain why breaking our echo chambers is the wrong place to start.

2

Why Not Break Our Echo Chambers?

T IS EARLY JANUARY 2019. Dave Kelly is venting about Medicare for All—a proposal made by Bernie Sanders to provide free health care to all Americans as part of his presidential campaign. In his unmistakable Philadelphian accent, Dave said: "I don't want the government to solve my problems. . . . I got myself into them, and I'll get myself out of them." As you may remember, Dave was deep inside a conservative echo chamber when I introduced him at the outset of this book. Nearly everyone he followed on social media leaned to the right, and he seldom encountered political viewpoints that were very different from his own. But for the past month, Dave has been part of a unique experiment designed to see what happens when people are exposed to opposing views on social media. Each day, he sees twenty-four messages from a range of liberal policy makers, pundits, advocacy groups, and media organizations. And for good measure, he's also seeing a few pictures of cute animals to make the experience a bit more bearable.

In mid-2018, the United States was embroiled in controversy about the separation of immigrant children from their parents—a policy enacted by the Trump administration to deter illegal migration to the United States from Mexico. When we first spoke with Dave, he sympathized with Democrats who criticized the policy. When we interviewed him five months later—after he had endured a month of liberal messaging—his views had shifted sharply. During that month, a caravan of migrants was making its way from Honduras, El Salvador, and Guatemala toward the United States. Thousands of people, many of them women and children, traveled more than 2,700 miles in the hope of reaching the U.S.-Mexico border. Conservative and liberal media presented very different stories about the caravan. Fox News highlighted Trump's description of the migrants as dangerous gang members from crime-ridden countries with "unknown Middle Easterners . . . mixed in."[1] Meanwhile, CNN, MSNBC, and other left-leaning outlets described them as hapless refugees fleeing violence and persecution.

Despite his exposure to the liberal narrative, Dave now subscribes to a popular conspiracy theory. "I don't think these are honest refugees," he says. "I think this is a political ploy. Someone put them up to coming here, and paid them to come here. . . . They're talking about families coming, but who drags a kid on a 2,000-mile hike?" After participating in the experiment, Dave has developed more conservative views about other political topics as well. Though he was once mildly concerned about climate change, he now recites another conspiracy theory—this one about the Camp Fire that struck Northern California in late 2018. "I think the governor of California should be arrested," he says. "He's directly responsible for those fires. I think he did it on purpose."

Similarly, Dave—once a lukewarm Trump supporter who had originally supported Gary Johnson, the Libertarian candidate— now jumps to the president's defense. Former FBI director Robert Mueller's investigation into the president did not come up once during our first interview, but Dave now tells us that "it's 100 percent politically motivated." In his opinion, there was "more collusion on the Clinton camp side with Russia than there was on Trump's side." Dave was somewhat put off by Trump's bombastic style when we first interviewed him, but he now defends Trump's character on even the most salacious issues—such as his alleged affair with the pornographic actress Stormy Daniels. "Maybe it was a crappy thing to do," Dave says, "but let's face it, we're never gonna be able to . . . elect someone who's completely clean, because those people don't want to get into politics."

Breaking the Echo Chamber

The story of why my colleagues and I asked Dave Kelly and hundreds of other people to step outside their echo chambers begins on November 3, 2016. On that day, the probability that Hillary Clinton would defeat Donald Trump in the presidential election reached 87.4 percent, according to the popular polling website fivethirtyeight.com.[2] That figure was very easy to believe. The smartest political scientists I knew all agreed that Trump had violated every taboo in the campaign playbook. Also—from what I could tell by scanning my social media feed each night—Trump was not creating the palpable excitement that had propelled Barack Obama to victory eight years earlier. The day after Trump's improbable victory, the postmortem began quickly. Pollsters pointed to the margin of error. Others blamed James Comey's inquiry into Clinton's famed email server. Still others argued that people's overconfidence in a Clinton victory had decreased voter turnout.[3] These explanations all had merit, but my mind kept returning to one simple fact: how had so many of us never seen a shred of evidence that Trump could really win? What were we not seeing that made us so surprised by Clinton's defeat?

The concept of the echo chamber provided an elegant explanation. If my social media feed had not contained posts from so many left-of-center college professors, I might have realized that Trump actually was generating the same type of emotional energy that Obama had. Or perhaps I would have seen more clearly just how unlikable so many voters found Clinton. There was quite a bit of precedent for this explanation as well. Soon after World War II, sociologists Paul Lazarsfeld and Robert Merton discovered what is now considered an axiom of social science: the principle of homophily.[4] The two professors—who had been studying how new media technologies were shaping political beliefs—observed that people tend to form social connections with those who are similar to themselves. To discover that "birds of a feather flock together," their team spent years carefully mapping social networks by interviewing people.[5] Lazarsfeld and Merton would be awestruck by the social network data generated each day on Twitter, whose logo, appropriately enough, features a feathered bird.

Like many other computational social scientists, I charged ahead with the hubris that the puzzle of social media echo chambers could be solved with a few hundred lines of code. Though I was able to map echo chambers with unprecedented scale fairly easily, I soon realized that I faced a much bigger problem. If we want to really understand how social media echo chambers shape our political beliefs, we need to solve a "chicken or the egg" problem: do our social media networks shape our political beliefs, or do our political beliefs determine who we connect with in the first place? To figure out how social media echo chambers work, my colleagues and I were going to need to break them.

Bad Bots, Good Bots

Social scientists usually solve "chicken or the egg" problems with an experiment. In this case, we could recruit a group of Republicans and Democrats to tell us about their political beliefs and then invite half of them to our lab to watch messages from the opposing political party. But would this really tell us what would happen if we asked someone to step outside their echo chamber? If a laboratory experiment created a moderating effect, how could we know whether that effect would disappear once people returned to their echo chambers—or amid the mind-numbing distraction of memes, sports news, or celebrity voyeurism on social media? What if it takes a long time for people to realize how their echo chamber shapes their views, or to learn to see both sides of a story?

What was really needed, we concluded, was what social scientists call a field experiment. In a field experiment, researchers assign people to treatment and control conditions within a real-life setting and keep track of changes in their behavior before and after the intervention.[6] The ideal field experiment, for our purposes, would be to expose people to opposing views in their own social media feeds for a lengthy period of time. Computational social scientists have conducted very interesting field experiments on social media platforms about issues such as whether peer pressure might influence people to vote. But in the wake of the Cambridge Analytica scandal (discussed in chapter 1) and an earlier controversy about an experiment designed to study the spread of emotions on Facebook, collaborating with industry seemed like a nonstarter.[7] Trying to convince the platforms to run an experiment on the sensitive topic of political polarization in late 2017 was a fool's errand simply because it carried too much legal risk—not to mention the public relations maelstrom it might create.

Suddenly, an unlikely solution emerged: bots, automated accounts that share messages on social media platforms. At the time, bots were notorious for spreading misinformation or divisive messages produced by malicious actors such as the Internet Research Agency (IRA), which has been linked to the Russian government.[8] But it occurred to us that bots could also be repurposed for valuable research. Instead of spreading misinformation, bots could expose people to different points of view. If an experiment with bots could be designed in an ethical manner—and if bots were not disguised as real people—maybe they could be repurposed for scientific research.[9] We decided to build two bots: one that retweeted messages from prominent Republicans and another that shared messages from prominent Democrats. We could pay a large group of Democrats and Republicans to follow the bot from the opposing political party, we reasoned, and survey them before and after the experience to study how it changed their views.

Unfortunately, we were not able to run our experiment on Facebook, because the platform restricted academic research so heavily after the controversies I described above. So we elected to run our experiment on Twitter, even though it has far fewer users than Facebook and a much more public format.[10] In late October 2017, we recruited 1,220 Americans who used Twitter at least three times per week and identified with either the Democratic or Republican Party to answer a range of questions about their political beliefs and behaviors. We asked the respondents a series of ten questions about social policy issues such as racial inequality, the environment, and government regulation of the economy. These questions allowed us to classify each person on a continuum that ranged from extremely liberal to extremely conservative. Those who favored less government regulation of the economy and cared less about racial inequality, for example, were categorized as more conservative on this scale. In addition to measuring their beliefs with a traditional public opinion survey, we also asked respondents to share their Twitter handles with us. This allowed us to track their behavior before and after the experiment and also account for the strength of their echo chambers before they followed our bots.

The bots were designed to expose people to the full range of messages from the other side. Building upon a previous study, we created a database of prominent liberal and conservative Twitter accounts that were carefully selected to represent a range of different viewpoints within each political party.[11] The accounts included those of opinion leaders (elected officials, pundits, activists, and other thought leaders) and organizations such as media companies and advocacy organizations. Each hour, our bots randomly selected one of these accounts that had tweeted within the previous hour and retweeted its message. Thus, a Republican following our liberal bot might see messages from Nancy Pelosi, Planned Parenthood, or MSNBC. A Democrat, by contrast, might see messages from Mitch McConnell, the Heritage Foundation, or *Breitbart News*. We gave the bots nondescript names and generic profile pictures.[12] When the bot retweeted a message, the name and profile picture of the account that originally tweeted the message was most prominent—as is Twitter's custom—and the name of our bot appeared in smaller font on the upper left side of each tweet.

Though our bots created a new opportunity to study echo chambers "in the wild," all field experiments face a thorny problem: people are not lab rats. It's not easy to recruit a diverse group of people, randomly assign them to treatment conditions without their knowing it, and make sure that they actually receive the treatment that you want to give them. If we told people that our experiment would expose them to dozens of messages from people with opposing views each day, some might balk—and we might be left with a study of unusually tolerant people. If those people were also intrinsically more likely to change their minds, our study would overestimate the impact of taking people outside their echo chambers. To solve this problem, we did not tell people they were being offered money to follow a bot that would retweet messages from those with opposing political views. Instead, we told them they would receive $11 for following a bot that would retweet twenty-four messages each day for one month, without telling them anything about the messages themselves.

Even if we could recruit people who were not predisposed to change their minds, how could we know that some of them—maybe the less tolerant people—might simply ignore our bot's tweets? Or, even worse, take a month-long hiatus from Twitter? In medical trials, blood tests can determine whether a patient has taken an appropriate dosage of a treatment. But social scientists often have to be more creative than bench scientists. We already had one way of checking whether people were paying attention: we wrote code that monitored who was following our bots each day. But this did not tell us whether the respondents were actually paying attention to our messages. Enter cute animals. To measure how much study participants complied with the treatment we were trying to give them, we offered them up to eighteen additional dollars if they could both identify an animal that our bots retweeted during the study period (but was later deleted) and answer questions about the content of our bot's messages. These questions were factual in nature, not easily searchable, and designed not to privilege participants with greater knowledge of current affairs.[13]

Though cute animals solved some of our problems, we faced one more: the Hawthorne effect. The name for this phenomenon was taken from a study of factory workers in the late 1920s. When the workers discovered that they were being studied, they quickly became more productive.[14] If a Democrat in our study learned that we were exposing her to messages from conservatives, we worried that she might express more conservative views simply because she thought that the experiment was supposed to make people more tolerant. Or the same person might describe herself as more liberal as a way of expressing her displeasure with our experiment, not because her views actually changed.[15] To mitigate the risk of the Hawthorne effect, we took two steps. First, we used very different recruitment dialogues to invite people to complete our survey and invite some of them to follow our bots. Doing this, we hoped, would make respondents—many of whom take dozens of surveys each month—less likely to realize that the two tasks were part of the same study.[16] Second, our bots retweeted pictures of nature landscapes during the first few days of the study to further mask our plan.

In mid-November 2017, we sent everyone in the study a survey that asked the same questions about social policies we had asked them one month earlier. By comparing how much people who followed our bots moved on our liberal-conservative scale to the movement of those in our control condition, we were finally able to learn what happens when people step outside their echo chambers. Though common wisdom told us this would make people more moderate, our results were much more depressing. Figure 1 describes the effect of following our bots for one month for both Republicans and Democrats. The horizontal axis indicates whether people became more liberal or more conservative in response to our treatment. The vertical axis shows how much attention people paid to our bots, as measured by how many of our questions about the bot's tweets they were able to answer.

As the figure shows, neither Democrats nor Republicans became more moderate when they followed our bots. In fact, the findings pointed in the opposite direction. On average, Republicans who followed our Democratic bot for one month expressed markedly more conservative views than they had at the beginning of the study.[17] And the more attention they paid to our bots, the more conservative they became. The results were less dramatic for Democrats. On average, Democrats who followed our Republican bot became slightly more liberal, though this effect was not statistically significant. We cannot rule out the possibility that the overall effect of exposure to our bots was zero for Democrats. Still, the size of this effect increased the more Democrats paid attention to our bots, which suggests that the small effect might have become statistically significant if we had recruited a much larger group of people to join the study. Even if we could not definitively address that issue, the overall message was clear: Exposing people to views of the other side did not make participants more moderate. If anything, it reinforced their preexisting views.

When my colleagues and I first saw these findings, we were worried that we might have made a coding error. We spent hours retracing our steps but kept getting the same results. Our

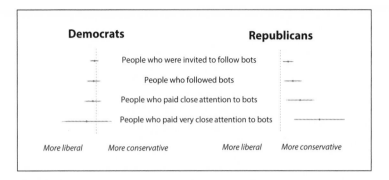

FIGURE 1: The effect of disrupting social media echo chambers for one month on opinions about social policy issues among Democrats and Republicans who visit Twitter at least three times per week

Note: Attention to our bots was monitored by asking study participants a set of questions about the content retweeted by the bots at the end of each week during the study period. For definitions about how the categories of participants were created, see the appendix.

findings were also very consistent across different subgroups in the study. It did not seem to matter whether people were very devoted members of their political party or moderates who were mostly indifferent to politics. People reacted similarly to following our bots regardless of whether they were in strong or weak echo chambers before joining the experiment. The results were the same for people from different racial groups too. It did not matter if people were male or female, were old or young, lived in a city or a rural area—or any of the more than one hundred other variables we analyzed. We also carefully scrutinized the bots to determine if they had retweeted too many extreme messages. They hadn't. We also weren't the only ones to discover that exposing people to opposing views on social media could make them double down in their preexisting views. Two years after our study, an independent group of researchers from the Massachusetts Institute of Technology and Yale replicated our study on a different population and found the same puzzling effect.[18] Though more studies are needed to further verify these findings in other contexts, it was clear that the common wisdom about echo chambers deserved some scrutiny.[19]

Solving the Puzzle

Why didn't taking people outside their echo chamber make them more moderate? Since the mid-twentieth century, social scientists have argued that exposing members of rival groups to each other—under the right settings—should reduce prejudice between them.[20] Bringing members of rival groups into contact, these scholars claimed, gave them experiences that contradict stereotypes that arise when people are isolated from each other. This research has been conducted in dozens of countries, at different time periods, and with many different types of people.[21] Though studies of intergroup contact in online settings such as Twitter had not yet been done—and though many studies stressed that contact between members of rival groups must be positive to reduce tensions—the idea that Republicans and Democrats would moderate their views if they stepped outside their echo chambers is highly intuitive.[22]

At the same time, other studies indicate that exposing people to new information can backfire. Social psychologists and political scientists have discovered that attempts to discredit rumors about public health or politics, for example, can lead people to double down on their inaccurate beliefs.[23] For example, studies have shown that trying to convince people who believe that vaccines cause autism can make them more concerned about inoculating their children.[24] But our study was not attempting to correct factual inaccuracies—instead, we were exposing people to an entirely different worldview.[25] And though previous studies briefly exposed people to one corrective message in a laboratory setting, our study exposed people to many different messages—from many different people—in a real-life setting.

At the same time, the messiness of this real-life setting made our results much more difficult to interpret. We did not know what happened when people began to see a steady stream of messages from the opposing party in their feeds. Were certain messages, events, or individuals more polarizing than others? Were most people doubling down on their preexisting beliefs for a single reason, or were different people responding in different ways? More broadly, how did the experience of following our bots fit into the daily lives of the people who participated in our study, and did their online experiences shape their off-line behavior as well?

Computational social science has created invaluable opportunities to study large groups of people and run new kinds of experiments. But solving the puzzle of why people were doubling down on their preexisting beliefs wasn't going to require larger data sets. Instead, it was going to require wider data: we needed to see what it is like to step outside the echo chamber from the perspective of the people we asked to do so. Too often, computational social scientists treat people like abstract data points—obscuring the space between our digital footprints. Instead, we wanted to get to know the people we studied—hear stories about their upbringing, friends, and family members and find out how social media and political polarization fit into the bigger picture of their lives. Most importantly, we wanted to know how following our bots influenced their views.

We first considered recontacting some of our study participants for an in-depth interview. We could have asked them what it was like to step outside their echo chamber, and how the experience shaped their views. But we quickly realized this was a bad idea. First of all, we would be betting that people were conscious of their response to our study and would be able to tell us why it happened. Yet social scientists have long known that people usually provide inaccurate and post hoc rationalizations of their attitudes or behavior.[26] Second, this strategy risked having people provide us with the answers they thought we wanted to hear instead of what they had actually experienced. Finally, we would be asking people to remember what it was like to follow a bot almost one year after they had done so. Can you remember which social media messages influenced your views one year ago? I can't.

Instead of reconnecting with people from our original study, we decided to conduct a new one. This new study would be the same as the first one, but with a much smaller group of people whom we could get to know much better before, during, and after the experiment.[27] In mid-2018, we conducted in-depth interviews with forty-four Republicans and forty Democrats for at least one hour. Later, we invited half of them to follow our bots for one month. After this period, we reinterviewed everyone in order to compare the people who followed the bots with those who did not. Our interviews began with a series of questions about why our research participants first started using social media and how they used it each day. Once we developed a rapport, we began to ask a series of questions about politics and four of the issues we used to create the liberal-conservative scale in our first study: the economy, immigration, racial discrimination, and climate change. We also asked them a series of questions about what they thought about people from the opposing political party. Finally, we asked a series of questions about how the participants' online experiences shape their lives off-line.

The period of our study coincided with some major events in the news. These included the controversial nomination of Brett Kavanaugh to the Supreme Court; the caravan of migrants described at the beginning of this chapter; the final stages of Mueller's investigation of President Trump; and the Camp Fire, one of the largest forest fires ever to strike the state of California. The period also included the shooting of a twenty-six-year-old Black security guard in Illinois by police while he was pursuing a criminal; the assassination of the *Washington Post* journalist Jamal Khashoggi in Turkey; a major government shutdown in the United States; and the death of former U.S. president George H. W. Bush. We asked questions about each of these events in our second interview to compare how following our bots shaped the views of the people in our study who did and did not follow our bots.

Our in-depth interviews provided key clues about why exposing people to opposing views led them to double down on their preexisting beliefs. The interviews not only let us get to know people through conversations that ranged as long as two and a half hours; they also inspired us to look much deeper into participants' online behavior. We collected hundreds of thousands of data points produced by each respondent online—including the texts and images they shared and the profiles they created to describe themselves. By comparing these data to the information we acquired in our interviews, we were able to compare how people present themselves online and off. We also asked everyone we interviewed to complete the same online surveys we had sent to people in our original bot study. This allowed us to see how each individual fit into the bigger picture of our previous experiment and compare whether people expressed different views to us in our interviews and a confidential online survey. Together, these different streams of data allow me to present rich case studies of individual social media users before, during, and after our experiment—but also much broader insight about how political polarization unfolds on social media.[28]

In the next chapter, you'll meet two women—one Democrat and one Republican—who helped us begin to solve the puzzle, even though the two of them could not be much more different.

3

What Happens When
We Break Them?

PATTY WRIGHT is a sixty-three-year-old woman who lives in a small town in upstate New York. She and her husband worked for a farming supply company until she was forced to retire because of a chronic medical condition. They raised three children in their quaint town, which is known for its foliage each fall. Patty has the slow but staccato speech that is characteristic of people from her region of the country. She tells it like it is. But she also misses the way things were. "When we were young . . . you were proud," she told us. "You were damn proud to be an American. You were proud to talk about your president . . . because you knew he was trying hard for you." For Patty, everything changed in the late 1960s. "I was a senior when they [U.S. soldiers] were coming home from the Vietnam War," she said. "There was a change in the way things were done." In previous wars, she explained, soldiers returned home as heroes, but "the guys [who] came home from Vietnam . . . were treated so poorly." Veterans who returned to towns like hers were hit hard by post-traumatic stress disorder and struggled to find jobs.

In Patty's view, veterans of the Vietnam War also returned to a different kind of country. The conflict had a radicalizing effect on many people in her generation—inspiring some to become advocates for social justice and others to become neoconservatives who believed in peace through strength. But the period left Patty with a negative opinion about politics altogether. "Other countries . . .

looked at us and they thought 'wow . . . it's great to be an American,'" Patty reminisced. "And today they look at us and see how our political system is, and [they think] we're pathetic." Patty's disenchantment with politics had grown so deep by the time we first met her that she avoided the topic whenever possible.

People who follow politics closely often assume that others share their passion for the subject. But as the political scientist Philip Converse recognized many years ago, most people are actually like Patty.[1] Distaste for politics is pervasive among Americans—so much so that the sociologist Nina Eliasoph was able to identify dozens of ways Americans like Patty train themselves to redirect conversations away from politics or avoid discussing current events.[2]

Patty is not typical of most Americans in that she is a relative newcomer to social media.[3] "I'm not very computer savvy," she told us. Her son helped her set up a Facebook account years ago, she explained, to stay connected to her grandchildren and her brother's foster children. Quickly captivated by posts about these kids on Facebook, Patty began to realize the benefits of other social media sites as well. She joined Pinterest to keep track of cooking recipes, and she set up a Twitter account because it helped her keep up with news about celebrities. She followed some of her favorite TV shows, such as NBC's *The Voice*. She also followed her favorite country music star and several other popular singers. Eventually, her interest in social media spread beyond entertainment and celebrities to include businesses she likes.

When we first met Patty, she had designed her social media networks to insulate her from politics. She spent most of her time following celebrities, and news about politics only trickled into her timeline from two of the accounts she followed: those of her local news station and NBC's *Today Show*. Patty watched the *Today Show* each morning at 7:00, and she occasionally turned on her local news station or CNN to get information about the tumultuous weather in her area—or natural disasters unfolding far away. Patty avoided Fox News because she was disgusted by its bias. But she had no love for liberal-leaning channels either. "I've watched a couple of them, like [Don] Lemon," she said, referring to the prominent CNN news anchor. "I mean, back when we watched the news it was unbiased. And today it's not like that. . . . They should keep their views separate." Patty's frustration with media bias was another reason why she gravitated toward social media, which, she told us, helped her avoid the biased political coverage she found on TV. Still, Patty was inside a left-leaning echo chamber when we first met her, even if it was a weak one.

When we asked Patty whether she belongs to a political party, she said, "I'm not conservative; I'm not liberal—I'm in the middle." But when we asked her which party she usually votes for—as public opinion surveys often do to identify which way people lean—she named the Democrats. As we got to know Patty better, however, we discovered that many of her views were more in line with those of the Republican Party. For example, Patty believes that the United States has accepted too many immigrants. "I don't think the United States should pay for [immigrants'] health care right off the bat and give them [a] tax break," she told us. Patty and her husband are poor. They worked hard for every penny they earned, she explained, until she got sick with a chronic condition. But immigrants, according to Patty, were getting a better deal on health care and taxes: "I mean, we've been here a long time and we don't get that. . . . This isn't a free zone." Like many Republicans, Patty also worried that immigrants threatened American culture. "You can't even call it Halloween anymore," she told us. "You have to call it Harvest. We have to change all of our culture because we don't want to upset them."

Though Patty was a victim of the skyrocketing cost of health care in her area—and across the United States in 2018—she had very little interest in discussing economic issues with us when we first met her. When we asked whether she thought there is too much government regulation of the economy, she responded, "I don't know, really." When we asked her a more general question about why people become rich or poor in America, she quipped: "I don't know. I've never been in the rich folk." In many ways, Patty seemed to be the type of disenchanted Democrat who might appreciate President Trump's "drain the swamp" style of populism.[4] When we asked her what she thought of Trump, however, her liberal sensibilities became more apparent. "I don't like him," she told us. "He's nasty. He needs to act presidential." However, Patty did not have any kind words for Democratic leaders either. And unlike so many Democrats in late 2018, her negative opinion of Trump did not extend to his handling of every issue. For example, Patty gave Trump credit for improving the economy and creating new jobs during his first two years in office.

Patty Learns How to Party

Several weeks after we interviewed her for the first time, Patty received an invitation to follow one of our bots that was designed to appear as though it were coming from another group of researchers, not us. We did this to discourage Patty from experiencing a Hawthorne effect—that is, giving us the type of answers she thought our experiment was supposed to produce—or simply venting about the experiment itself. Like most of the people we invited to follow our bots for pay, Patty agreed. As we steadily increased the number of conservative messages within her Twitter feed, I was very curious to know what would happen. Patty seemed like precisely the type of unenthusiastic Democrat who could be nudged, if only slightly, toward the right. Some of her views were already in line with conservative talking points, I reasoned, and she had not yet formed opinions about many political issues.

It turns out Patty was not as persuadable as I thought she might be. Like many unenthusiastic Democrats in our first study, one month of following our bot—and paying enough attention to its messages to correctly answer questions about the messages it retweeted—sent her further to the left. And the difference in her views was significant.

In our first interview, Patty described herself as a being "in the middle," leaning slightly toward the Democrats. After a month of following our bots, however, Patty described herself as a "pretty strong Democrat." Although she still acknowledged that some of her views were not completely in line with those of her party, she described her views as "totally different" from those of the Republican Party. When we asked Patty about immigration and the economy, she also gave much more progressive responses. Though she had expressed somewhat anti-immigrant views in our first interview with her, she was strongly opposed to Trump's border wall when we spoke with her months later. The wall had not come up in our first interview, but she was now offering a popular liberal talking point: we need partitions on some parts of the border, but not a continuous physical barrier.

Patty also developed markedly more liberal views about the caravan of migrants that was approaching the U.S.-Mexico border at the time. Dave Kelly—the conservative I profiled earlier in this book—latched onto conservative conspiracy theories that the migrants were being paid by wealthy Democrats. But Patty now subscribed to a liberal conspiracy theory: she didn't believe that there was a caravan at all. "I don't know if I believe everything that they say, that there's so many [people], or if it's just fake," she told us. In stark contrast to Dave, Patty now thought that the caravan had been invented by the Trump administration to drum up support for a border wall. "It's like they constantly beat a dead horse. They stick to something, and it's like they blow it all out of proportion, just to get a rise," she told us.

Patty's views on economic issues also drifted toward the left. She did not have strong opinions about government regulation of the economy when we first met her. Yet after a month of following our bot, Patty's views evolved in line with those of her party: "I don't think it [regulation] slows [the economy] down," she told us, "I think it helps it." She even gave us several examples of regulation that she believed were beneficial to her home state. Her views on economic inequality had also evolved. Though she had blamed immigrants for much of her family's economic struggles when we first met her, she now mentioned structural factors that produced inequality. She even mentioned the Earned Income Tax Credit, a policy designed to reduce the tax burden of very poor families. "We never had that when I was bringing up my children," she said, and it "would have been a godsend."[5]

As I read the transcripts of our interviews with dozens of other unenthusiastic Democrats and Republicans who followed our bots, I discovered that most of them had a similar experience to Patty during our study. They not only came to identify more strongly with their political party, but they developed new partisan views about issues that they had previously known little about. For Patty, this was most evident in her attitudes about the economy, though we also observed shifts in her views of issues she had cared about when we first met her, such as immigration. None of these shifts was extreme—for example, our experiment certainly did not turn Patty into a sign-waving supporter of sanctuary cities—but they were nevertheless easy to see. And we saw these shifts not only during our in-depth interviews, but also in the confidential online surveys we sent people before and after they followed our bots. For example, not only did Patty express more liberal attitudes overall, but her attitudes on the economy became more liberal than her attitudes about other issues.[6]

So what happened? Unenthusiastic partisans like Patty do not carefully review new information about politics when they are exposed to opposing views on social media and adapt their views accordingly. Instead, they experience stepping outside their echo chamber as an attack upon their identity. Patty did not focus on the moderate messages retweeted by center-right Twitter accounts. Rather, she was captivated by the uncivil or ad hominem attacks on Democrats by several of the more extreme conservatives that our bot retweeted. The worst of these attacks were previously obscured by her echo chamber, but now Patty was experiencing the full scale of partisan warfare for the first time. Unlike the unenthusiastic partisans we interviewed in our control condition, Patty came to realize that there was a war going on, and she had to choose a side. The attacks even inspired her to post about politics on Twitter for the first time. "I don't post anything nasty [about] the Republicans," she told us. "I read their views, and I am fine. But if I post anything about being a Democrat, then I get nasty posts." These types of attacks from extreme conservatives made things personal.

Wading into partisan warfare on social media—in its full, awful splendor—not only triggered Patty's liberal identity, but also inspired her to learn how to toe the party line. Discussing how she had been using social media after following our bot for a month, Patty said, "It's a lot more detailed online than it is on the TV." TV gives you a partisan viewpoint, she explained, but social media are more interactive: they allowed her to search for liberal counterpoints to the steady stream of messages she was viewing from conservatives each day. For Patty, like most of the other unenthusiastic partisans who followed our bots, exposure to the other side did not help her see that there are two sides to every story.[7] Seeing her side attacked and being attacked personally provoked Patty to learn how to defend herself with liberal talking points. Patty was learning how to party.

Janet

Janet Lewis is a hairdresser in her late thirties who lives with her husband in a suburb outside Gainesville, Florida. Her two grown children live nearby. Unlike Patty, Janet is a passionate Republican who spends hours each day reading about politics, and she discusses current events with many of her clients. In this way, Janet is different from most Americans: she is part of the small but extremely vocal minority described by Converse as politically engaged. When we first met her, it was immediately clear that she goes out of her way to discuss politics and enjoys persuading others to embrace her views. Like many other people who enjoy proselytizing about politics, Janet is very active on social media.[8] She originally joined Facebook to connect with distant family members, like Patty. But unlike Patty, Janet spent hours each day tracking politics on Facebook, and eventually on Twitter as well. In 2018 alone, our analysis showed that she produced nearly 2,000 tweets—most of them about current events.

Janet came of age in the 1990s in a family of Baptists who voted for Democrats but eventually shifted to the Republican Party because of its stronger emphasis on Christian values. "I didn't really keep up with . . . politics. I just really didn't care about that stuff," she told us, displaying her Southern accent more frequently as she described her childhood. The turning point for Janet came in her late twenties, when Barack Obama was first elected president: "I was okay 'cause I thought: 'Well, you know, he's young. We're gonna give him a chance—he may do just great.' But I just kept watching everything he was doing, and it just made me madder and madder." Eventually, the very sight of Obama upset her. "The more I saw his face," she told us, "the more fake he just seemed to be—more and more."

Janet's anger was fueled by a deep distrust of almost every policy promoted by the Obama administration. She was extremely upset by Obama's foreign policy, for example, and worried that America was losing its reputation for military strength. "He would go over to Saudi Arabia, or whatever, and apologize for America," she said. She also felt that many of the administration's policies privileged undocumented immigrants over American citizens: "The Democrats are saying, 'Just open the door . . . just come on in. Just heck with the law.'" "I don't wanna sound bad," said Janet, "but . . . I have to pay for *their* health care. I have to pay for *their* food stamps. You know, we're just barely [getting by] as it is. This is not fair." Her Baptist roots also made her deeply troubled by Obama's policies on gay marriage. By the end of his second term, Obama had created an existential dread in Janet: "The way he was leading our country, it made me get into politics . . . because I figured . . . we're not gonna have our country if I don't."

Trump's gloves-off style offended many of the moderate Republicans we interviewed. But Janet embraced it. For her, Trump personified the potent anger she felt toward a ruling party that ignored her daily struggles while pretending to fight for the so-called little guy. As Trump created unprecedented volatility in American political debate, Janet could not get enough of it. She attended several of his rallies and became an ardent Trump defender on Facebook. "I started getting into Twitter a couple years ago when Trump got elected," she told us. "He communicates to us through Twitter. . . . I wanted to see what he was twittering about," she joked. "I never had a Twitter account until he became president." Our review of her timeline confirmed that she quickly became one of Trump's most ardent supporters on Twitter soon after joining the platform.

Unlike Patty, Janet considered it very important to pay attention to the news when we first met her. When we asked her how she keeps track of current events, she named three conservative websites: "I do *FoxNews.com*, *Breitbart*, and the *Drudge Report*." Janet visits Twitter approximately once an hour each day. "The majority of my followers," she told us, "and [the] people I follow, are conservative." A deeper analysis of her Twitter network confirmed that Janet occupied a strong conservative echo chamber. After following Trump on Twitter, she began following several of her favorite Fox News hosts. She also followed a variety of conservative activist groups. Among the few nonpolitical accounts she followed was one of her favorite fast-food chains.

Janet also subscribed to widely discredited conspiracy theories.[9] For example, she believes that Obama is a Muslim and that illegal immigrants voted in recent elections in droves. But Janet was not completely unable to criticize her own side. When we asked her whether she worries about fake information in the media, she said, "That is very, very hard because it is on the conservative side, too." She explained that she often uses sites such as snopes.com to get to the bottom of things. She told us about a story she had read about former NBA star Michael Jordan. Jordan, the story claimed, had asked Nike to discontinue its line of Air Jordan sneakers in protest of the company's support for a player who had kneeled while the national anthem was played before an NFL game. "I looked," she told us. "That's not true. He did not."

It Feels Good to Be Right

When Janet agreed to follow our liberal bot, her situation was much different from Patty's. While Patty was mostly detached from politics and indifferent to current events, Janet took strong conservative positions on nearly every issue we discussed with her. If Patty was gradually convinced that there was a war going on and she had to choose a side, Janet was already a two-star general who was suddenly called to duty on the front line. When she arrived there, however, the situation was much worse than she had thought.

The first thing that shocked Janet was the sheer magnitude of attacks on her side, and on Trump in particular. "It never ends," she told us, in awe of the panoply of Trump criticism from the left. "I'm getting really, really tired of people cutting down my president, you know? It just gets old." She was already aware of some of the criticism before stepping out of her echo chamber, of course, but our bot exposed her to a whole new series of attacks that she had not witnessed before. She was particularly upset about a message retweeted by our bot that described a series of anti-Trump missives by the popular actor Samuel L. Jackson. "He was probably one of my favorite actors," she told us. "Not anymore." The bot also exposed her to many different anti-Trump memes intended to be humorous, such as a giant street float that depicted the president as a screaming child in a diaper. "Everybody laughs about it," she said, but "I get very angry—it makes me mad, and I think most conservatives [are] very angry because we are the ones who put him in office."

The second thing Janet noticed was the lack of attention—particularly positive attention—to her side from Democrats. She did not expect a lot of positive coverage of Trump, but she was shocked to discover there was none at all. She was also deeply disturbed by the lack of positive coverage of conservative issues more broadly. "For instance, the pro-life rally had over one million people," she told us, referring to the anti-abortion March for Life in late January 2019. "They [the mainstream media] said they only had 1,000 [people] and they didn't even put it on . . . but when the Women's March came it was all over the pages. . . . Those are the kind of things that irritate me," she said, referring to the large anti-Trump rally for the empowerment of women that had occurred the day after his inauguration.

The March for Life was just the tip of the iceberg. At the time we interviewed Janet, liberals were enraged about a viral video that appeared to show a high school student from a Christian school in Covington, Kentucky, taunting a Native American man who was demonstrating for indigenous rights in Washington, D.C. "They said the teenager was harassing him, and all you had to do was look at the video and see he was not," Janet told us. Soon after our interview, Janet was validated: new videos emerged, showing that the student had been harassed by a group of Black Hebrew Israelite protesters before their encounter with the Native

American man. Janet was also perplexed by liberal outrage about a viral image of a young mother and her two children fleeing after a tear-gas canister was shot near them at the U.S.-Mexico border. "When I see them down there throwing rocks at our border patrol and trying to climb over the fence and taunt people," she said, "it makes me very mad." And she was particularly angry about double standards: "It's like, Obama did that too when he was in office, but nobody said anything about it. He did throw tear gas too."

When I heard Janet's claim I was dubious. By that point, I knew that she subscribed to conspiracy theories about Obama. And Obama had championed immigration in numerous ways—fighting for the right of the DREAMers (a group of undocumented young people) to stay in the United States, for example. Obama also championed diversity as America's foundational value. He had criticized the human rights abuses and maltreatment of prisoners conducted by the administration of President George W. Bush in Iraq, Guantanamo Bay, and the CIA's so-called black sites. I didn't think that there was any way his administration would have used tear gas on hapless migrant populations stranded at the border of our country. I promptly consulted snopes.com—the same fact-checking website that Janet had used to check the story about Michael Jordan—to confirm my suspicion that Janet was the victim of fake news. I was wrong. According to U.S. Customs and Border Protection, border patrol agents used tear gas 1.3 times per month during the last five years of Obama's presidency.[10]

And while I was getting an education in misinformation, Janet was getting more targets to attack. Though moderates like Patty seldom interacted with our bots, impassioned partisans like Janet routinely attacked the messages they retweeted. Describing anti-Trump posts by the Democratic Party leaders Chuck Schumer and Nancy Pelosi, she said, "Sometimes I go onto people's accounts. Like if I read . . . something hateful, then I'll get on their account and then tell them what I think of them." "I have to make sure I remind them," she continued, "that he [Trump] was elected—so when they [make fun of him], they're hurting a lot of other people, not just their people." Janet's responses were often snide dismissals of what she felt was clear-cut liberal hypocrisy (for example, the point about tear gas that I just described). At other times, she shamed people for tweeting messages she considered un-American.

The strong partisans we interviewed felt that it was their duty to defend their side. But doing so also seemed to make them feel good. When we asked Janet about her attacks on leading liberals such as Schumer and Pelosi, she said, "I don't know if they read it or not, but at least it makes me feel better that I've voiced my opinion." She felt even better, she told us, when fellow conservatives cheered her on—which happened frequently. "When I scroll down [and see] there's a lot of people that believe the same way I do," she told us, describing likes or supportive comments about her posts, ". . . it just makes me feel good." This affirmation not only seemed to make Janet's conservative identity even stronger, but it also led her deeper into a conservative echo chamber. Six months after following our bot, Janet—like many strong partisans we studied—was following even more people from her own side on social media. I realized that Janet's echo chamber was not simply exposing her to the same type of information that she had seen before she joined our study. It was also insulating her from the most extreme attacks upon her party from the other side.

Hard Reset

Let's pause for a moment to remember what is supposed to happen when people step outside their echo chambers, according to the popular narrative. First, confronting opposing views is meant to provoke introspection. People are supposed to realize that there are two sides to every story. In addition to creating a better competition of ideas, stepping outside our echo chambers is supposed to help us humanize each other, and realize there is more that unites us than divides us. With time, these experiences are supposed to make all of us more moderate and better-informed citizens, who dutifully perform our responsibilities to consider a range of evidence as we develop our opinions. Some people even assume that the experience will make us push back against extremists on our own side by pointing to reasonable arguments on the other side.

For me, the stories of Patty, Janet, and the many other people we interviewed make this narrative seem like a fairy tale. After a month of following our bots, neither woman was reflecting upon policy ideas presented in the messages our bot retweeted by moderates such as the *New York Times* columnist David Brooks or Governor Steve Bullock of Montana. In fact, most people who followed our bots did not discuss the new ideas they encountered about social policies at all. Those who stepped outside their echo chambers were certainly not humanizing each other more effectively, either—much less criticizing extremists on their own side. Instead, stepping outside their echo chambers seemed to sharpen the contrast between "us" and "them."

For unenthusiastic partisans like Patty, such attacks seemed to activate underdeveloped or dormant political identities. For passionate partisans like Janet, stepping outside the echo chamber made the differences between "us" and "them" seem even bigger. For both types of people, stepping outside the echo chamber was not creating a better competition of ideas, but a vicious competition of identities.

Though we set out to understand why people dig in when they are exposed to opposing views on social media, our research had once again raised much deeper questions: Why does exposure to the other side activate people's identities, instead of inspiring social media users to engage with new ideas? Why don't people

CHAPTER 3

like Patty simply ignore the partisan warfare that awaits them
outside the comfort of their echo chambers? And why do people
like Janet press even further into battle once they leave their echo
chambers, even when they realize that their efforts to influence
the other side are probably futile?

4

The Social Media Prism

N MID-JULY 1973, one of the world's leading social psychologists walked through the woods of Middle Grove, New York, searching for the ideal location to start a forest fire. While many of his contemporaries were conducting bland research on lab rats, Muzafer Sherif yearned to understand how human identities shape violent conflict. Having grown up amid the ancient rivalry between Turks and Armenians, Sherif wanted to know how groups of people can develop intractable differences, even when they are very similar. Sherif planned to start a fire as part of an unusual study he was planning in this sleepy, forested town in upstate New York. With a modest grant from the Rockefeller Foundation, Sherif had created a fictitious summer camp and invited forty eleven-year-old boys to attend. The boys had been selected to be as similar to each other as possible: they were all White and Protestant, and they were about the same age with no abnormal psychological traits. None of the boys had known each other before the experiment. Sherif's plan was to allow the boys to socialize and make friends with each other, but then randomly assign them to teams that would compete in a series of contests. Once the boys had been arbitrarily assigned to be "Pythons" or "Panthers," Sherif predicted, the mere existence of a collective identity would lead them to develop animosity toward each other. The experiment was designed to illustrate how humans' intrinsic need for belonging could produce the type of tragic intergroup hatred that Sherif had witnessed as a child.[1]

But Sherif was wrong. Despite becoming Pythons and Panthers, the boys continued to play together amicably—mostly ignoring their assigned identities. In a hasty attempt to save the experiment that he spent years planning, Sherif instructed two research assistants to sneak into the summer campers' tents to steal some of their possessions. But Sherif's attempt to goad the boys into conflict also failed. The boys calmly discussed the situation, swore to each other that they were innocent, and sensibly concluded that the camp's laundry service had lost the clothing items that had been stolen. When the campers later began to cast suspicion on their "camp counselors" (the researchers), Sherif—who had been drinking—pulled his two research assistants into the woods and began excoriating them. When he raised his fist as if to hit one of them, the young graduate student reportedly said, "Dr. Sherif, if you do it, I'm gonna hit you."[2] Fortunately, the older man came to his senses and stormed off angrily. And while the three researchers were comically oblivious to the children's peaceful example of conflict resolution, they eventually decided that no one needed to set a forest fire that night—a stunt that had been intended to determine if the boys could overcome their differences to address a shared threat.

The story of Sherif's unusual research does not end there. Undeterred by the failure of his experiment in upstate New York, Sherif created another fictitious summer camp one year later in Robbers Cave, Oklahoma. Once again, he recruited a group of very similar young boys. But in this now infamous experiment, the boys were not allowed to make friends with each other before being assigned to different teams. Instead, the two groups were segregated on opposite sides of a lake. The Rattlers and Eagles were not told about each other's existence when they arrived, and they engaged in the wholesome activities characteristic of U.S. Boy Scout camps in the mid-1970s. Yet after a brief period of bonding, each group was told about the existence of the other and informed that the two groups would be competing against each other on the following day.

Though Sherif's first experiment had been a bust, his new experiment quickly devolved into something resembling William Golding's *Lord of the Flies*, a popular 1950s novel in which children stranded on an island resort to murder to resolve their conflicts. Even though the boys had no reason to dislike each other a priori—and had once again been selected to be as "normal" as possible—they quickly began taunting each other without provocation. After the Eagles defeated the Rattlers in a tumultuous game of tug-of-war, the Rattlers burned the Eagles' flag. Members of each group soon refused to dine next to each other and conducted late-night raids to steal personal belongings from the other team that eerily resembled those of Sherif's research assistants in the previous year.

To his delight, Sherif's second experiment confirmed his hypothesis: All that is necessary for groups of people to develop antagonism toward each other is a collective identity. The only difference between his failed experiment and this one was that the Eagles' and Rattlers' identities had time to grow when the two groups were isolated from each other. Decades of subsequent research showed that people who are assigned membership in social groups will consistently prefer members of their own group and punish those outside its boundaries.[3] The phenomenon is not unique to children, either. The human tendency to prefer members of our own group has been observed in every culture on Earth.[4] Scholars have also shown that in-group favoritism can be created even when people are assigned membership in groups that have even less meaning than the Eagles and the Rattlers. Across many different studies, social scientists have discovered that members of such meaningless groups will penalize out-group members, even if doing so comes at a cost to their own side.[5]

As the political scientist Lilliana Mason notes, perhaps we should not be so surprised that political parties—armed with sophisticated campaigns, media professionals, and long periods of time to coordinate their activities—can create such deep-seated animosity between Republicans and Democrats if similar animosity can be created so easily with completely arbitrary identities such as Eagles and Rattlers.[6] And if these same political parties are so effective at inflaming our passions, perhaps we should not be surprised that their power seems to increase when we find ourselves trapped within echo chambers—not unlike summer campers on opposite sides of a lake in rural Oklahoma.

The Not-So-Rational Public

One of the most ancient ideas in Western thought is that rational deliberation will produce better societies. The notion that societies function more smoothly when people form their opinions based on a wide range of evidence has become part of the bedrock of democracy. Like so many of the ideals we hold dear today, this idea gained momentum during the Enlightenment. Reason had helped scientists conquer so much of the natural world, philosophers such as Denis Diderot argued—so why not use it to build better societies as well? A key venue for this progressive idea was the salon. Invented in Italy and later popularized in France, salons were small-group discussions about current events organized by influential elites. Equal parts wit and erudition, salons were a critical precursor to modern democracy, some historians believe, because they provided people with a forum to discuss shared challenges. But other historians think salons were mostly just an excuse to drink wine and have sex.[7]

Even if salons were not the crucible of democracy, that is how many social scientists describe them.[8] According to the German sociologist Jürgen Habermas, salons laid the groundwork for the systems of mass communication that emerged in the twentieth century.[9] Newspapers, radio, and television allowed for the emergence of the public, Habermas argued, because they provided societies with forums expansive enough for large groups of people to deliberate about the issues of their day. By spreading information more efficiently, Habermas argued, these new technologies facilitated a better competition of ideas. Such beliefs—which echo those of other prominent scholars of the public sphere—provided the foundation for modern theories of public opinion.[10] In recent decades, political scientists such as James Fishkin have popularized the idea of deliberative polling, which brings together small groups of people to discuss how to solve social problems. This practice, Fishkin argues, can lead people to moderate their views, identify optimal solutions, and even become more enthusiastic about politics.[11]

It is not surprising, then, that early observers of the internet celebrated the potential of social media to scale up salon culture, creating a massive and open marketplace of ideas.[12] Social media sites were not only open to anyone, these observers argued, but they also lacked the conventional gatekeepers (television producers, newspaper editors, and so on) who tightly policed the boundaries of the public sphere. What is more, social media offered people seemingly endless access to information they could use to form their views. And social media could also allow users to discuss such information with a much more diverse group of people than they might encounter in off-line settings.

This heavily idealized vision about social media may now seem whimsical. But the same logic that propelled these prophecies—that connecting people more easily will lead to more effective democracy—continues to motivate many technology leaders. For example, Mark Zuckerberg, Facebook's CEO, reportedly believes that Facebook users can effectively deliberate about what should be labelled as fake news, even though the term itself is a political football.[13] Similarly, Jack Dorsey, Twitter's CEO, has considered tweaking his platform's algorithm to expose people to more diverse views because he believes that would increase moderation.[14] Maybe you have used such logic as well. Have you ever wondered why your heady, carefully researched posts on social media aren't gaining as much traction as the pictures of your kid, cat, or dog do?

As the stories of Patty and Janet in chapter 3 taught us, social media are less like an eighteenth century salon and more like a sprawling football field on which our instincts are guided by the color of our uniforms instead of our prefrontal cortexes. In fact, the tendency for our political identities to guide our opinions—instead of the other way around—was identified years before our study in a clever experiment by the psychologist Geoffrey Cohen.[15] Cohen recruited liberal and conservative students to evaluate hypothetical welfare policies. One of the policies offered very generous benefits, in line with the typical preferences of Democratic voters. The second policy was much more stringent, consistent with typical Republican preferences for economic redistribution. But in the study's treatment condition, Cohen attributed each hypothetical policy to the "wrong" political party. Democrats strongly endorsed the policy that they were told was supported by their party, regardless of whether the benefits described were generous or stringent. Similarly, Republicans preferred the policy that they were told was endorsed by their party, notwithstanding its content.

This experiment and many subsequent studies indicate that Americans are actually much less polarized about social policy issues than most people realize.[16] Though rates of disagreement about social policies have remained relatively steady over the past few decades, our attitudes toward each other have become much more negative. Since 1960, the American National Election Study has asked thousands of Americans whether they would be upset if their child decided to marry someone from the opposing political party. In 1960, only 5 percent of Republicans and 4 percent of Democrats reported that they would be displeased in this scenario.[17] But in 2010, the shares were 27 percent of Republicans and 20 percent of Democrats.[18] And in 2018, the shares were nearly 50 percent of both Republicans and Democrats.[19] In a masterful ethnography of political conflict in the U.S. South, sociologist Arlie Hochschild argues Democrats and Republicans not only dislike each other, but have also created "empathy walls" that prevent them from humanizing the other side.[20]

Social science has produced a litany of troubling indicators of how easily our political identities override our rational instincts, our ability to empathize with each other, and even our ability to connect with each other around nonpolitical issues.[21] For example, one study showed that Democrats and Republicans will accept lower financial compensation in online labor markets to avoid working with each other.[22] Other studies reveal that Democrats and Republicans award hypothetical jobs and college scholarships to members of their own party, even if those candidates are less qualified than others from the opposing party.[23] Political identity has even become so central to our sense of self that it shapes who we are attracted to. When a group of political scientists randomized people's party affiliation and asked respondents to judge how physically attractive those people were, they discovered that respondents rated members of opposing parties less favorably—even when they were judged to be very attractive by other respondents when the people were labeled as belonging to the same party as the respondent.[24] And the differences between members of the two parties don't end there. Republicans like Ford pickups, and Democrats prefer the Toyota Prius. Liberals like lattes, and conservatives prefer drip coffee. Research shows that Democrats and Republicans now watch different television shows and prefer different music too.[25]

Because of the mounting evidence that our political identities shape the way we understand the world around us, social scientists have mostly abandoned the idea that people dispassionately deliberate about the merits of each other's arguments.[26] But there is another, even deeper, problem that social scientists have not yet solved. Democrats and Republicans are not Eagles and Rattlers. And social media platforms are not a summer camp, to say the least. As the stories of Patty and Janet showed, our political identities are not simply a jersey that we put on each time we log onto social media.[27] Instead, our identities evolve as we interact with information in our news feed and with other social media users. The critical question, then, is how do social media platforms shape who we are and what we think of others?

Social Media and the Quest for Status

Let's pause for a moment to do an exercise. If you gave me access to all of your social media accounts—if you let me analyze every post, picture, or video—would I get a good sense of who you are? Take a moment and look through the last dozen messages you posted to Facebook, Twitter, Instagram, or whatever platform you use most often. How do you decide what should be included in this ever-expanding digital archive of your life? More importantly, what do you not post on social media? If you are like most people, the answer is "a lot." And if you've ever used an internet dating app, you might have experienced the consequences of such behavior firsthand. The point of this thought exercise is not to try to convince you that blind dates were better before social media (they were not) but to shine a light on one of our most basic human instincts. We humans are unusual creatures because we care so deeply about what other people think of us. Consciously or unconsciously, we expend unreasonable amounts of energy—from a dog's perspective, at least—presenting different versions of ourselves in varied social settings to figure out which ones "work."

Our obsession with social status long predates social media, of course, and some people care much more about gaining status on social media than others do. But the key point I want to make here is that we care so much about our identities because they give us something that we all strive for: a sense of self-worth. This idea can be traced back to the early writings of sociologists such as Norbert Elias and Erving Goffman and all the way up to cutting-edge neuroscience.[28] The general conclusion of this research is that we choose identities that make us feel good about ourselves, and we avoid those that make us feel shame or embarrassment. One of the main reasons we look for membership in social groups such as political parties is that they can provide us with self-esteem that we cannot obtain on our own.[29] While this can occur because of the positive self-affirmation that results from bonding with other people, it is also often driven by the process of drawing boundaries between ourselves and others we deem to be less capable, honest, or moral.[30] The sense of superiority that we derive from categorizing people into groups of "us" and "them" fulfills our intrinsic need for status.

One of the most frustrating things about identities for those of us who study them for a living is that they are constantly evolving. Unlike the summer campers profiled at the beginning of this chapter, people are not randomly assigned membership in the Republican or Democratic Party. Though we've learned so far that people develop identities that improve their self-esteem, we have not yet analyzed how people read the signals of other people in order to do so. This is where sociology becomes indispensable. Sociology is the science of social relationships. Sociologists study how social contexts shape people's beliefs, behavior, and—most importantly for the current discussion—identities.

A seminal example of how social contexts shape the way humans develop our identities is the sociologist Charles Horton Cooley's notion of the looking-glass self.[31] According to Cooley, we develop our concept of self by watching how other people react to the different versions of ourselves that we present in social settings. This idea recasts identity not as a jersey we wear, but as the outcome of a complex process of social experimentation.

CHAPTER 4

We constantly present different versions of ourselves, observe which ones elicit positive reactions from others, and proceed accordingly.[32] For example, I could not describe myself as a talented break-dancer without expecting a significant amount of ridicule from my friends and family members. However, I've come to learn that people are surprisingly tolerant of my self-deprecating style of humor—or at least I think they are. And that last part (that I think other people appreciate my tendency to make fun of myself) is key. Although we scan our social environments, consciously or subconsciously, we are often quite wrong about what other people think.

Goffman discovered our tendency to misread the reactions of others by conducting ethnographic observations of people with marked physical deformities such as elephantiasis, a condition characterized by gross enlargement of limbs or other body parts.[33] People who carry such stigmata, Goffman learned, come to expect discrimination from others. When they change their behavior in anticipation of such discrimination, however, it often makes others more uncomfortable—or simply makes it easier for people to ignore stigmatized people altogether. Such errors in reading the social environment, Goffman showed, create many other types of self-fulfilling prophecies that can be scaled up to explain broader patterns of prejudice experienced by members of many different stigmatized groups.[34]

Goffman believed that we read our social environments through a combination of verbal and nonverbal cues, including facial expressions, other types of body language, and tones of voice. In contrast, social media enable an entirely different "presentation of self," to borrow one of Goffman's famous phrases.[35] Our ability to hide certain aspects of our identity and highlight others is highly constrained in real-life interactions, but social media give us much more flexibility to present carefully curated versions of ourselves. As communications scholar Alice Marwick and information scientist danah boyd observe, social media allow us to present nearly every detail of our lives if we choose to do so, or to remain completely anonymous—at least on certain platforms.[36] Very few people choose either of these extremes. The most interesting sociological questions are why we present one version of ourselves instead of another.

In addition to giving us more control over our presentation of self, social media also allow us to monitor large parts of our social environment with unprecedented efficiency. Our news feeds—which provide frequent updates from everyone we follow—are not simply a convenient way of getting information about issues that we care about. They also enable us to make social comparisons with unprecedented scale and speed.[37] A team of psychologists led by Erin Vogel studied how frequently people make social comparisons on and off social media. The researchers found that people who use Facebook engage in far more frequent social comparisons than those who do not.[38] In related research, the psychologist Claire Midgley conducted a series of studies in which she observed people using Facebook. Midgley also tracked the frequency of social comparisons people make, as well as who they compare themselves to and what effect this has on their self-esteem.[39] She found that social media users tend to compare themselves to people who are more socially distant from themselves and also those who have higher status. After people make such upward comparisons, Midgley discovered, most people experience decreased self-esteem.[40]

Our news feeds also offer built-in tools for monitoring our social environments. Most social media sites provide instant metrics we can use to learn whether our presentation of self is working. In this way, status is deeply embedded in the architecture of social media sites.[41] We can monitor whether people respond positively or negatively to the content we share by tracking likes, retweets, or shares. Sometimes we post content that people react to so negatively that they go out of their way to comment negatively on our posts. We even have a name for making posts that get more negative comments than positive endorsements: getting "ratioed." Social media platforms also communicate our status by prominently displaying the number of followers or friends that each user has. The Twitter and Instagram elite are even distinguished by a shiny blue check mark that verifies their identity as VIPs, while the rest of us have to wade through these platforms like a bunch of savages.

And though some people couldn't care less about whether they gain lots of followers on social media or whether their posts get lots of likes, research indicates that most people do care. In 2015 a group of communications scholars asked 141 Facebook users to share their news feeds with the researchers. Next, they asked these people how each post made them feel. People reported experiencing more positive emotions after making posts that received a large number of comments or responses from their friends.[42] Some scholars argue there may even be a neurological basis for this type of finding.[43] One team of neuroscientists recruited a group of teenagers to view a mockup of the popular photo sharing site Instagram from inside an fMRI machine. Teenagers who viewed posts that received a lot of likes from other Instagram users exhibited greater brain activity in neural regions associated with "reward processing, social cognition, imitation, and attention."[44]

The Power of the Prism

Many people believe that social media platforms are addictive because they provide us with an endless stream of visual stimuli, carefully designed by marketing experts in Silicon Valley to make it impossible for us to put down our smartphones and tablets.[45] Having carefully reviewed the literature—and studied thousands of people as they use social media over multiple years—I think that our rapidly shortening attention spans are only part of the story. The deeper source of our addiction to social media, I've concluded, is that it makes it so much easier for us to do what is all too human: perform different identities, observe how other people react, and update our presentation of self to make us feel like we belong.[46]

The great tragedy of social media, which has critical implications for political polarization, is that it makes our tendency to misread our social environment even worse. We use social media platforms as if they were a giant mirror that can help us understand our place within society. But they are more like prisms that bend and refract our social environment—distorting our sense of ourselves, and each other. The social media prism exerts its most profound influence when people are not aware that it exists. In the following chapters, I delve back into our interviews with social media users to explain how the social media prism works. I begin by taking the concept of the social media prism to its logical extreme—showing how status seeking on social media creates a vicious cycle of political extremism.

5

How the Prism Drives Extremism

I T IS LATE ON A TUESDAY NIGHT, and Jamie Laplace is wrapping up his night shift as a medical assistant at a large hospital near Huntsville, Alabama. He pulls out his aging iPhone, scrolls past a series of tweets about Coldplay (his favorite band), and pauses on a video of Steve Bannon, President Trump's former campaign manager. The video had inspired a number of negative reactions from liberal Twitter users. But Jamie chimed in with his own—considerably less civil—tweet. "Nice STD, Steve," Jamie tweeted, referring to a large red mark on Bannon's ruddy cheek that resembled a cold sore from the herpes virus. Jamie kept scrolling, paused to insult a few other prominent conservatives, and then headed home.

A cursory review of Jamie's Twitter feed reveals that he is one of the most extreme liberal users of the platform. But when we first met Jamie, none of his online antics came up. "I only have a Twitter account to find out if a new album is getting released," he told us. "I could care less about people seeing my opinion. I only have Twitter for, you know, up-to-date sports scores, or if Coldplay puts out a new album. . . . I just use Twitter as an information source—that's all that it is to me." Jamie, I later learned, was lying to us. The mismatch between the person he described himself to be and the sarcastic social media provocateur I came to know him as was shocking. Jamie's talent for deceit was so well-honed that he even trolled the survey firm we hired to recruit him. He told the firm that he was a "strong Republican."

Though Jamie is certainly not a Republican, he lives among them. He was born to liberal parents in one of the reddest regions in the country. Most of his aunts and uncles do not share his views. "Now that Trump's been [elected] president," he complained, "our family is literally torn—we can't even get through a football game together." Watching sports is not the only challenge for Jamie and Democrats in this bright red state. "I have friends that I've known my entire life that I would jump off a bridge for," he told us, "but I don't speak to them anymore because they vote for Donald Trump." This caused deep frustration and loneliness for the single atheist in his late thirties who was working night shifts for less than $40,000 per year after dropping out of college a decade earlier. He occasionally runs into friends from high school, he explains, but things quickly go south when politics comes up: "Ah man, you always struck me as sort of cool, but there you are just falling for [Trump's] nonsense. . . . You're probably not going to call to get a beer during Christmas break anymore."

Though Jamie lied to us about his online trolling, he was forthright about his strong liberal views. He describes Republicans as the "bad guys," for example. "Anything they're for, I'm automatically against," he told us. When we asked him if he is similar to Republicans in any way, he said, "No, not in the slightest." Like so many other passionate liberals, Jamie was furious about Trump. Asked if he could find anything to like about Trump, he responded, "No, not at all." He paused. "I guess . . . if I had a gun to my head . . . if I was being tortured to death and had to come up with something . . . I think that [he] did prison reform, which needed to be done." But then he quickly retreated: "Like, congratulations, you did one thing for non-millionaires. I'm sure that if we dug further into it, they're getting money out of it some shape or way." Jamie did not even appreciate one thing that might appeal to many poor Americans like him: Trump's election meant a little more money in his paycheck each month. Instead, Jamie mistakenly believed that lower- and middle-class people did not receive a substantial break from Trump's 2017 tax reform.[1] "What I'm getting ready to get back is way worse than what I got under eight years under Obama," he told us.

How do social media platforms influence the views and behavior of political extremists like Jamie?[2] There has been no shortage of answers to this question among pundits, policy makers, and technology leaders, but there is relatively little academic research about political extremists or trolls.[3] And with good reason. Political extremists do not like to be studied, and when social scientists have been able to survey or interview them, many of them—like Jamie—hide important details about their lives.[4] For this reason, nearly every study of social media extremism focuses upon the behavior of people on the platforms.[5] Yet this strategy, as Jamie's story shows, also provides a very incomplete picture of extremism. In this chapter, I explain how the social media prism distorts how extremists see themselves and others, which creates a self-fulfilling prophecy that pushes people further apart.

Lonely Trolls

One of the most common things I observed after studying extremists on social media is that they often lack status in their off-line lives.[6] I have already described how Jamie struggled to fit in with his conservative friends in Alabama, and thousands of miles away a very similar story was unfolding. Ed Baker is a widower in his early sixties who lives in a motel in Nebraska. Almost every day he wishes that he could return to Fort Collins, the heavily gentrified city in Colorado where he was born, raised, and went to college. He spent the 1980s living a comfortable life working in the financial sector with his wife, who died a few years before we met him. But like so many other people in that field of work, Ed fell on hard times—moving between jobs as giant financial firms crowded people like him out of work. When he was forced to tap into his 401(k) plan early to survive, he became livid with the Obama administration. By the time we met him, Ed was on food stamps. He could no longer afford to live in his hometown, which was rapidly gentrifying because the location's outstanding opportunities for outdoor activities and relatively low taxes attracted wealthy technology entrepreneurs.[7] But despite his move, Ed remained unemployed and desperate. "Here in this small town," he explained, "I'm overqualified for everything."

Ed wakes up and falls asleep to the free DirecTV service that comes with his extended stay at the motel. Most days, he wakes up to *Fox and Friends*—the popular morning news program that Trump reportedly watches each morning as well. In Trump, Ed sees his savior. He blames Obama for the high cost of medical care during the final stages of his wife's life and thinks that Trump is uniquely qualified to solve this and many other problems facing the United States. "I think he's great," he told us. "He reminds me of Ronald Reagan." Ed sends a handwritten letter to Trump every week, asking him to create jobs in the small Nebraska town where Ed is living. "I get a nice letter back," he told us, "Thank you for your concern, we appreciate that. We'll do our best to get this to the president." Ed is particularly impressed by Trump's business acumen and has spent some of his savings on Trump's book *The Art of the Deal*. But perhaps more importantly, Ed believes that Trump ran for office to help people like him: "I'm convinced that he's doing as much as he can do . . . for the American people. I admire him for that. I'd love to work for him in one of his hotels. And, I don't have a red ["Make America Great Again"] hat because I can't afford one right now, but I would walk around with that [if I did]."

Because Ed is isolated from the increasingly liberal Colorado city that he loves, and has few friends and family members to connect with off-line, Twitter and Facebook are a social oasis for him. Though most of the conservatives we interviewed for this book think that Trump tweets too often or should be more careful about what he tweets about, Ed delights in Trump's social media style. "He cracks me up," he told us. Describing the way Trump aggressively attacks his opponents—such as North Korea's leader, Kim Jong-un—he said, "I love the nicknames . . . Rocket Man. . . . He [Trump] cracks me up." In addition to praising Trump by retweeting such attacks, Ed uses social media to vent his anger toward liberals. When we first met him, he was deriding the "Mexican mafia Democrats" who he believed were preventing Trump from building a wall along the U.S.-Mexico border. Like many other conservative extremists, Ed frequently targeted Hillary Clinton or her family, even years after she lost the presidential election. Whenever he encountered a post about Robert Mueller's investigation of Trump, for example, Ed left a reply about the corruption of the Clinton Foundation—or stories about the women he believes Bill Clinton raped.

Ed told us he engages in extreme behavior on social media because it is cathartic and helps him cope with social isolation. But it was also clear from speaking with him that such behavior gives him a powerful sense of status.[8] During our interview he repeatedly mentioned that he had "a couple thousand" followers, and he was particularly proud to count several prominent conservative leaders among them. When I analyzed Ed's social media account several months later, however, I discovered that he only had about two hundred followers. What is more, the high-profile conservatives he thought were following him were actually people with copycat accounts. For Ed and many of the other political extremists we interviewed, social media enables a kind of microcelebrity—even if his influence was exaggerated, or even if many of his followers did not seem like real people who were genuinely interested in his views. Another extremist we interviewed likened the effect of such status to substance abuse: it makes you feel better about yourself, even if you know it might be bad for you.

Besides earning status from people on their own side, many of the extremists we interviewed simply delighted in getting other people worked up. Our ability to influence others, however artificially or temporarily, is valuable to people who feel that they have very little control over their own lives. A team of political scientists in the United States and Denmark conducted a series of studies in both countries to determine who spreads political rumors or fake news online.[9] What they found was somewhat surprising: the people who spread such falsehoods were not simply motivated to see their own side win; rather, the researchers found they have a need for chaos—a desire to see the entire system suffer. This need, the scholars speculated, emerges from the experience of marginalization itself—something I saw very clearly in the case of Ed, Jamie, and most of the other political extremists we interviewed.

The Troll You Did Not Know

One thing that distinguished Ed from the other extremists we interviewed is that he did not hide his online extremism. This was certainly not the case for Ray White, whose Twitter feed contains such vile content that it made me wish I'd chosen another kind of book to write. The content is so vile, in fact, that you might want to skip this paragraph if you are squeamish like me. When you visit Ray's Twitter page, which does not mention his real name, the first thing you see is a lot of shit. Unfortunately, I mean that literally: human excrement. The post that caught my eye first was a meme that depicted a refuse collection truck with a long, snaking hose connected to a portable toilet on one side and a picture of Obama's face on the other. As I quickly scrolled down, things got even worse. Hillary Clinton and influential liberal members of congress such as Nancy Pelosi and Alexandria Ocasio-Cortez were all surrounded by shit or pictured performing sexual acts in meme after meme.[10] I quickly closed the page, disgusted. Why on earth would anyone do that? When my stomach was strong enough, I returned to Ray's timeline and discovered that he shared an average of ten posts a day that contain some painstakingly photoshopped liberal and the occasional moderate Republican like Mitt Romney—mixed in for good measure, I suppose.

Now here's the part that might surprise you. Though Ray's online behavior was by far the most reprehensible of anyone in our study, he was one of the most polite and deferential people we interviewed. The first person who interviewed him on our research team was a female graduate student. He addressed her throughout the phone call as "miss," and went out of his way to condemn political incivility. Describing Democrats, he said, "I avoid getting into conversations with them, because I know what it's going to lead to. Just screaming and arguing. . . . I don't like to argue with people, because my father, God rest his soul, taught me something many, many moons ago when I was a young boy. He said, 'Son, in life, [there are] two things never to discuss with people in public.' I said, 'Dad, what's that?' 'Number one, politics. Number two, religion.'" Despite his reprehensible social media posts, he told us in a later interview: "I'm the kind of person that—you don't need to use vulgarity, profanity, racial comments toward somebody, to get your point across. . . . I don't like that." Even though non-White Democrats were Ray's most frequent target on social media, he also went out of his way to distance himself from racists. "I grew up in the city," he told us. "Most of my friends were African American, Spanish, Latin, Chinese, Korean. We all got along like brothers. Racism, to me . . . I don't want to go off on a tangent here on that. . . . It's despicable."

The first time I listened to the audio recording of our interview with Ray, I was taken aback. This could not be the same guy whose Twitter timeline made me question my decision to write this book. "There must have been some type of data merging error," I thought to myself. But after remerging the data several times, I concluded that there was no mistake. "Maybe he was trolling our survey firm," I wondered. After all, Jamie—the liberal troll we met at the beginning of this chapter—had told our survey firm that he was a strong Republican. Maybe Ray had filled in someone else's Twitter account to protest an attempt to invade his privacy. I returned to Ray's Twitter feed to investigate. His Twitter biography described the same job he had mentioned in our interviews with him. He followed several small organizations listed within his ZIP code. And most tellingly, his tweets contained several of the same distinctive sayings he used in our interviews.

Having convinced myself that the interviewee really was Ray, I immediately returned to the interview transcript, searching for one of my favorite questions we asked our study participants: "If I were to look at your social media accounts but never meet you in person, do you think that I would get a good sense of who you are?" Ray's answer was "Absolutely." Ray, I realized, was hiding in plain sight. When we asked him later in the interview to reflect on the differences between his encounters with Democrats in real life and on social media, he told us that sometimes he'll have polite conversations with people he works with in his office, "but [later] that night . . . they'll be online . . . and they turn [from] Dr. Jekyll [into] Mr. Hyde and start using all kinds of abrasive, vulgar, obscene language that they can't use in the office, but they'll do it online." "Imagine if his coworkers saw *his* social media page," I thought to myself. Ray continued: "There's a lot of people that get on [social media] and do this. You want to know why? They're lonely. They're looking for attention. So they can't get attention in their town, or they go out to a bar or tavern and can't meet somebody. So they get online, and they express their frustration online, and when people respond to it, this makes them happy . . . and I say, 'What's wrong with some of these people? What the hell are they thinking about?'" That lonely person expressing frustration online? It turns out to be Ray. Reviewing the demographic data that he provided to our survey firm and real estate records, I discovered that Ray is a single, middle-aged office manager who lives with his eighty-five-year-old mother. Like many of the other extremists we interviewed, Ray had created an entirely different world for himself online.

The Cult of Extremism

Another thing that surprised me as I continued to compare the online and off-line behavior of political extremists was how carefully they coordinated activities with each other. One troll we interviewed told us about a list of extreme conservatives who pledge to follow each other. "They'll send a list of what we call patriots, like-minded people," he told us. "MAGA ["Make America Great Again"] people, whatever. . . . And I'll go through a list and follow people, and people follow me back. It's kind of a circle that goes around." This phenomenon was not limited to conservative extremists. For example, we interviewed an extreme liberal from Texas who told us about a secret Facebook group he organizes for liberals who live in his conservative region of the state. The group boasts more than three hundred people, he said, and some members "meet for lunch once a month in the capital." The group does not engage in very uncivil behavior, he explained, but it does provide a very meaningful sense of belonging for people who feel ostracized for their political views.[11]

I also learned that extremists bond with each other by launching coordinated attacks on people with opposing political views. Though it may seem that social media extremists are most concerned with taking down the other side through superior argumentation—ideally laced with wry humor or sarcasm—my research suggests that these attacks also serve a ritual function that pushes extremists closer together. During multiple periods in our research, I observed extremists ganging up on each other. I had a unique window into this process, since several of the extremists we interviewed were among the users we paid to follow bots that exposed them to opinion leaders with opposing views. During our bot studies, I set up notifications on my phone to alert me every time anyone interacted with our bots, so that I could monitor the study in real time. On many occasions I observed both conservative and liberal extremists reply to a message that our bots had retweeted with a snide or abusive comment, only to watch others in the study pile on. This happened so often that three of the most extreme conservatives in our study began following each other. The trio teamed up to attack many of the messages our liberal bot retweeted for an entire week, often pushing each other to make increasingly extreme criticism as time passed.

This type of behavior underscores a common theme I observed among all of the political extremists we interviewed. Though many spend long hours attacking the other side online—including one man who replied angrily or sarcastically to 107 of the tweets our bot made over one month—they know they are not changing anyone's mind. For example, the same troll who replied to so many of our bot's tweets recounted one of his most recent arguments on Twitter. The argument was about the death of a migrant girl in U.S. custody from dehydration at the Mexican border. Though many liberals on Twitter were blaming the Trump administration for failing to provide adequate care for the child, our respondent blamed the girl's mother: "Everybody's playing [this] like it's our fault that the parent took the girl over a desert and she got sick and died. Even though they airlifted her to the hospital and everything else, they couldn't save her. And suddenly, it's America's fault." Though he spent multiple days arguing with liberals about this issue, he recognized that his efforts to influence them were futile: "I have to respond to something like that because it's ridiculous. Not that it's going to matter, because the people who believe it's our fault are going to believe it's our fault no matter what the evidence is." We heard similar stories from nearly every political extremist we interviewed. Partisan warfare, it seemed, is often more about status signaling and bonding than persuading others.

The interviews and quantitative surveys we conducted, as well as years of social media content produced by the people in our study, also allowed me to probe deeper into how such bonding occurs. Interestingly, several of the extremists we interviewed were political converts. "I supported Hillary Clinton for her first run as president," a conservative extremist named Sandy Brown told us. "When she didn't get the nomination, I voted for Barack Obama because I thought it would be good for the country to have some Black representation and heal racial wounds. . . . He sounded intelligent, caring, rational." But she quickly regretted this decision: "I followed him. I supported him, and I think the turning point for me was when he turned against the police and created a racial divide in the country. That basically was the breaking point for me to start questioning . . . why do things never change no matter who I vote for? I've been voting for forty years. Things are just getting worse, and I could see it. I could see the country going downhill. That's when I started going online and looking for new information." A close inspection of her Twitter feed from years before we met her revealed that Sandy had initially made some mildly critical posts about Obama, after he criticized the leaders of Ferguson, Missouri, where Michael Brown Jr.—an unarmed Black man— was shot by local police officers. Though her previous Twitter posts received little or no response, her criticism about Obama went viral among conservatives. Suddenly, her posts were garnering dozens of likes, and she attracted many new followers as well. The more critical she became, the more engagement she received. Midway through Obama's second term, Sandy had moved to the Republican side of the aisle.[12] Two years after Trump's election, she had become one of his most ardent defenders, even adding MAGA ("Make America Great Again") to her Twitter handle.

Even if most extremists weren't apostates, many of them engaged in another purification ritual: attacking moderates on their own side. A good example of this is Ellen Cohen, a forty-nine-year-old real estate agent from Newark, New Jersey, who is a passionate vegan and environmentalist. Like many extreme liberals, Ellen follows some prominent conservatives to push back against their messages. However, Ellen told us, "I can't really follow Kellyanne Conway . . . because I want to punch her in the face." Some of Ellen's most extreme anger is reserved for Democrats who criticized her preferred presidential candidate in the 2020 campaign. She told us that moderate Democrats had "sabotaged Bernie Sanders's opportunity to get the nomination." "That was very disappointing," she told us, "because I think that's what caused us to be stuck with Trump." Deeply embedded in a network of vegan activists on Twitter, Ellen routinely chastised members of her own party who did not share her views on animals. These types of attacks were even more common among the conservative extremists we studied, who routinely attacked anyone who criticized Trump—such as Justin Amash, a Republican member of the House of Representatives who left his party and decided not to run for reelection in 2020.

The symbolic meaning of the bonds that extremists make with each other became even more apparent to me when I learned how closely extremists monitor their followers. Though social media sites do not alert users when people stop following them, several of the extremists we interviewed used third-party apps to identify such individuals. People who unfollowed the extremists we studied—particularly several of the conservative extremists—were often subject to even more aggressive attacks than the moderates I just described. For me, this type of retribution further underscores how deeply trolls value the status and influence they achieve online, and how much it upsets them when people on their own side sever ties with them.

The more I delved into communities of political extremists on social media, the more they seemed to have cult-like dynamics. As the famed sociologist Max Weber noted more than a hundred years ago, most extreme religious groups exist in constant tension with established mainstream churches.[13] Proving one's membership in a cult often becomes a sort of ritual in which members reward each other for take increasingly extreme positions to prove their loyalty to the cause.[14] For Sandy, the former Obama voter who became an ardent Trump supporter, this required frequent rehearsal of her conservative bona fides. For Ellen, this often takes the form of attacking other Democrats for policies that—in her view—are scarcely different from those of her true enemy: Republicans. For still others, it means attacking extremists who challenge their loyalty to their side more forcefully than anyone else. In each of these cases, my research indicates that political extremists are pushed and pulled toward increasingly radical positions by the likes, new follows, and other types of engagement they receive for doing so—or because they fear retribution for showing any sympathy toward the mainstream. These types of behavior mirror the famous finding of the social psychologist Leon Festinger about a doomsday cult from the 1950s: the further people become committed to radical views, the more difficult these commitments become to undo, and the more people come to rely on the status and support system that cults create.[15]

Extremism through the Prism

One of the key functions of the social media prism, as I argued in chapter 4, is that it reflects the social landscape back to us. But in so doing, the prism inevitably distorts what we see, and for many people it creates a delusional form of self-worth. The type of uncivil behavior I described in this chapter results from this process, taken to its extreme. Many people with strong partisan views do not participate in such destructive behavior. But the people who do often act this way because they feel marginalized, lonely, or disempowered in their off-line lives. Social media offer such social outcasts another path. Even if the fame extremists generate has little significance beyond small groups of other outcasts, the research my colleagues and I conducted suggests that social media give extremists a sense of purpose, community, and—most importantly—self-worth.

The social media prism pushes extremists to adopt increasingly radical positions via two interrelated processes. First, it normalizes extremism. As extremists get dragged deeper into the status-seeking, gang-like behavior described in this chapter, the majority of their interactions are with people who share their extreme views. Over time, this type of repeated exposure creates what the sociologist Robert Merton once called "the fallacy of unanimity": extremists begin to think that most people share their unusual views. But in addition to distorting extremists' understanding of themselves, the prism bends the identities of people on the other side too.[16] More specifically, the social media prism makes people from the opposing party seem more extreme than they really are. When extremists go on the attack, they often do battle with the most extreme members of the other side. Just as the prism normalizes extremism on one's own side, it also thus exaggerates the extremism of the other side—a phenomenon that the political scientist Jaime Settle also observed in her large-scale study of Facebook users.[17] Unfortunately, these two types of distortion combine to create feedback loops of extremism. At the same time that the prism makes one's own extremism seem reasonable—or even normal—it makes the other side seem more aggressive, extreme, and uncivil.

The power of the social media prism to create and sustain communities of extremists is deeply concerning. But what about everyone else? In the next chapter I'll explain why the most pernicious effects of the prism operate upon the far larger group of social media users who are appalled by online extremism and eager to find middle ground.

6

How the Prism Mutes Moderates

IT'S MID-2017, and Sara Rendon is up late, scrolling through her Twitter feed after coaxing her two young children to go to bed. She pauses on a post by someone complaining about the National Rifle Association. "My dad was a cop," she told us. "And I grew up in a house with guns. . . . I was fortunate to have someone who was highly trained to use [them]." Sara is now in her thirties and married to an accountant who owns a gun and periodically visits a local shooting range: "I posted something about how my husband had a gun that he uses for a hobby . . . not saying that there shouldn't be any regulation whatsoever, but just [that it's] people's right to own them." Within minutes, Sara's phone lit up with notifications from Twitter: "People started posting terrible things . . . like horrible things. . . . Someone said they were going to report me to child protection services because we had guns in the house." Then, things got much worse: "Someone [told me] they hoped my daughter found our gun and shot me."

The experience left a deep impression on Sara. "It was really pretty upsetting," she told us. "I'm pretty thick skinned . . . I'm from New York. . . . We yell at each other all the time," she explained. "But when it came to stuff with my kids I was like, 'I'm not dragging them into this.'" Sara was particularly worried about the safety of her family: "I was afraid that if people went back in my [social media] history, I might've said something that gave away where we lived . . . and I didn't wanna take that chance." So she deactivated her Twitter account—eventually re-opening it as a protected account so she could control who follows her and who reads her posts. "I don't mean to sound like a martyr," she said. "It's kind of the risk that you take in a way when you put stuff out there. You know people are going to reply. . . . There's always going to be trolls, I'm used to some trolling." But when she worked up the courage to make her account public again a few months later, she quickly regretted doing so. After a very liberal person attacked one of her tweets, she looked at the user's profile and saw that she had survived breast cancer. "I responded and said, you know, I'm sorry you had breast cancer. . . . I had a double mastectomy myself. . . . And she [the user] wrote back, 'I hope you die.' So I was like, 'oh, that's nice' . . . that's the kind of conversations that take place on social media. It's why minds don't get changed."

Sara describes herself as a moderate Republican. "I've never been a party liner," she explained. Being raised by a father whose parents were from Puerto Rico and a Jewish mother made her particularly sensitive to the plight of immigrants and ethnic minority groups. "My grandparents came here from Puerto Rico," she told us. "They were not illegal immigrants, they were citizens. But they did not speak English. . . . And they were really taken advantage of. My grandmother worked in a sweatshop in New York City." Sara also witnessed unfair working conditions when she worked at a restaurant during high school to save money for college: "Tons of illegal immigrants worked there, and they were really hardworking, good people. . . . And they really got taken advantage of by the restaurant owner. . . . I saw people get injured and get fired for getting injured." In Sara's view, the current immigration system is a "disservice to the immigrants." "I wish there was a way for more of them to come here legally," she told us, "and not have to be . . . in the shadows."

Sara's income from the restaurant came in handy when she won admission to a prestigious Ivy League university. There, she was exposed to a range of new ideas that challenged the conservative ideals she had inherited from her parents. Unlike many Republicans, Sara's preferred source of news became the *New York Times*, and she often reads the *New Yorker*—a left-leaning magazine—as well. "I don't always agree with them politically," she said, but like many moderate Republicans, she has liberal views on social issues. She wishes that Republicans would spend less time focusing on the so-called traditional family and attacking gay people, for example. She also supports civil rights for people who identify as transsexual. Despite her Catholic upbringing, she even supports a woman's right to choose. However, the experience of college not only left her with a new worldview but also a mountain of debt. "It's a vicious cycle," she complained. "My dad being a police officer. We were pretty squarely middle class in a state with a very high cost of living . . . we didn't qualify for a ton of financial aid."

One of the main reasons Sara identifies as a Republican is because she believes her party does a better job of addressing the issues that people like her care about—specifically, the economy. She does not need to worry about money anymore: her family income is now around $200,000, and she lives in a comfortable Maryland suburb. Still, she thinks that Democrats want to take the country down the wrong path. "The Democratic Party focuses a lot on issues that I consider kind of diversionary," she told us. "I wanna talk about the economy. I have kids—I wanna think about my husband keeping his job, and I wanna think about saving for their college education." She found debates about racial bias in policing particularly divisive, especially given her father's career and her multiracial identity. But she was also annoyed by Robert Mueller's investigation of President Trump. "I have a couple of friends who are just obsessed with the idea that Russia is responsible for everything that happens in this country," she explained. "And I'm like, 'Oh, give me a break. . . . If Russia is as powerful as you seem to think, we all have problems.'" Over the years, Sara has learned not to wade into arguments with liberal friends from college. Their complaints about Trump aggravate her, she explains. "But I don't usually respond to it because there's nothing that I can say . . . that will ever convince them."

Sara ultimately unfriended most of her liberal acquaintances from college on social media, but she does not feel that this is an option for family members who do not share her worldview: "I want to be in touch with [my family members] because they still live in New York and I wanna see pictures of their kids and stuff. I won't unfollow them. But then when I see their posts, I get irritated." "I can't say anything for the sake of family harmony," she explained. One family member is particularly challenging: "My aunt, who I really like . . . she's extremely liberal . . . she hates Trump. And every time I see her, she has to make some kind of comment [about] how she doesn't know how anybody could have voted for a sexual assaulter and I'm just like, 'I should tolerate Vivian, I'm not gonna go there.'" But things heated up after the controversy surrounding the nomination of Brett Kavanaugh to the Supreme Court. On social media, her aunt posted, "No wonder we're putting a rapist in the Supreme Court when there's a rapist in the White House." This upset Sara deeply: "I'm like, 'I'm sorry. If that's the way that you really feel, I don't need to be connected with you on social media, because I think [it's] unhinged to call people who have never been convicted of any crime rapists.'" Eventually, the experience provoked Sara to unfriend several other liberal family members as well. She told us: "That was a dark period. . . . So what I finally decided—and I spoke to my husband about it, actually—[is that] I have to delete these people because I care about them, and it will damage my relationship [with them] permanently if I keep seeing them say things like this."

These complex social relationships mean that Sara is a very different person online and off. When we asked her if one would get a good sense of who she is as a person by studying her social media accounts, she said, "I don't think so." "I don't write that many tweets of my own," she explained. "It's mostly just things that I share—that I find interesting. And I think it would be a very limited snapshot, because it wouldn't be anything that I'm saying about myself." Given her many difficult experiences with liberal friends and family members, Sara's moderate political views—which are very important to her—are almost completely hidden on social media. "I still post political things sometimes," she explained, but most of her timeline is now filled with details about her other interests and hobbies. "I think that's just like a more positive use of [social media]," she told us. "Because politics . . . can be exhausting on social media."

The Moderate Majority

Do parts of Sara's story sound familiar? If so, you—like her—may be among the majority of Americans who could be defined as political moderates. Though measuring people's political views is the subject of much controversy among social scientists like me, one of the most common ways we identify them is to ask people to place themselves on a seven-point scale that ranges from extremely liberal to extremely conservative.[1] This measure has been tracked for decades by the American National Election Study and other large, nationally representative surveys. In 2016, only 3 percent of Americans identified themselves as "extremely liberal," and another 3 percent identified themselves as "extremely conservative." In contrast, a strong plurality of Americans (47 percent) said that they were "moderate," "slightly liberal," or "slightly conservative."[2] These figures are even more revealing when one recognizes that nearly one in five Americans told researchers that they either "didn't know" what their ideology was or "had not thought about it." Social media can make it seem as though ideological polarization is growing rapidly, but rates of partisanship are actually fairly stable, and they appear more related to the ways in which the Republican and Democratic Parties have reorganized their policy platforms to appeal to different combinations of voters, rather than shifts in the opinions of voters.[3]

Sara's sympathy for immigrants is also not as rare among Republicans as some Democrats might think. In 2018, the American National Election Study asked whether "having an increasing number of people of many different races, ethnic groups and nationalities in the United States makes this country a better place to live."[4] Among Republicans, 38.9 percent agreed with this statement, 28.8 percent said the increasing number would "[make] no difference," and only 32.3 percent disagreed. The same survey also showed that most Republicans share Sara's belief that background checks for gun purchases should be mandatory: 66.2 percent of Republicans favored mandatory checks, 19 percent opposed them, and an additional 12.6 percent indicated they "don't know." Similarly, some Republicans might be surprised by how many Democrats have beliefs that are out of step with pervasive stereotypes about their party. More than three out of five Democrats have positive feelings toward the police and rural people, for example. I do not want to overstate similarities between Republicans and Democrats (on many issues, the two parties remain deeply divided), but it is fair to say that most Americans are not as extreme as one might think after spending an hour or two on social media.

Encounters with Extremists

Sara's stories about harassment on social media are also very common. In a survey fielded by the Pew Research Center in 2017, approximately one in four Americans reported that they had been harassed online, and three out of four said that they had witnessed others receiving such treatment.[5] According to the same report, nearly one in three Americans has witnessed someone being physically threatened online. Such attacks are particularly common against women, as the sociologist Sarah Sobieraj describes in her book *Credible Threat*.[6] The leading reason people gave in the Pew study for being harassed online was their political views. I took a look at these data to examine whether moderates experienced harassment at higher rates than extremists. Sure enough, I calculated that people who identified themselves as "moderate," "slightly liberal," or "slightly conservative" were about 40 percent more likely to report being harassed online than those who identified themselves as "extreme liberals" or "extreme conservatives."

As Sara's story shows—and as the stories of many other people we interviewed confirm—moderates often experience harassment from an extremist from the other party. Consider, for example, the experience of Pete Jackman. Pete is a middle-aged accountant who works for a government agency in a large office building in rural Ohio. His passions include hockey, college football, and video games (which he enjoys playing with his young children). On social media, he mostly follows athletes, celebrities, and sports pundits. He describes himself as a "not very strong Democrat," and like most moderates, he does not take strong stances on most issues. As he likes to put it, "there's his side, her side, and the truth." Pete leans toward the left because he is very concerned about his young children becoming victims of a mass school shooting, and he is also somewhat concerned about climate change. But he takes conservative positions on several issues: for example, he is very concerned about illegal immigration, and he thinks that the effects of racial discrimination are overstated. He also gave Trump credit for his handling of the economy during his first few years in office.

Pete is no fan of Republicans, however—not simply because he is disenchanted about politics, but also because of an experience he had on Facebook shortly before we met him. "My cousin," he told us, "normally doesn't talk much about [politics], but lately he has been going off on Republicans. He's really upset with the current direction of things and hasn't been afraid of voicing it." The cousin's online activism hadn't gone unnoticed in their small Ohio town. "He's actually lost a friend because of it," Pete told us, ". . . but that hasn't stopped him from saying how he feels." One evening, Pete's cousin got into an argument on the public Facebook page of a local news organization with a conservative man from their area about school shootings. Pete's cousin was arguing that high school teachers should not be allowed to wield guns in their classrooms. After exchanging some unpleasantries with Pete's cousin, the conservative posted a picture of what appeared to be his hand, holding a gun. "'You need to shut the fuck up, or you're going to see how this thing works,'" Pete said, paraphrasing the man. "That really upset me."

Like most moderates, Pete has relatively little exposure to politics online—and even less exposure to Republicans. For this reason, the threat his cousin received left a deep impression on Pete. Like so many of the moderates we interviewed (on both sides), Pete's encounters with extremists from the other party have shaped his views of Republicans more broadly. The social media prism thus exerts profound influence upon a phenomenon that social scientists call false polarization.[7] This term refers to the tendency for people to overestimate the amount of ideological differences between themselves and people from other political parties. As a 2016 study by the political scientists Matthew Levendusky and Neil Malhotra shows, people tend to exaggerate the ideological extremism of the other party while underestimating that of their own party.[8] The same pattern appeared in a nationally representative survey conducted by the Pew Research Center. Even though data I showed above from the American National Election Study indicated that only 3 percent of Americans identified themselves as either "extremely liberal" or "extremely conservative," the Pew study found that 55 percent of Republicans think Democrats are "extremely liberal," and 35 percent of Democrats think that Republicans are "extremely conservative."[9]

As the stories of Pete and many others we interviewed illustrates, false polarization can be driven by online experiences in which a minority of extremists come to represent a more moderate majority. I broke down data from the Pew study that I just described to compare people who listed social media as their preferred source of news and those who did not. I found that the partisan perception gap—that is, the extent to which people exaggerated the ideological extremism of people from the other party—was significantly larger among those who used social media to get their news.[10] The link between social media usage and false polarization is also driven by the fact that extremists post far more often than moderates. A 2019 report from Pew showed that a small group of people is responsible for most political content on Twitter. Specifically, this report found that "prolific political tweeters make up just 6% of all Twitter users but generate 20% of all tweets and 73% of tweets mentioning national politics."[11] What is more, extremists represented nearly half of all prolific political tweeters. Though people with extreme views constitute about 6 percent of the U.S. population, the Pew report found that "55% of prolific political tweeters identify as very liberal or very conservative."[12]

There is even more evidence that people who use social media tend to develop more inaccurate perceptions of the beliefs and behaviors of those in the other party. Communications scholar Matthew Barnidge polled a representative sample of Americans about their social media usage and political views in 2015.[13] He found that people who use social media frequently perceive significantly more political disagreement in their daily lives than those who do not. In her study of political polarization on Facebook, the political scientist Jaime Settle observed a similar phenomenon. She showed people sample Facebook posts on a range of topics and discovered that the participants were far more likely to exaggerate the ideological extremity of people from the other political party than their own party.[14] In a separate analysis, Settle examined how social network structure shapes false polarization. Interestingly, she found that the amount of perceived polarization grows as the social distance between people increases. If people have no direct connections on social media— such as being a friend of another person's friend—they tend to perceive each other as even more polarized than those who have direct connection.

Moderates Have Too Much to Lose

Extremists, I've argued, turn to social media because it provides them with a sense of status that they lack in their everyday lives, however artificial such status might be. But for moderates like Sara and Pete, the opposite is often true. Posting online about politics simply carries more risk than it's worth. Such moderates are keenly aware that what happens online can have important consequences off-line. For example, Pete is a happily married man who gets along well with his in-laws and has a solid government job with extensive benefits. But, he said, "they basically tell you when you're hired . . . if you post to social media and you make disparaging comments about political figures, you can be fired." Though Pete often gets upset about gun control issues, he never voices his opinions online. "Because as you go up the chain," he explained to us, "Donald Trump is actually my boss. He's my ultimate boss, and I can be fired if I say negative things about him."

After his cousin was threatened by the gun-wielding extremist I described earlier in this chapter, Pete was torn. He strongly agreed with the points his cousin was making about school shootings, he explained, "but I can't even like it [his cousin's post] . . . or anything like that—even put an emoji or anything—because I'm afraid of how that will come back on me." He added, "I wanted to get involved, . . . [but] I just knew it was best for me not to—[even though] it was so hard for me not to." Pete noted that multiple people at work have been ostracized for expressing political opinions online. One woman, he told us, had stopped sitting with another of their colleagues at lunch after this person shared a post endorsing Hillary Clinton on Facebook. Pete is so concerned about his job that he even stopped following anyone on social media who is overtly political. "I'll still talk about [politics] with my family and even with my friends," he explained, but the only thing he wants people to learn about him from his social media profile is his passion for hockey and a popular jock-rock band from the 1990s.

In addition to having concerns about their livelihoods, many of the moderates we interviewed were worried that discussing politics on social media would upset their family members or friends. It turns out that most people have a connection like Sara's Aunt Vivian—a family member or friend who has starkly different views about politics than their own. In a 2016 Pew survey, 53 percent of Facebook users reported having connections to people who share a "mix of political views."[15] An additional 5 percent of people say that most of those in their online networks have political beliefs that differ from their own. Like Sara, the vast majority of people do their best to ignore posts about politics from people in their network with whom they do not agree. According to the same Pew survey, 83 percent of social media users do not engage with this type of message. Once again, when I took a closer look at these data, I saw that these proportions were even higher among political moderates. Many social media users also block, mute, or unfriend "Aunt Vivians," as Sara did. Roughly four in ten Americans have taken such actions against people in their social media networks after seeing posts about politics, according to the Pew survey. Among these, 60 percent said that the content offended them (as Aunt Vivian's frequent labeling of Trump as a rapist offended Sara), and 43 percent said that the offenders simply posted too much political content.

Political moderates also get pressure from their own side. Remember that extremists reserve much of their vitriol for people in their own party. For example, many moderate liberals have experienced harassment from people like Ellen, the extreme vegan I profiled in the previous chapter who regularly takes members of her own party to task for eating meat—or even supporting large-scale farming. And many moderate conservatives report being rebuked immediately when they criticize Trump—even in the mildest manner. This type of pressure not only comes from extremists whom moderates don't know, but also from members of their offline social network. While some people have an "Aunt Vivian" whose opinions they don't like, still others have a relative or friend from their own political party who has extreme views. Reaching across the aisle can jeopardize these relationships too.

Moderates Feel Hopeless

Not every moderate social media user enjoys a charmed life offline. Derek Hunter is a gay Black man in his mid-fifties who lives in Richmond, Virginia. His mother passed away when he was young, and he and his two siblings were raised by his grandmother in a poor town in Alabama. Describing his childhood, Derek told us, "It was about being respectful and [being] good kids. . . . You know, we did our homework." Despite his hard work, Derek was not able to attend college, opting for a career in the military instead. "I didn't really learn about politics until I left the state of Alabama," he told us, "when I grew up and joined the military." After serving his country, Derek held a series of jobs in warehouses and customer service. But he kept getting passed over for promotions. "It wasn't that I wasn't qualified," he explained, "it was just the color of my skin—and I know that's what it was, and I've dealt with this all my life."

Though Derek has suffered from racial discrimination throughout his career, he subscribes to an explanation of racial inequality that is popular among conservatives: that Black people earn less money because they hold themselves back. "The only threat I am is to myself," Derek told us. "If I choose not to do something that's going to get me ahead, that's on me." He also said: "A lot of black people are in fear of going to places because they think, 'They ain't going to hire me anyway . . . they ain't going to help me anyway because I'm black.' Well, if you get your black voice heard, somebody *will* help you." Derek identifies as a Democrat, but he takes conservative positions on some issues. He believes that the United States has accepted too many immigrants: "They take jobs. They take housing. I know some that get housing for free, food for free. . . . They come in and get all those benefits, and that takes away from the people who are already here—because there are a lot of people here who can't get those benefits, and they end up homeless." Derek's military background also instilled in him a strong respect for authority and for law and order.

But Derek has also suffered harrowing discrimination from police officers. "There's an apartment complex I was living in, and somebody broke into one of the apartments one night," he told us. "I called the police." The woman who had been robbed asked him to wait for the police officer, and he agreed. But "the officer comes up, draws his gun on me, tells me to get down on the ground. I was like, 'Sir, I just called you.'" When the police asked him to provide a statement to help with their investigation the next day, he told them "'no.' I said, 'Because y'all treated me like a criminal and now you want me to help you . . . would you have done something different if I was a White guy?' It was just ridiculous to me." On another occasion, Derek told us, he went through a traffic light near his apartment just as it was turning red. A police officer saw him, he explained: "He comes up behind my car on the right side with his gun drawn. . . . I was so nervous." It was not his first terrifying traffic stop. "I know to keep my hands on the steering wheel," he explained, but "I was afraid that his gun might actually go off." Despite this horrendous experience, Derek still has respect for police. He had been treated rudely by Black police officers during traffic stops as well, he explained, though they had not drawn their weapons. Derek also criticized protestors who rioted after a police officer shot Keith Lamont Scott—an unarmed Black man—in Charlotte, North Carolina, two years earlier.

But you won't read anything about Derek's views about policing on social media. And that's not because Derek does not post to social media very often: in fact, he's been using Facebook, Twitter, or Instagram each day for years. It's also not because Derek doesn't care about politics. He once volunteered to work on a local politician's election campaign. It's because Derek thinks that posting negative content about politics on social media is pointless. He thinks that social media users who believe that others care about their political views are kidding themselves. "It's like an imagination playground," he joked. It is completely understandable that Derek does not talk about his frightening experiences with the police on social media, but if more people could hear his story, it would add critical depth to the public debate about race and policing that sometimes appears to have no middle ground.

The Missing Moderates

Derek is not the only political moderate who feels that discussing politics on social media is pointless. According to a 2019 Pew Study, 46 percent of "adult social media users say they feel 'worn out' by the number of political posts and discussions they see on social media."[16] This number was up from 37 percent in 2016, and moderates were more likely to report being worn out than others during 2019.

Regardless of their political party, most moderates never discuss politics online. According to a 2019 Pew study of Twitter users, "the median user never tweeted about national politics, while 69% only tweeted about it once or not at all. Across all tweets from U.S. adults, just 13% focused on national politics."[17] And as I mentioned above, these people are mostly extremists.[18] This phenomenon is not limited to Twitter users, either. According to my analysis of data from a 2016 Pew survey, moderates are two to three times less likely than extremists to "comment, post, or discuss government and politics with others on social media," regardless of which sites they use.[19]

What does it mean that moderates are missing from social media discussions about politics? In my view, this is the most profound form of distortion created by the social media prism. We see extreme conservatives applauding the Trump administration's decision to separate children from their parents at the U.S.-Mexico border but not the sizable group of Republicans who found the practice "completely appalling"—to use the words of a gun enthusiast from South Dakota whom we interviewed. Or we see extreme liberals doxing the students from Covington High School featured in the 2019 viral video that appeared to show them harassing an elderly Native American man. But we don't see the left-leaning high school teacher from Kansas we interviewed who was extremely upset that people were encouraging the harassment of children and shocked that left-leaning media outlets did not apologize more loudly after it was discovered the students themselves had been harassed before the encounter.

Instead, the social media prism makes the other side appear monolithic, unflinching, and unreasonable. While extremists captivate our attention, moderates can seem all but invisible. Moderates disengage from politics on social media for several different reasons. Some do so after they are attacked by extremists. Others are so appalled by the breakdown in civility that they see little point to wading into the fray. Still others disengage because they worry that posting about politics might sacrifice the hard-fought status they've achieved in their off-line lives. Challenging extremists can come back to haunt moderates, disrupting their livelihoods, friendships, or relationships with family members they will see every year at Thanksgiving. For moderates, such interpersonal contact enables people like Sara to understand that Aunt Vivian does not really think that everyone who voted for Trump hates women or condones sexual assault—even if Sara still can't accept her aunt's calling for Trump's ouster without substantial evidence that he committed a crime. Unfortunately, as I'll discuss in the next chapter, such opportunities for mutual understanding are few and far between in an age of rapidly increasing social isolation. As Republicans and Democrats continue to sort themselves into separate ZIP codes, pastimes, and social circles, I worry that the power of the social media prism to fuel extremism and mute moderates will only continue to grow.

7

Should I Delete My Account?

JARON LANIER MAKES an immediate impression. He has long, unkempt dreadlocks that hang below his waist and intense eyes that appear to pop out of his head when he gets worked up about an idea. At age sixty, Lanier has more than four decades of experience in the tech world. He began taking college-level classes in computer science at the age of thirteen, and he founded one of the first virtual reality companies in the 1980s. He is also a prolific writer, social critic, and all-around Renaissance man. In his mid-fifties, Lanier was listed as one of the world's most influential people by *Time*. In 2018, *Wired* featured him as one of the twenty-five most influential people in the technology scene. He has written three books that warn of the dark side of technology—particularly when it becomes yoked to the principles of neoliberal economics. Over the years, his work has appeared in the *New York Times* and *Wall Street Journal*, and he's made numerous appearances on popular television programs such as the *Colbert Report*, *Nightline*, and the *View*.

It is not surprising, then, that Lanier's latest book, *Ten Arguments for Deleting Your Social Media Accounts Right Now*, quickly became an international best seller.[1] As you might expect from the title, the book is a polemic that sets Facebook, Twitter, and Google squarely in its sights. In a far-ranging argument, Lanier argues that social media sites are robbing us of our free will, spreading falsehoods, decreasing our capacity for empathy, making us unhappy, polarizing us, and—perhaps most devastatingly—destroying our very souls. Lanier offers little evidence for these sweeping claims, but the appeal of his argument is obvious: Why do we do this to ourselves? Is social media a net positive, or a net negative? Most people, Lanier argues, would be better off without it.

The previous chapters of this book do not give much grounds for optimism, so let's take Lanier's provocation seriously: should we all delete our social media accounts immediately? Some people have already responded to this clarion call. In 2018, the Pew Research Center fielded one of the first surveys of Americans' relationships to social media platforms. Among the most attention-grabbing results from the survey were the following two figures: 42 percent of Facebook users took a break from the site during 2017–18, and 26 percent deleted the Facebook app from their phone during the same period.[2] These headlines rang loudly across the internet after Pew published its report. The hashtag #deletefacebook trended for several days on Twitter, indicating that this was one of the most widely discussed topics on the platform. A handful of celebrities announced their plans to delete their Facebook accounts, including the singer Cher; the comedian Will Ferrell; and Tesla's CEO, Elon Musk. Lanier's book was certainly not the only impetus for this movement. Facebook was embroiled in multiple controversies at the time—particularly the public relations nightmare created by the Cambridge Analytica affair (discussed in chapter 1)—and many people seemed fed up.

Meanwhile, social scientists were studying the sources of public dissatisfaction with our platforms.[3] In an unprecedented experiment, a group of economists recruited almost three thousand Americans over age eighteen who spent at least fifteen minutes using Facebook each day to complete a survey.[4] Later, the researchers offered half of these people $100 to deactivate their Facebook accounts for one month and carefully monitored those respondents to make sure they did not reactivate their accounts. The results added more fuel to the public relations fire engulfing Facebook at the time, since study participants who deactivated their accounts reported being happier—and, more importantly for our purposes, less angry toward members of the opposing political party.[5]

Despite all the fervor, Facebook emerged largely unscathed. The number of people who use Facebook frequently held steady from 2018 to 2019, according to a follow-up study by the Pew Research Center.[6] Google searches for "how to delete my Facebook account," which had surged, dropped to imperceptible levels after the peak of the movement in mid-2018. And shortly thereafter, searches for "how to undelete my Facebook account" soared. And what happened to the people paid by the researchers to stop using Facebook for a month? More than 95 percent of them returned to Facebook within the first hundred days after the study.[7] Moreover, a closer look at the 2018 Pew report I just described shows that most of the people who temporarily deactivated their Facebook accounts, or deleted the app from their phones, were young. Specifically, people ages 18–29 were four times more likely to report deleting their accounts than those ages 65 and older. Where these young people enlightened devotees of Lanier? Had they seen his viral *New York Times* video op-ed titled, "Jaron Lanier Fixes the Internet"?[8]

Evidently, the answers to both questions were no. Though millennials and members of Generation Z abandoned Facebook in droves, these young people were flocking to other platforms. Instagram usage surged. Twenty-six percent of all Americans used the platform in 2014, and this figure nearly doubled by 2019.[9] Among the members of Generation Z, these numbers are much higher: 72 percent of Americans ages 13–17 reported using Instagram in 2018, 69 percent reported using the chat platform Snapchat, and 51 percent remained on Facebook—perhaps to distract their parents from the risqué posts they produced on newer platforms such as TikTok, the video-sharing platform du jour at present.[10] How many of those people who fled Facebook for Instagram realized that the former acquired the latter in a major corporate takeover in 2018? Though the numbers of daily users of Facebook and Instagram may yet dwindle in the United States, both platforms continue to expand in other countries at a breakneck pace.

Breaking Up Is Hard to Do

Why do people have so much trouble leaving social media? For members of Generation Z, the answer is obvious: Not only did they grow up with the internet (like the millennials before them), but many of them never knew a world without social media. Most members of Generation Z don't remember the United States before it was awash with smartphones—many of them pointed toward young people, broadcasting their childhood in unprecedented detail. Maybe we should not be so surprised that this generation has become more deeply immersed in the internet and social media than any other. A 2018 Pew study found that 95 percent of U.S. teens had access to a smartphone, up from 73 percent four years earlier.[11] And they use those phones all the time. The same study revealed that 45 percent of teens use the internet "almost constantly" (up from 24 percent in 2014), and an additional 44 percent reported using it "several times a day." Ninety percent of U.S. teens also reported playing video games, and many of these now feature social networking components that allow users to play together on teams.[12]

For young people, leaving social media does not simply mean going back to the way things were—it means giving up their way of life.[13] Sara Rendon, the moderate young Republican described in chapter 6, briefly left social media after she was threatened by extremists for supporting her husband's right to bear arms. But she soon came back to Twitter and Facebook because she felt that they were the only way for her to get regular updates about her siblings, nieces, and nephews who lived far away. Other people interviewed for this book who took temporary leaves of absence from social media reported similar fears about missing out. Often this fear extends beyond friends and family members and into the social media communities where people spread information about their interests, hobbies, or fields of employment.

And while some people are sucked back in because they miss some type of social connection that social media create for them, others are pushed back onto platforms by friends, family members, or colleagues. Many people who try to leave social media are quickly reprimanded when they do not "like" or comment about posts in which they had been mentioned or tagged. Still others are criticized for not liking the accomplishments of their friends or empathizing with people in their lives who suffer a loss. People who delete their accounts are often also viewed as holier than thou—akin, perhaps, to the type of people who used to brag about not watching television when I was young. Still others are pushed back onto social media because of professional obligations. Maintaining an online presence has become increasingly important for succeeding in many different fields, especially among those who are self-employed or do not have large advertising budgets.

The most important reason we are not able to delete our accounts, I think, is what I've been arguing throughout this book. Social media have become so deeply woven into the fabric of our lives that they are beginning to shape our identities. Facebook, Twitter, and other platforms allow us to present different versions of ourselves; monitor how other people react to them with unprecedented speed and efficiency; and revise our identities accordingly. For tech apostates like Lanier, the source of our addiction is much more mundane: the endorphins that are released when we see bright flashy things on our screens, or the sheer convenience of purchasing consumer products that are usefully placed in our social media feeds. I don't completely disagree—Silicon Valley has clearly hacked some of the dopamine receptor channels in our brains—but I don't believe that quitting social media is like quitting smoking, as Lanier contends. Instead, deleting our accounts would require a fundamental reorganization of social life. Social media are now so much a part of our friendships, families, and professional lives that it would require unseen coordination to fight against these tools that satisfy our deepest social instincts so seamlessly.

"Okay," you may be thinking, "maybe we can't delete our accounts, but can't we still separate politics from the more warm and fuzzy parts of social media that keep us connected to family, or entertained by meme-worthy reality TV stars?" Once again, I fear the answer may be no. A growing number of people now rely upon social media as a source of news. In 2019, according to the Pew Research Center, 55 percent of American adults reported getting news from social media "often" or "sometimes," up from 47 percent in 2018.[14] And by 2018, social media had become a more popular source of news for Americans than printed newspapers.[15] Though television and radio remain the leading source of news for most Americans, social media are rapidly becoming the most popular news source for young people. Americans ages 18–29 are nearly twice as likely to get their news from social media, compared to those in older age brackets.[16] There is also considerable evidence that young people are repurposing Instagram and TikTok—originally designed to share beautiful images or humorous video clips—for political purposes.[17] In fact, one of the first studies of political communication on TikTok suggests its users make more political statements than those who use other platforms.[18]

Even if we set aside the question of whether people can stop discussing politics on social media, there is another daunting question: where else can such discussions occur? Social scientists have been warning about rapidly growing rates of social isolation for decades.[19] The sociologists Byungkyu Lee and Peter Bearman recently conducted a large-scale historical analysis of what they call "political isolation" in the United States.[20] They compared data from more than a dozen surveys fielded between 1985 and 2016 that asked Americans to list the names of people with whom they discussed politics. The researchers discovered that our political discussion networks have shrunk by approximately 30 percent over the past three decades. During the same period, the number of people in our discussion networks from different political parties has also decreased—even in networks where people discuss nonpolitical issues.

Broader demographic trends may help explain these shifts. In his influential book, *The Big Sort: Why the Clustering of Like-Minded America Is Tearing Us Apart*, the journalist Bill Bishop warned of rising geographic segregation between Republicans and Democrats. In 1976, he writes, 26 percent of Americans lived in counties where one party's candidate won a presidential election by more than twenty percentage points.[21] By 2014, that number exceeded 48 percent. Though some social scientists warn that Bishop's measures exaggerate the scale of this shift, there is also evidence of demographic segregation in other areas.[22] The political scientists Gregory Huber and Neil Malhotra looked for clues about political isolation by studying online dating.[23] These scholars not only discovered that people on a large online dating platform usually date members of their own party, but they also confirmed the finding of a study I mentioned in chapter 4: that people strongly prefer to date others from their own party.[24]

Even if Republicans and Democrats continue to sort themselves into different neighborhoods and dating circles, won't they still see each other at Thanksgiving—where Sara Rendon sees her Aunt Vivian each year? The economists Keith Chen and Ryne Rohla asked this question using physical location data collected via smartphones.[25] The researchers tracked the average length of time people spent at Thanksgiving dinner several weeks after the divisive 2016 presidential election in more than six million locations across the United States. They found that Thanksgiving dinners were 30–50 minutes shorter if they were attended by a mix of people from Republican- and Democratic-leaning voting precincts. These findings hold even after many other factors, such as distance traveled, were taken into account. All told, Chen and Rohla estimate that Americans lost thirty-four million hours of bipartisan Thanksgiving dinner discourse because families with heterogeneous political beliefs apparently had less patience for each other's views.

Much as it pains me to write this—given that I have spent so much of my career studying how social media platforms distort our politics—I think social media will remain the public square of American democracy for some time to come.

Why the Platforms Cannot Save Us by Themselves

If we can't delete our accounts, perhaps we can promote change from the inside out, lobbying Facebook, Twitter, and other platforms to combat polarization for us. Like Lanier, other Silicon Valley apostates have recently penned strongly worded indictments of the social media industry. Roger McNamee, a legendary technology investor and early advisor to Mark Zuckerberg, recently published *Zucked: Waking Up to the Facebook Catastrophe*. Nir Eyal, who made his reputation by publishing a guide for technology companies about building addictive technology recently wrote its antidote: *Indistractable: How to Control Your Attention and Choose Your Life*.[26] Similarly, Tristan Harris—a former Google employee who won acclaim for criticizing that company's focus on creating addictive technology—has launched an entire movement to force technology companies to stop robbing customers of their time, passions, and common sense by creating technology that creates a "race to the bottom" instead of a race to the top.[27]

These former Silicon Valley leaders argue that social media companies wield unimaginable power over human psychology. Social media platforms, they claim, are not only shaping what products we buy but also our most intimate thoughts and desires.[28] But do they really have the power to shape our innermost thoughts? Are we just simple dupes, victimized by algorithms or addictive platforms that control our beliefs and behavior without us knowing? People who are searching for scapegoats to blame for the deterioration of public debate may find these ideas seductive—and they are particularly compelling when they come from the same people who helped build the platforms. But why are we counting on the people who helped to create the problem to find the solution? Does working as a software engineer at a technology company really qualify you to explain how platforms shape our political views? A careful review of social science research suggests the answer is a resounding no.[29] There is very little evidence to support much of the popular wisdom about polarization on our platforms today that comes from inside Silicon Valley.

One popular idea, for example, is that radicalization on social media is driven by the algorithms that determine what appears in our news feeds. Because these algorithms are driven by user engagement—whether people click on one message and continue to click through to subsequent messages—they amplify extreme content that provokes angry responses. Even worse, critics argue, is that Silicon Valley companies do this unwittingly, since many algorithms are guided by deep learning—technology that can produce fairly accurate predictions about why someone might click on an ad. But these predictions are made through so many complex computations that the people who built them often cannot explain why they work.

The idea that algorithms are driving radicalization gained traction after several articles appeared about this issue in the *New*

York Times.[30] One of these articles tells the story of Caleb Cain, a liberal college dropout who went down a rabbit's hole of extremist content on YouTube, watching thousands of videos "filled with conspiracy theories, misogyny, and racism." The piece details how Cain was steadily transformed into a fully-fledged member of the far right who eventually purchased a handgun to protect himself after he began to receive death threats from liberals. Kevin Roose's article was particularly compelling because it included graphs of the young man's viewing history that allowed readers to see his shift from the extreme left to the extreme right. Google promptly rebutted the story, not only questioning the evidentiary basis for the author's claim, but also pointing to its efforts to prevent radicalization such as Jigsaw—a secretive unit within the company that it claims has prevented countless people from becoming violent extremists.

Though we should be very skeptical of responses from technology companies on this point, there is surprisingly little evidence to support the idea that algorithms facilitate radicalization. A large study of this issue by a group of computational social scientists found that some YouTube users advanced from moderate content to more extreme content, but the study estimated this happens to only 1 out of every 100,000 users.[31] Similarly, an earlier study of 10.1 million Facebook users concluded that the overwhelming majority of ideological segregation on this platform was driven by the individual decisions of users about what to engage with, rather than the algorithms that determined the order in which users see messages.[32] More recently, political scientists Kevin Munger and Joseph Phillips conducted an extensive analysis of radical political content on YouTube.[33] Though they discovered a large amount of such content in their analysis, they also found that most of the traffic to these videos came from new users—which suggests that radicalization may result from unmet demand for more extreme content, and not the radicalization of users. Even more surprisingly, Munger and Phillips showed that the most extreme content on YouTube has been viewed considerably less often in recent years.[34] Much more research on the relationship between algorithms and radicalization is needed—ideally using better data from social media companies—but for now machine learning does not seem to be a smoking gun.

Another popular criticism frequently leveled at Facebook, Twitter, and other social media platforms is that they failed to stop malicious foreign actors from spreading fake news and sowing discord. Though such criticisms are widespread—echoing across the floors of Congress and media studios around the world—there is actually very little evidence that these misinformation campaigns succeeded in dividing Americans. The political scientist David Lazer led a team of researchers who linked Twitter accounts to voter files (records that states keep about who is registered to vote). By merging these data, the researchers were able to estimate how many people encountered fake news during the 2016 campaign. Lazer's team estimated that less than 1 percent of Twitter users were exposed to 80 percent of the fake news that the team could identify, and that 0.1 percent of users were responsible for sharing 80 percent of such messages.[35] Another study by economists Hunt Allcott and Matthew Gentzkow found the average American saw—and remembered—approximately one fake news article in 2016.[36] A subsequent study by the political scientists Andrew Guess, Jonathan Nagler, and Joshua Tucker found similar patterns by linking a public opinion survey to a tool that tracked the browsing histories of survey respondents. The researchers found that only a small fraction of Facebook users shared fake news, and most of that news was shared by elderly conservatives.[37]

At the same time, it is possible that even a small amount of fake news could do a lot of damage. But there is not yet high quality evidence that interacting with messages from foreign misinformation campaigns actually makes people change their political views or behavior.[38] I assembled a team of researchers at Duke

University and the University of North Carolina at Chapel Hill to study the impact of accounts associated with the Russia-linked IRA identified by Twitter and U.S. intelligence sources.[39] We searched for these accounts in an extremely detailed data set that we created in 2017 that tracked the online behavior of more than 1,200 Americans and asked them two waves of questions about their political views. This allowed us to determine not only who interacted with trolls, but also whether or not such interactions shaped a range of different outcomes—from what people thought about individual government policies to what Republicans and Democrats thought of each other. Though we were only able to examine people who affiliate with one of these two parties on a single platform (Twitter) in late 2017—and could only focus on the impact of direct interactions between these people and IRA accounts—we were able to study how foreign misinformation campaigns shape public opinion.

Once again, our research findings challenged the prevailing wisdom: we could not detect any significant effects of interacting with IRA accounts on any of the political attitudes and behaviors we studied. Moreover, we found that the people who interacted with IRA accounts were mostly those who already had strong partisan beliefs—precisely the type of people who would be least likely to change their minds in response to trolling. This finding fits into a broader trend that many people don't know about: most mass media campaigns have minimal effects.[40] Political campaigns are not a hypodermic needle that injects opinion into the masses. Instead, most people ignore the campaigns—and the few who do engage with them already have such strong beliefs that their overall impact is negligible.[41] It is still possible that fake news and foreign misinformation campaigns can influence voting behavior. But studies indicate that even the most sophisticated targeted campaigns to persuade voters in the 2016 election probably had little or no impact—and possibly even a negative impact upon voters who were mistargeted. Voters who are accidentally shown ads intended for others, for example, are less likely to vote for the candidates advertised than those who were not targeted.[42] Perhaps even more surprisingly, there is also very little evidence that microtargeting ads influences consumer behavior. Though being targeted by an online advertising campaign surprisingly close to one's interests is certainly creepy, research indicates such campaigns have very little influence on what we buy.[43]

Still another area in which Silicon Valley companies are blamed for political polarization is the concept of the echo chamber. But if Facebook and Twitter exposed people to those with opposing views—as many of the Silicon Valley apostates described above prescribe—the analysis I've presented throughout this book indicates that this strategy might backfire. There is also an even deeper issue here, however. The most recent studies indicate that the prevalence of the echo chamber phenomenon has been greatly exaggerated. A 2019 study from NYU's Center for Social Media and Politics concluded that 40 percent of Twitter users do not follow any political accounts (that is, accounts of elected officials, political pundits, or media outlets).[44] The researchers found that of the remaining respondents, most consume information from a mix of liberal and conservative sources. The only people stuck deep inside echo chambers, they concluded, were the minority of people on the extremes of the liberal-conservative continuum.[45] Even more surprisingly, another recent study of the browsing histories of more than fifty thousand internet users concluded that people who use social media are exposed to more opposing views than people who do not.[46]

I also worry that we overestimate the capacity of social media companies to combat political tribalism. In recent decades, new technologies have created self-driving cars and other remarkable breakthroughs that I did not think I would see in my lifetime. But these same achievements have also created extreme hubris— or at least false confidence that the same technologies that learn the rules of driving a car can counteract political polarization.

In fact, the best available evidence suggests that machine learning has a long way to go before it can predict complex human behavior, much less change it. In a landmark study, the sociologist Matthew Salganik challenged hundreds of experts in machine learning to predict the outcomes of children who grew up in impoverished families.[47] His team gave the experts half of a data set that contained hundreds of variables about thousands of people across multiple points in time. Each team built a model to predict which people would escape poverty using the best available machine learning techniques. Surprisingly, the best model did not improve upon decades-old statistical techniques and explained only about 10–20 percent of the variation in life outcomes among children in the study. One could easily argue that childhood poverty and political polarization are very different outcomes, but for me, Salganik's study indicates that we have a long way to go before a machine learning engineer can simply turn a dial deep inside Facebook's source code to mitigate political polarization.[48]

Even if social media platforms could make changes that would reduce polarization, would they really do it? Consider the following thought experiment. Suppose we could identify a small tweak to Facebook's platform that would reduce the number of uncivil exchanges between Republicans and Democrats by 7.5 percent, though it would also decrease ad clicks by 5 percent. Would the company's leadership and board members go for it? To its credit, Facebook has made laudable efforts to increase voter turnout and organ donation and to raise money for charities, as I described in previous chapters. But would implementing the most effective solutions to political polarization be an easy pill for shareholders to swallow?

Even if we imagine that simple technological fixes do exist and that social media companies are willing to implement them, would people trust the current platforms to implement them? According to a 2018 Pew survey, 55 percent of Americans believe that technology companies have "too much power and influence" in today's economy, and 65 percent think that "they often fail to anticipate how their products and services will impact society."[49] A later survey revealed that about two-thirds of Americans are not comfortable with social media companies' allowing political messaging firms to employ their users' data.[50] Perhaps most importantly, this survey showed that Republicans are much more distrustful of social media platforms than liberals. Though 72 percent of all Americans think that social media platforms censor political viewpoints, this figure is considerably higher among Republicans. Even if liberals could be convinced to trust social media companies to address political polarization, Republicans might be a harder sell. Even worse, Republicans might perceive attempts to reduce political polarization as part of a conspiracy to suppress conservative voices online—a belief that has become so prevalent that it has been raised by elected officials in recent government hearings.

It's Up to Us

If we can't count on Facebook, Twitter, Google, or any of the other big platforms to solve political polarization from the top down by themselves, what can we do? In the final chapter of this book, I describe exciting new research that we've conducted in the Polarization Lab about what a better kind of social media might look like, and how we could create a new platform for better public conversations about politics. In the meantime, it will be largely up to us—the people who use social media—to improve our current platforms from the bottom up. In the next chapter, I offer a road map for hacking the social media prism. I describe new research in the social sciences and introduce technology that we can use to understand how the prism distorts our understanding of ourselves, each other, and—perhaps most importantly—political polarization itself.

8

Hacking the Prism

L ET'S BEGIN WITH THE GOOD NEWS: political polarization is not as bad as most people think. The concept of false polarization first emerged in the United States in the mid-1990s, amid the culture wars that pitted the family values of the Republican Party against the Democrats' belief in redistributing wealth to the poor. The two parties traded increasingly negative attack ads about each other's candidates, and elected officials engaged in a series of seemingly intractable debates about abortion, welfare, and crime, among other divisive issues. Newt Gingrich, a Republican who served as the Speaker of the House of Representatives, led the first campaign to impeach a U.S. president (Bill Clinton) for lying about having a sexual affair. Cable television amplified partisan conflicts like never before.[1] These developments might seem tame by today's standards—especially after reading about the extremists I described in chapter 5—but at the turn of the twenty-first century, many people worried that the growing culture wars might never stop.

But in reality, the culture wars were not growing. Though Americans were divided about contentious issues such as abortion, the sociologist Paul DiMaggio and his colleagues discovered that the rates of disagreement about this and many other divisive issues did not increase between the 1970s and 1990s.[2] Meanwhile, the social psychologist Robert Robinson was leading a team that was about to make a parallel discovery.[3] Robinson's team recruited college students who took liberal or conservative positions on abortion and racial conflict. In addition to measuring each student's opinion on a range of questions related to each issue, the team also asked the students to estimate what people from the opposing party thought about each issue. The results would not have surprised DiMaggio and his colleagues: both liberals and conservatives drastically overestimated the difference between their views and those of the other side. They also underestimated the amount of difference in views within their own side.

Robinson and his team revealed that false polarization was rampant among college students, but what about the rest of the country? In 2016, the political scientists Matthew Levendusky and Neil Malhotra searched for evidence of false polarization among a nationally representative group of Americans. On average, the researchers found that perceived differences between the two parties were roughly two times larger than the actual differences.[4] This held across a range of topics that Robinson's team had not studied—including immigration, tax reform, free trade, and campaign financing. Later research showed that the perception gap between Democrats and Republicans broadened at the same time as the culture wars were escalating in the mass media. Though false polarization was negligible in 1970, the political scientists Adam Enders and Miles Armaly found that it grew by nearly 20 percent over the next forty years.[5] What is more, they discovered that false polarization explained why Democrats and Republicans came to view each other so negatively over this time period. The more people misperceived the views of people in the other party, the more they disliked the members of that party. The latest research suggests that Democrats and Republicans also overestimate how much people from the other party dislike them.[6] When we think that people in the other party dislike us more than they actually do, it makes us more likely to dislike them. A key strategy for reducing political polarization is to find ways to help members of opposing political parties correct the misperceptions they have about each other.

Closing the Perception Gap

If previous research is our guide, closing the perception gap between Democrats and Republicans should be a top priority for reducing polarization. Fortunately, many social scientists have studied how such gaps emerge.[7] My first book analyzed how the mass media warped public opinion of Muslims after the September 11 attacks, for example, by amplifying the voices of emotional extremists at the expense of the more moderate majority.[8] In *The Outrage Industry*, Jeffrey Berry and Sarah Sobieraj show that such angry outbursts were almost completely absent from major U.S. newspapers in the 1950s.[9] By 2009, however, the average newspaper article included nearly six statements of outrage. Mass media not only amplify extreme voices, they can also create misperceptions about the scope of polarization. Levendusky and Malhotra scanned dozens of newspapers, television show transcripts, and magazines to count the number of mentions of polarization, uncivil discourse, or lack of compromise.[10] The researchers discovered a twofold increase in such mentions between 2000 and 2012. When they exposed people to such messaging in an experiment, they discovered that their subjects were more likely to overestimate the amount of political polarization in the United States.

One of the most important messages I'd like readers to take away from this book is that social media has sent false polarization into hyperdrive. In chapter 5, I presented data from nationally representative surveys, as well as stories of individual social media users, to explain why extremists enjoy an outsized role in discussions about politics on social media. In chapter 6, I showed how the gap between perception and reality also causes widespread apathy or political disengagement among moderates—

which only increases the amount of real estate that extremists occupy on our platforms. Though I only presented evidence from the United States, the power of social media to distort the political landscape is even more evident when we use a cross-national perspective. In 2016, a group of fourteen scholars examined the gap between perceived and actual polarization in ten countries.[11] Though the researchers found mixed evidence about whether consuming information in legacy media (for example, television news, newspapers, and magazines) contributes to the perception gap, they discovered that online news consumption was the strongest predictor of false polarization in nearly every country.[12] Social media also exacerbate the mass media's contribution to false polarization. Journalists often use social media to monitor public opinion, and this distorts their reporting on polarization even further.[13] It's a vicious cycle.

How can we disrupt the feedback loop between the social media prism and false polarization? This is no easy task, to be sure. But in this chapter, I present three strategies we can use to hack the social media prism. First, we can learn to see the prism and understand how it distorts our identities, as well as those of other people. Second, we can learn to see ourselves through the prism and monitor how our behavior gives the prism its power. Finally, we can learn how to break the prism by changing these behaviors and discovering how to engage in more productive conversations with the other side. Using each of these three strategies may seem challenging. But the latest social science research indicates that implementing them might not be as hard as you think. Still, developing mindfulness and changing our behaviors—particularly when we are passionate about politics—is easier said than done. This is why my colleagues and I in the Polarization Lab spent years developing new tools to make this process easier. In the pages that follow, I will explain how these resources can help you implement the three strategies I will now describe in detail.

Seeing the Prism

Perhaps the most daunting challenge in hacking the social media prism is that it is usually invisible. To become aware of the gap between perception and reality, we usually need to have an experience that reveals it to us—for example, meeting someone who does not conform to a stereotype we have about people like them. Because Republicans and Democrats rarely discuss politics in everyday life, most of our misperceptions go unchallenged. And as I discussed in chapter 6, the majority of people who discuss politics on social media have extreme views. The more we are exposed to such extremists, the more we risk confusing them with the moderate majority. In other words, the most pernicious effects of the social media prism operate at a subconscious level. This is why learning how to see the social media prism is so important.

Another reason why learning to see the prism is critical is that research indicates making people aware of misperceptions has a strong depolarizing effect. In a 2015 study, the political scientists Douglas Ahler and Gaurav Sood asked 1,000 Republicans and Democrats to answer questions that cued common stereotypes associated with each party.[14] For example, they asked Republicans to estimate what percentage of Democrats are Black; atheist; union members; and gay, lesbian, or bisexual. Next, they asked Democrats to estimate how many Republicans are evangelical Christians, age sixty-five or older, reside in the South, and earn more than $250,000 a year. Remarkably, these scholars found that respondents overestimated the actual proportion of partisans in each of these categories by an average of 342 percent.[15] In a follow-up experiment, the researchers corrected these misperceptions, showing respondents the actual number of people from the opposing party who fit into each category. People who saw this information reported more favorable attitudes toward the opposing party than those who did not. A series of subsequent experiments by the psychologists Jeffrey Lees and Mina Cikara revealed that the depolarizing effect of correcting misperceptions extends into broader policy issues as well—such as attitudes about redistricting for electoral offices or anonymous campaign contributions.[16]

These studies inspired our Polarization Lab to create new technology to combat false polarization. If you visit polarizationlab .com, you can take advantage of the latest tools we've created to help you learn more about where the people whom you interact with fall on the ideological spectrum. The next time you are shocked by a political statement someone makes on social media, use our tools to help you see this person in broader perspective. You may be surprised to discover how often the people you think are rank-and-file members of the other side are actually some of the most extreme people on the platform. And the next time you find yourself criticized on social media by someone from the other side, taking the time to carefully reflect about who this person is—and what their motivations are—can help you calibrate your response. Engaging with people who are the type of extremist I profiled in chapter 5 may be counterproductive, since they gain status within their cult-like communities for provoking attacks from people on the other side. However, if you've been criticized by people whose views put them in the center or only slightly on the other side, debating with them might be a valuable opportunity to find common ground.

Seeing Yourself through the Prism

The second important strategy for hacking the social media prism is to learn how it refracts you. Take a moment to learn where you fall on the ideology spectrum by using the tools on polarizationlab.com. Then, take some time to study how accurately your behavior on social media reflects your political views. If your behavior reflects your views perfectly then you are in the minority. Most of us present very different versions of ourselves online and off-line, as I described in chapters 4–6. Extremists, for example, tend to minimize the strength of their own ideological extremism and exaggerate that of others.[17] The social media prism also makes many moderates seem apolitical. This might be the case for those people who—like Sara Rendon, the moderate Republican discussed in chapter 6—avoid discussing politics because they are worried about offending their relatives or losing their jobs. It might also be the case for people like Derek Hunter, the moderate Democrat who I also discussed in chapter 6, who avoids discussing current events because he believes that discussions about politics on social media are simply not productive.[18] Either way, understanding how people on social media see you—regardless of who you really are—is very important. Research indicates becoming more aware of how your political views relate to those of others can have a depolarizing effect no matter where you fall on the spectrum.[19] Realizing that the identities we are trying to project are not consistent with the ones other people see may help us realize that other people are not always what they seem either.

The key thing I urge you to consider is whether the version of you that is projected through the prism is what you want other people to see. If it isn't, don't despair. More than a century of social science suggests that we are very bad at seeing what we look like through the eyes of others. We believe we know what other people think of us, but we are often very wrong. And as I've argued throughout this book, social media can make this process even harder.

In early 2020, scholars from Cornell University partnered with a data scientist at Facebook to study how often the self-presentations we aim to project accurately map onto what other people see.[20] The research team tracked discussions on 800,000 public Facebook pages—that is, pages where anyone can post a comment or reply to other people, even if they are not friends on

Facebook. The researchers surveyed 16,000 of the people who either posted a message on one of these pages or replied to something on one of them. They asked each of the people who posted what their intentions were for their message: for example, whether they were trying to express an opinion or state a fact. The team also asked people who replied to those messages what they thought the original poster's intentions were. The researchers discovered that people misperceive each other's intentions all the time. For example, people who think that they are simply sharing facts about an issue are often perceived by others as expressing an opinion. Even worse, the researchers discovered, when such perception gaps exist, conversations are much more likely to become uncivil.

This research should provide a warning to those of you who regularly share information about politics on social media. But I believe that the most important distortion the social media prism creates is through those who—like Sara or Derek—don't post about politics at all. As I argued in chapter 6, the lack of moderate voices on social media may contribute more to political polarization than the abundance of extremists on our platforms, because the absence of the former enables the latter to hijack the public conversation. I beg the moderate Democrats and Republicans who read this book not to delete your accounts: we need you. Look, I get it—I don't want to have uncomfortable conversations about politics with my relatives at Thanksgiving dinner any more than you do. And like everyone else, I present a carefully manicured version of myself on social media. No one who reads my Twitter feed will learn what I am watching on Netflix or other information that is unbecoming to a college professor. But all of us must carefully balance the desire to preserve our self-image with the consequences of these choices for the public good. We all need to think carefully about the issues we consider to be important enough to weigh in on. Moderate people need to decide which issues are so important to them that they won't allow extremists to speak on their behalf. We all need to balance our desire not to upset friends, family members, or colleagues with the urgent need to beat back polarization on our platforms.

You may be a very passionate partisan who regularly does battle with people from the other party on social media. In volatile times like ours, such passion can be a very good thing—shining a light on inequality or hypocrisy, or motivating others to act against unfair policies. But unexamined partisanship is also destructive. Before you charge into battle, ask yourself what really motivates you: Is this an issue that you are willing to die on a hill for? Or are you just seeking the status derived from a clever takedown of a political opponent? If it is status on social media that you want, take a moment to carefully examine the people liking or retweeting your messages: Who are they? Are they people whose opinions you value, or are they just status-seeking extremists out to win a few more followers? Finally, think about the consequences of your behavior for people on the other side. Is attracting a few more followers worth upsetting people on the other side? Are you really "owning" your opponents, or does your behavior only further contribute to stereotypes about your side? And if you are only preaching to the social media choir, could your energy be better spent trying to persuade people on the other side of the aisle?

Shifting our goals away from creating self-worth or ensuring that our side is winning runs counter to our deepest social instincts. But in the final section of this chapter, I explain why the latest advances in social science indicate that reaching across the aisle might not be as hard as you think.

Breaking the Prism

From the first few chapters of this book, you already know what you should not do to begin reaching across the aisle. In chapter 2, I showed that stepping outside your echo chamber and immediately exposing yourself to a broad range of people who do not share your views might just make you more convinced that your side is just, honest, or right. If you are a passionate partisan like Janet Lewis, the hairdresser who lives in Gainesville, Florida, and was introduced in chapter 3, you may discover the beliefs of people on the other side are even more extreme than you thought. Or if you are like Patty Wright, the unenthusiastic Democrat I introduced in the same chapter, stepping outside your echo chamber may heighten your feeling that there is a war going on around you. But if the stories of these two women were not convincing, you can try the experiment that Janet and Patty participated in yourself. Visit polarizationlab.com to find a link that allows you to follow the same type of bot that Patty and Janet saw for one month.

Rather than stepping boldly outside your echo chamber (if you are actually in one), social science suggests that taking some baby steps might be in order. Carolyn Sherif, wife of the hot-tempered, forest-fire-starting social psychologist Muzafer Sherif described in chapter 4, did some pioneering work on how to persuade people that probably came in useful with such a mercurial spouse. When we are exposed to a new argument—say, an opinion about climate change—Carolyn Sherif argued that our response will be conditioned by the distance between this argument and our preexisting views.[21] If the argument is far from our preexisting view—as would be the case when, say, a liberal Rachel Maddow viewer encountered an argument by archconservative Rush Limbaugh—then the likelihood of persuasion will be very low. If, on the other hand, the argument is within what Sherif called our "latitude of acceptance" (a range of attitudes about a given issue that an individual finds acceptable or reasonable even if they don't agree with them a priori), then people will be more motivated to engage with the viewpoint and perhaps even move closer to it.[22]

The notion that we can find some type of common ground on social media today may seem like a pipe dream. Or perhaps the idea of listening to the other side makes your blood boil. But an interesting study by researchers at Harvard University's John F. Kennedy School of Government indicates that it might go better than you'd think. In a series of studies, Charles Dorison, Julia Minson, and Todd Rogers asked Democrats and Republicans to read, listen to, or watch statements by politicians from the opposing political party.[23] These included highly partisan statements such as President Trump's inaugural address. Before they were exposed to these materials, the research team asked participants to estimate how angry, fearful, or sad such statements would make them, as well as how much they thought they would agree with the messages in the statements. The researchers found that people not only consistently overestimate how negative the experience will be but also underestimate how much they will agree with messages from leaders on the other side of the aisle. People who were exposed to such statements even expressed more willingness to be exposed to similar statements in the future, compared to those who did not see the statements.

It might still seem that people on the other side live in an entirely different world. How can we hope to have a meaningful conversation when the current political moment is plagued by debates about fake news and alternative facts—that is, the meaning of reality itself? Such seemingly intractable arguments belie an underappreciated fact: the majority of Americans actually want political compromise, as the political scientist Jennifer Wolak writes in *Compromise in an Age of Party Polarization*.[24] It is vital to remind ourselves that the most visible people discussing politics are not most people. As I showed in chapters 5 and 6, a small percentage of people with extreme views account for the majority of all posts about politics on social media. If you find the views of most people you encounter from the other side to be appalling, you might not be seeing people within your latitude of acceptance. The tools at polarizationlab.com can also help you identify other social media users within your latitude of acceptance.

Once you've begun following accounts within your latitude of acceptance, I do not recommend starting conversations with people from the other side right away. Instead, take some time to study what those people care about, and more importantly how they talk about it. Research by the sociologist Robb Willer indicates that the best way to bridge partisan divides is to communicate using arguments that resonate with the worldviews of the people you are trying to persuade. In a 2015 study, Willer and Matthew Feinberg showed liberals and conservatives a series of statements about same-sex marriage and military spending.[25] They found that liberals are more approving of defense spending if military service is framed as something that can help the poor and disadvantaged achieve equal standing with wealthier Americans. This argument emphasized core liberal values such as fairness and equality. Willer and Feinberg were also able to convince conservatives to support same-sex marriage at higher rates by framing the issue in terms of patriotism and group loyalty, two key conservative values. "Same sex couples," the message argued, "are proud and patriotic Americans."[26]

Unfortunately, the researchers also discovered that people are not very good at communicating in the language of the other side. In their 2015 study, Willer and Feinberg asked liberals and conservatives to write messages about same-sex marriage and immigration that they thought would appeal to people on the other side. Next, the researchers asked people from both parties to rate the appeal of each other's messages. Even though the researchers offered a large cash prize to the respondent who wrote the most appealing messages, only 9 percent of liberals and 8 percent of conservatives wrote messages that were considered persuasive by the other side.

Why is learning to communicate in the language of the other side so difficult? One reason is that Republicans and Democrats spend so little time listening to each other.[27] So if you're willing to begin listening, then you are a step ahead of most other people. And if you listen to people within your latitude of acceptance, you might begin by keeping a list of issues on which you think the other side may have a point. Be patient with yourself if you do not find productive conversation partners right away. If you have extreme views, it may take longer for you to find counterparts on the other side with whom you can agree to disagree. If you have more moderate views, this process might occur more quickly. A recent study by a team of psychologists found that moderates are more accurate than extremists at gauging the ideological extremity of the other side—in other words, moderates are less susceptible to the downward spiral of false polarization.[28]

If you've spent a week or two listening to views from the other side, pat yourself on the back. Few people ever listen to the other side, but even fewer actually engage across party lines on social media. And there is good reason for this: Some people wonder if doing so is worth the effort, or if people from the other side will just shoot down their arguments or (even worse) make fun of them. More confident people wonder if pointing out the obvious flaws in the arguments of those on the other side would just embarrass their opponents. Once again, social science research provides room for hope. In a series of studies, Charles Dorison and Julia Minson—two of the Harvard researchers who showed that people think being exposed to the other side is worse than it actually is—again exposed Democrats and Republicans to a series of messages from the opposing side.[29] This time, however, they asked people to anticipate their own anger, frustration, or anxiety as well as how they thought people from the other side might feel if they were in the same situation. People once again overestimated how upsetting viewing material from the other side would be, but they also overestimated how negatively people from the other side would react to seeing opposing views. Minson provides a cunning interpretation of their findings: "If you think you are right, you assume that your political opponents will be embarrassed and anxious when the flaws in their arguments are exposed. What people misjudge, however, is that their opponents are likely to feel the same way."[30]

If you are looking for a productive point of entry into a conversation with someone on the other side, you might also consider taking a few more baby steps. One thing that most Democrats and Republicans have in common is that they do not like politics. Remember those studies that I mentioned in chapter 4 that documented a steady increase in the number of Americans who say that they would feel uncomfortable if their child married a member of the other party? The political scientists Samara Klar, Yanna Krupnikov, and John Ryan decided to scrutinize such trends more carefully. They conducted an experiment in which some people in a nationally representative panel of Americans were shown the classic question social scientists used to gauge interparty animosity—the one about their child marrying a member of the opposing party.[31] But other people in the experiment were asked how they would feel if their child married someone who "talks about politics rarely."[32] Though people with extreme views still reported feeling uncomfortable with the idea of their child marrying someone from the other party, the vast majority preferred a child-in-law who does not discuss politics, regardless of their political party. So if you are looking for a way to break the ice when you step outside your echo chamber, consider other topics—sports, for example. Or consider something completely unpolarizing like whether or not people should use the Oxford comma (on second thought, don't do that).

If you just can't wait to dive into politics, consider performing some introspection about your own side before questioning the beliefs of others. In early 2019, a major news organization asked me to write an op-ed about how Americans could fight political polarization more effectively on social media. To answer this question, I decided to study which liberal and conservative opinion leaders (elected officials, journalists, and pundits) are most appealing to people on the other side. What is it about their posts that resonate across the aisle? Using data that my colleagues and I had collected from a large survey of Twitter users, I was able to count the number of times Democrats liked tweets by Republican opinion leaders and Republicans liked tweets by Democratic opinion leaders. What I found was not altogether surprising, but I think it is extremely important: the opinion leaders whose tweets resonated most with members of the other party were those who frequently criticized their own side.[33] Turning a critical eye on one's own party may convince people to open up the cognitive space necessary to begin listening, or see the possibility of compromise more clearly.

Another promising strategy is to avoid talking about polarizing opinion leaders altogether. According to a 2018 Pew Research Center study, only 4 percent of Americans have "a great deal of confidence" in elected officials.[34] Only 15 percent have a great deal of confidence in journalists, and 4 percent have high confidence in business leaders. What about university professors like me? Only 18 percent of Americans have a great deal of confidence in us. And the handful of opinion leaders who are heroes to people on one side are most often enemies to those on the other. Looking back over hundreds of hours of interviews that my colleagues and I conducted for the research in this book, I can say one thing with extreme confidence: the worst way a Democrat could begin a conversation with a Republican would be to ask why that person voted for Trump (similarly, the worst way a Republican could begin a conversation with a Democrat would be to criticize Obama or Joe Biden). If you do not recognize that someone could vote for Biden and still be offended by people who criticize the police—or that someone could vote for Trump but have grave concerns about climate change—then you are missing an important opportunity to structure conversations around issues instead of the polarizing individuals who too often define them.

Avoiding polarizing elites ties into my next recommendation: whenever possible, try to put your ideas before your identities. In chapter 2, I showed that exposing people to messaging from the other sides sharpens the contrast between "us" and "them," because it turns up the volume of partisan rancor. Does your social media profile include terms such as "progressive," "conservative," or other strong cues about which party you support? If so, consider how such terms might pigeonhole you in the mind of someone on the other side. Or if you are a Democrat concerned about an issue such as climate change, consider the value of criticizing Republicans versus making appeals to our shared interests (you get bonus points if you can communicate such interests in a way that will resonate with the conservative worldview). Snapping the feedback loop between our identities and the information-processing regions of our brains means recognizing that people on the other side may not approach evidence in the same manner that we do. Or, that they might appreciate certain types of evidence more than others.

Of course, snapping the feedback loop between our ideas and our identities is not always possible and is sometimes ill-advised. Social media users of color such as Sara Rendon or Derek Hunter often face prejudice from others who assume that they already know the users' views because of the color of their skin. Many social media users may not want to put their ideas before their identities because the issues they are most passionate about revolve around their identities. After a gruesome viral video captured the murder of George Floyd by a Minnesota police officer, many Americans came to believe that racism is the most important issue facing our country—if they had not already been swayed by earlier murders of unarmed Black men by law enforcement officers. In their current form, social media platforms do not provide the type of environment necessary for Democrats and Republicans to discuss such questions about identity in a productive manner. Still, I believe that our country needs conversations between people like Sara (the moderate Republican who is the daughter of a police officer and half Puerto Rican) and Derek (the moderate Democrat who still believes in law and order even though he suffered the horrific harassment from police officers that I described in chapter 6). In the final chapter of this book, I discuss how we can create a better platform for these and other vital cross-party conversations. If we could redesign social media from scratch to make it less polarizing, where should we begin?

9

A Better Social Media

I N MARCH 2020, the number of Google searches that included the term "unprecedented" soared higher than ever before. As the sheer scale of the COVID-19 pandemic set in, the watershed events that had occurred in the previous few years—the divisive 2016 election, two major investigations of a sitting president, and what could be described as the most dysfunctional period in the history of the U.S. Congress—felt like a distant memory. Only two months later, the virus had claimed more than sixty-five thousand American lives. And while the loss of lives was utterly devastating, the economic cost of the pandemic was also heart-stopping. After many companies closed or cut back their output, unemployment levels spiked near record highs. It became a cliché to say that the pandemic had stretched into every corner of American life, and hundreds of millions of Americans sheltered in place while they watched the grim news pour in, with each day feeling more unprecedented than the last.

I don't think Muzafer Sherif, the temperamental social psychologist I profiled at the beginning of chapter 4, could have imagined a more perfect common enemy to force Democrats and Republicans to set aside their differences. Like the forest fire Sherif once planned to ignite to create solidarity between the summer campers he studied, COVID-19 seemed poised to burn everything to the ground. Not only did the pandemic devastate health and the economy (things that everyone cares about), but saving both required unprecedented societal coordination in the form of social distancing. History teaches that crises—even those much less daunting than the COVID-19 pandemic—provide warring factions with the opportunity to hit the reset button.[1] To give one of many possible examples, the decade after the end of World War II witnessed unprecedented international cooperation and prosperity. Such crises also strengthen collective identities, both good and bad. In fact, some scholars argue that the Cold War between the United States and the Soviet Union kept U.S. political polarization in check for years.[2]

But there was something unique about the COVID-19 pandemic. During World War II, Republicans and Democrats huddled together in foxholes, where their shared fate was immediately apparent. But during the pandemic, Americans were intentionally avoiding as many other people as possible. According to data from Safegraph, a company that aggregates GPS data from smartphones for advertising purposes, the median number of minutes Americans spent inside their homes each day shot through the roof in March 2020.[3] The bars, restaurants, and other social venues that occasionally allowed Republicans and Democrats to interact were mostly shut down. By early May 2020, more than 100,000 small businesses had already closed their doors permanently, and many more soon followed.[4] Though some businesses eventually reopened, smartphone data from the summer of 2020 showed that many of their customers continued to stay home—perhaps because they were concerned about their health or that of others, or because they no longer had any disposable income.[5]

As Americans quarantined in their apartments, condos, and houses, the internet lit up. Remarkably, internet infrastructure survived the massive influx of users both new and old, who flocked online at (you guessed it) unprecedented rates. Within the first few weeks of social distancing, the amount of daily traffic to Netflix and YouTube increased by more than 15 percent.[6]

Social media usage increased even more. During the same time period, Facebook usage skyrocketed by 27 percent. Americans also flocked to new platforms. Zoom connected parents working from home with their colleagues, while they struggled to set up Google Classroom for their children—whose entire education had suddenly moved online. Use of Nextdoor.com, which connects people to their neighbors for discussions about community issues, increased by 73.3 percent. Houseparty, an app that connects friends for video chats during which they can play games together, saw a 79.4 percent increase in users.

How did the surge of social media activity shape political polarization on our platforms? Within days of the first reported cases of COVID-19 in the United States, pundits launched volatile debates on social media about closing the country's borders, the adequacy of testing regimes, and whether enough protective medical equipment was available.[7] These debates continued throughout the first two months of social distancing. But as some states announced plans to reopen their economies despite increasing infection rates within their borders, the discussion on social media grew more fervent. Liberal pundits warned that the second wave of infection would be worse than the first. Conservative pundits responded that the cure should not be worse than the disease, with some people worrying that suicides might outnumber COVID-19 deaths because of high unemployment. In my neighborhood, liberals shamed conservatives for allowing their children to play with others on Nextdoor.com. Facebook and Twitter were also quickly awash with misinformation about the coronavirus, ranging from claims that China created the disease in a lab to fabricated pictures of dolphins swimming in Venetian canals.

Meanwhile, nationally representative surveys of Americans painted a much different picture. Though Democrats expressed support for wide-scale protective measures against COVID-19 more quickly than Republicans did, a strong bipartisan consensus quickly emerged in favor of social distancing in early 2020.

Democratic leaders objected to the Trump administration's decision to close the country's borders in late February, yet by late March, 96 percent of Republicans and 94 percent of Democrats supported the move.[8] Though many Republican leaders objected to shelter-in-place orders from local governments, surveys revealed strong public support for these measures as well. In mid-March, a large survey revealed that 84 percent of Republicans and 89 percent of Democrats supported canceling gatherings of more than ten people.[9] The bipartisan consensus about the need for social distancing and other new measures persisted even as many governors announced plans to reopen their states' economies. A representative survey in late April of voters in Georgia, Tennessee, and Florida—three of the states that opened first—found that only 12 percent of voters supported reopening the economy at that time.[10] Another survey found that the number of Americans who described their country as "very divided" dropped from 62 percent in October 2018 to just 22 percent in April 2020.[11]

Unfortunately, there was very little sign of unity on social media. Instead, the social media prism was hard at work. The extremists we met in chapter 5 were busy playing the blame game. Jamie Laplace, the liberal medical assistant from Alabama whose story I told at the beginning of that chapter, tweeted that Fox News anchors who initially downplayed the seriousness of the crisis should be put in jail. Meanwhile, Ed Baker, the lonely conservative who falls asleep watching DirecTV each night in a Nebraska motel, was claiming that the Chinese government not only had started the pandemic, but was also scheming to disrupt the U.S. supply chain in its wake. What about the moderates we met in chapter 6? Sara Rendon, the moderate conservative worried about upsetting her liberal aunt, did not post a single tweet during the first two months of the pandemic. And Pete Jackman, the moderate liberal whose cousin received a death threat? He was busy tweeting about video games. Once again, the social media prism was refracting the most extreme people on the political spectrum and muting moderates, two processes that reinforce each other, emboldening extremists to express increasingly radical beliefs and disenchanting moderates—many of whom will mistake such extremism as typical of the other side, as we've seen throughout this book.

Social Media in the COVID-19 Era

By summer 2020, surveys showed that the fragile consensus among Americans about how to respond to the pandemic had already fallen apart.[12] Though I had hoped that the pandemic would encourage American social media users to set aside their differences and reevaluate the purpose of our platforms, it now seems that the social media prism is as powerful as ever. The crisis has not changed the rules of the game or the behavior of its most prominent players. On Facebook, Twitter, and Instagram, extremists continue to flex their partisan identities, treating nearly every interaction as an opportunity for their side to win or the other side to lose. Even worse, opportunities for Republicans and Democrats to humanize each other in off-line settings—which were already becoming rare before the pandemic—will only become less frequent as the virus changes how many people think about social interaction with strangers.

In chapter 8, I discussed how we can hack the social media prism to beat back polarization on our platforms. But I think that the only way we can create lasting improvement is to create a new playing field. Calling for a new form of social media may seem like a moon shot given Facebook's enormous market share. But taking the long view teaches us that platforms come and go. Friendster, the first broadly successful social media site, was once so popular that Google offered to buy it for $30 billion.[13] Only two years later, MySpace supplanted Friendster, eventually becoming the most visited site on the internet by 2006.[14] And while Facebook once seemed unlikely to spread beyond the elite college campuses where it was born, it would of course go on to exceed the expectations of Silicon Valley's most bullish prophets.

In more recent years, Facebook has also shown signs of vulnerability. It took five years for Facebook to knock MySpace off the top of the social media hierarchy. But only four years after that, Instagram rocketed onto the scene, attracting fifty million users in its first two years of existence.[15] Instagram usage surged so quickly that Facebook wisely acquired the platform in April 2012, allowing the photo-sharing site to maintain its distinctive identity. But Facebook and Instagram's combined monopoly on the selfie market would not go unchallenged for long: by December 2013, Snapchat users were sending more than 400 million messages per day, and by April 2015, the platform had more than 100 million users.[16] Similarly, TikTok came out of nowhere. It arrived in the United States in 2018 and surpassed 100 million users just two years later.[17] Though Facebook remains the dominant platform today, it continues to shed young people—whose preferences will ultimately determine the landscape of the market.[18]

What will come next? A new platform probably will not supplant the dominant platforms and serve as a forum for more productive discussions about politics. But just as social media users have splintered onto new platforms according to their interests, hobbies, and professional needs, I think that there is room for a new platform for political discussion. Would everyone use it? Of course not. But decades of social science research indicate that most people get their opinions about politics from friends, family members, or colleagues who proactively seek information about politics, regularly engage with others about such information, and care enough about issues to try to influence people in their social network who trust their opinions.[19] What would better social media look like for these people, particularly those who are appalled by the current state of polarization on our platforms?

CHAPTER 9

A New Kind of Platform

Imagine, for a moment, that we could peel back the layers of social media and isolate the ones that give the social media prism its power. When I first did this thought experiment several years ago, I had the urge to contact friends who work at social media platforms to see if they would be interested in conducting an experiment that could shed some light on this issue. After all, they were already experimenting with various parts of their platforms. Twitter apparently did extensive research before expanding the number of characters it allows users to write, staggering the rollout of this change to assess its impact.[20] Instagram did the same thing with its "like" button, allowing users in some countries to see the number of likes their posts received but not displaying this information to others. The company learned that this change might discourage status seeking or bullying on the platform. Facebook runs so many experiments on its platform that data scientists within the company were forced to build an entirely new type of software to compare dozens—or even hundreds—of experiments to each other. However, the vast majority of these experiments are designed to improve advertising and user retention. The type of experiments my colleagues and I in the Polarization Lab wanted to run were quite different.

We wanted to ask fundamental questions about the architecture of social media. More specifically, we wanted to explore interventions that could disrupt the feedback loop between identity, status seeking, and political polarization that I have described throughout this book. As I mentioned at the end of chapter 8, we hoped to create a place where people like Sara Rendon and Derek Hunter could have a productive conversation about race and policing. The first thing our lab was interested in exploring was what might happen if you could create a space where people can put their ideas before their identities. What would happen, we wondered, if you brought Republicans and Democrats together to discuss politics on a new platform where they were completely anonymous? Would moving the game to a new playing field allow people to find common ground more easily?

There is, of course, a very dark side to anonymous conversations on the internet. Anonymous websites such as 4chan.org host some of the most disturbing content on the internet.[21] Similarly, many anonymous Twitter trolls make outlandish statements that they would probably never make in person. Other platforms such as Yik Yak—a defunct platform that allowed people to converse anonymously with other people nearby— were also accused of encouraging uncivil or abusive behavior.[22] At the same time, other social media forums thrive precisely because of anonymity. Though anonymity can minimize the social consequences of bad behavior, it also gives people the opportunity to explore alternative views outside the social relationships that often prevent them from doing so.[23] A prime example is Change My View, a Reddit community whose users are invited to post a statement about a controversial topic so that others can attempt to persuade them to reconsider their position. Users award each other "deltas" if they changed their minds about an issue. Change My View (which spawned another app called Ceasefire) is not limited to political topics, though many of the discussions on these forums included spirited—yet highly rational—debates about social policies among sizeable groups of people.[24]

Studying whether anonymous conversation increases or decreases polarization would simply carry too much risk for large companies like Facebook or Twitter. Besides, our goal was to take Republicans and Democrats out of their environment and create a new playing field. So we decided to create our own social media platform, one that would allow us to experiment with different features of platforms in a highly ethical manner. We wanted the platform to be polished enough to effectively simulate the experience of real users interacting with each other. We also wanted it to be attractive enough that people would actually want to use it. We did not want the platform to have a name that would give away its purpose. If we called it "the anti-echo chamber," for example, we worried that our platform might attract the presumably small group of people who are willing to change their views—a criticism that is often leveled against proponents of Reddit's Change My View.

We decided to give our platform a generic name: DiscussIt. We advertised it as "a place where people anonymously discuss various topics." We hired a graphic designer to produce a sleek logo, and we spent more than a year writing, testing, and debugging the software for the platform. In the end, we created a mobile app that paired two people so they could discuss issues anonymously on a chat platform. After installing DiscussIt, users were shown a series of images that explain how to use the platform and told that they would be assigned an issue to discuss with a chat partner. DiscussIt informed them that their own names would be replaced with pseudonyms. All users were then assigned to a discussion topic and told that they would be matched with another user as soon as possible. Once users were matched, the app assigned them an androgynous name such as Jamie or Casey and directed them to the main chat interface. Users could then discuss topics in real time or asynchronously. The app periodically nudged people if they became nonresponsive, and I led a staff of graduate students who served as a user support team to further simulate a real social media platform. We even had to create a limited liability company to give our app the bona fides it needed to pass muster at the Apple AppStore.

To test whether DiscussIt could successfully reduce polarization between Republicans and Democrats, we designed a field experiment.[25] In early January 2020, we hired a survey firm to recruit 1,200 Democrats and Republicans to complete a survey about their political views as well as their attitudes toward people on the other side. Our survey also included a battery of questions about immigration and gun control, the two issues we asked people to have a conversation about on DiscussIt in this study. One day after respondents completed the survey, we randomly assigned some of them to a treatment condition in which they were invited to earn $17 to "test a new social media platform for a few hours." Those who consented were given an invite code and instructed to plug it into the app's log-in screen. Unbeknown to the study participants, our app used this code to pair them with another person in the study who was from the opposing political party.[26] One week later, we sent all study participants a follow-up survey that included many of the questions asked in the first survey.

The results of the experiment make me cautiously optimistic about the power of anonymity. People who used DiscussIt exhibited significantly lower levels of polarization after using it for just a short time. Many people expressed fewer negative attitudes toward the other party or subscribed less strongly to stereotypes about them.[27] Many others expressed more moderate views about the political issues they discussed or social policies designed to address them. A lot of people became less polarized on all of these measures. Most surprising to me, however, is that an overwhelming majority of people told us they enjoyed using our social media platform, even though they had no incentive to do so. In a survey we administered within our app after users completed their discussions, 89 percent of people indicated that they had enjoyed their conversation. These engagements were not uniformly positive, but I was further encouraged by the people who emailed our user support team to ask how they could continue using our app after the testing session ended. Several users even asked how much the app would cost when it is released to the public.

If the quantitative results of the experiment were encouraging, then reading the transcripts of people's interactions was doubly so. People shared heartbreaking stories about friends and loved ones who had taken their own lives with handguns, as well as terrifying stories about being the victims of crime. One person even recounted in harrowing detail how she had survived a mass shooting. Others connected over nonpolitical issues. Two middle-aged parents sympathized with each other about raising teenage children, and others commiserated about friends or family members who blocked them because of their political views. Not every conversation was so congenial. One chat became so toxic that we decided to shut it down before it concluded. However, the vast majority of chats were not only civil but also highly productive. Many people outlined sophisticated policy proposals, and one pair even laid the groundwork for a grassroots campaign to prevent suicides in rural communities and became Facebook friends to make sure that they could continue their conversation after their trial of DiscussIt ended.

Our experiment also gives me hope that anonymous forums might facilitate more productive conversations across racial lines. One of our chats paired a White man who is a Republican and a Black woman who is a Democrat to discuss gun control. The man began the conversation by sharing his anger about the murder of two police officers in his home state of California. The woman responded with sympathy, telling the man that her son is a police officer. But the woman went on to denounce recent incidents of police violence against unarmed Blacks as well. The conversation continued respectfully, and ultimately both participants moved toward slightly more moderate positions on handgun control, according to our follow-up survey. As I read this chat transcript, I began to wonder if this type of progress would have been possible if the participants had been aware of each other's racial background. Would the man have shared his views about the murder of police? Would the woman have had the opportunity to tell him that she shares his fear and anger? Would they have found any common ground at all? These questions are for future researchers to grapple with, but it's worth noting that most of the 108 conversations in our study that connected Whites and Blacks had depolarizing effects that were on par with the other 660 conversations we analyzed. And race may only be the starting point. Could focused anonymous conversation also eliminate prejudice or status hierarchies associated with gender, class, or whether or not people have blue check marks next to their names (or other indicators of online celebrity)? People should not have to be anonymous to be heard or respected, but anonymity may give disadvantaged groups the power to decide how much they want to share about their identity. I'm hopeful that carefully designed anonymous conversations can help build the foundation for the deeper form of respect and mutual understanding that we need so badly.

Platforms with a Purpose

The DiscussIt experiment is one of the few success stories in fighting political polarization on our platforms that I know of. But could a platform like DiscussIt really scale? Even if people were willing to jettison parts of their identities for more productive debates in the short term, would they continue to do so as the platform expanded to include thousands—or even millions—of users over weeks, months, or years? Would the dialogue remain so civil after trolls or extremists arrived? And would the promise of more-productive conversations about politics be compelling enough to make people keep coming back? Or would a platform like ours make an inglorious exit to the graveyard of social media?

To answer these questions, we need to revisit the core argument I've made throughout this book about why people use social media in the first place. In chapter 4, I argued that people keep coming back to social media because they help us do something that makes us distinctively human: create, revise, and maintain our identities to gain social status. Social media allow people to present different versions of themselves, monitor how others react to those versions, and revise their identities with unprecedented speed and efficiency. But we humans are notoriously bad at judging what other people think of us—and the fleeting interactions we have with each other on social media make matters even worse. As I described in chapters 5 and 6, the social media prism fuels extremism, mutes moderates, and leaves most of us with profound misgivings about the other side. But we won't stop using social media any sooner than we will stop caring about our identities and social status. Instead, we need to think more about how the design of our platforms shapes the types of identities we create and the social status we seek.

What is the purpose of Facebook? The company tells us its mission is to "bring the world closer together."[28] But the platform began as a sophomoric tool that Harvard undergraduates used to rate each other's physical attractiveness. What is the purpose of Twitter? Its motto is to "serve the public conversation," but it was reportedly built to help groups of friends broadcast SMS-style messages to each other.[29] What is the purpose of Instagram? We're told it is to "capture and share the world's moments." But the app was originally called "Burbn" (as in the drink) and was built to help people make plans to hang out with their friends.[30] What is the purpose of TikTok? I'm not even going to go there. Hopefully, my point is already clear: Should we really expect platforms that were originally designed for such sophomoric or banal purposes to seamlessly transform themselves to serve the public good? Should we be surprised when they create the kind of leaderless demagoguery from which anyone can invent a kind of status, no matter how superficial or deleterious to democracy? Is it any wonder that people find themselves so rudderless on social media, when there is no common purpose for posting in the void?

Imagine if we created a platform on which status was tied to a more noble purpose. Imagine a platform that gave people status not for clever takedowns of political opponents but for producing content with bipartisan appeal. Once we articulate the purpose of our platforms more clearly, we can build such principles into the architecture of the entire system. Instead of boosting content that is controversial or divisive, such a platform could improve the rank of messages that resonate with different audiences simultaneously. Instead of recommending that people follow others who already share their views, a platform could expose them to those within their latitude of acceptance. We could define this range by asking people to complete a questionnaire about their views before they sign up for the platform. To fight false polarization, we could even build in the type of tools we have developed in the Polarization Lab. "Like" counters could be replaced by meters that show how people from across the ideological spectrum respond to people's posts in blue, red, and purple. Artificial intelligence could be used to ask people who are about to post uncivil or ad hominem content to reflect upon their goals or to help people rephrase their messages using values that appeal to the other side.

Needless to say, not everyone would use a platform where you gain status for bridging political divides. But that may be a good thing. The trolls and extremists who gain notoriety on other platforms for taking down political opponents could not be entirely banned from the type of platform I'm envisioning, but it would be a much less rewarding place for them to play.[31] Instead of gaining attention for taking people down, their posts would be downranked because they only appeal to one side. Regulating extreme content would also become easier. Once platforms have a purpose, such as bridging partisan divides, it will be much easier to make policies to define acceptable and unacceptable behavior. Instead of moderation policies that are so broad that they are difficult or even impossible to enforce, a platform built to depolarize users could moderate any posts that were ad hominem or uncivil. These terms would still be difficult to define, but I think that a platform guided by top-down principles that are transparent for all users to see when they sign up will always be more effective than a platform that relies upon norms to emerge from the bottom up—particularly when the bottom is composed of extremists whom moderates are unable or unwilling to police.[32] These policies—combined with undisclosed identity verification to further prevent trolling and extremism—could create the conditions necessary for anonymous conversation across party lines that is not only civil, but also productive.

Enforcing such policies would not be easy, or cheap. While the idea of a decentralized platform to reduce polarization from the bottom up is romantic, I don't think that it is realistic. Decentralized social media platforms such as Mastadon and Diaspora have struggled to attract new users while they try to keep the lights on.[33] A full-fledged effort to create a platform to depolarize us would require a significant investment from a major funder. Governments would be ideal candidates, and proponents of publicly funded platforms such as the internet activist Ethan Zuckerman have argued that they could be funded by a digital advertising tax.[34] Though depolarizing efforts should be an easy sell in highly polarized countries such as the United States, I will not hold my breath until they become a reality. If governments don't step in, there is money to be made by entrepreneurs willing to bet that a place where people can build reputations as effective bipartisan communicators will be more attractive to businesses, governments, and nonprofit organizations alike. There is already precedent for such a fundamental redesign of social media from companies such as Stack Overflow, where software developers gain reputational points for providing the best answers to each other's questions. Though this site originally served as a simple forum for the discussion of complicated technical issues, it has become so important to the technology industry that headhunters now sift through the platform to identify people who not only have technical talent but also enjoy the respect of their peers. As the United States confronts the most daunting challenge to its social fabric in a generation, developing a reputation for bridging partisan divides may become an increasingly valuable social asset. And if the opportunities for Democrats and Republicans to engage with each other in off-line settings continue to decline, a new social media platform may be one of the few places where such reputations could be made.

It is also not too late for existing social media platforms to adopt many of the principles outlined above as well. Facebook, Twitter, and other platforms could optimize the order of posts in their users' timelines based on the amount of approval they generate from people on both sides of the aisle, instead of simple engagement metrics alone. Recommender algorithms could be trained to identify each user's latitude of acceptance—based on the content they like or who they follow—and encourage people to connect with people whose views are different, but not too different, from their own. Together, these two reforms could promote content that nudges social media users to engage with each other around issues where there is room for compromise, instead of getting worked up about the content that is enraging their own side on any given day. Our current platforms could also create new incentives for people to engage in such productive debate— for example, leaderboards that track how often prominent users generate content that appeals to people from both parties. Or, they could invent new forms of status—such as badges for people who effectively attract diverse audiences, instead of highlighting those who have achieved celebrity for their achievement outside of politics. Facebook, Twitter, and other dominant social media platforms could also experiment with creating new spaces on their platforms for people who want to reach across the aisle and offer their users the opportunity to connect using the same type of focused, small-scale conversations that we created on our simulated social media platform in the Polarization Lab.

Regardless of whether solutions come from the top down or the bottom up, the effort to depolarize our platforms could benefit from a much deeper engagement with social science. As we unlock the keys to make our platforms less polarizing, we can use insights from social science to make them a reality. Instead of implementing untested interventions proposed by technology leaders, pundits, or policy makers, we must build the methods of empirical observation of human behavior into the architecture of our platforms, as some social media companies have already begun to do. Along the way, we must recognize that the immense challenges we face will continue to evolve over time. We must continue to test all of the solutions I've prescribed throughout this book in the coming years and decades. And if the rapidly evolving field of computational social science discovers the recommendations I've proposed no longer work, I'll be the first one calling for a change of course.

APPENDIX: RESEARCH METHODS

In the main text of this book, I described three large field experiments conducted by me and my colleagues in the Polarization Lab between 2018 and 2020. In this appendix, I provide a much more detailed discussion of the research methods we employed in each study for readers who wish to learn more about the specific sampling procedures, modeling assumptions, and analysis techniques used—and for those who seek a lengthier discussion of the strengths and limitations of our work. Each section of the appendix describes one of the three studies described in the main text. In the first study—the quantitative bot experiment, described in chapter 2—we recruited 1,220 Democrats and Republicans to follow a Twitter bot we created that exposed them to messages from the other side. The second study—the qualitative bot experiment, described in chapters 2 and 3—was a follow-up in which we conducted 155 in-depth interviews with a new group of Republicans and Democrats before and after they followed the same type of Twitter bot employed in the first study. In the third study—the simulated social media platform experiment, described in chapter 9—we recruited 7,074 Democrats and Republicans to complete a survey about their political views and invited 2,507 of them to interact with each other on a new social media platform that we created.

APPENDIX

The Quantitative Bot Experiment

We hired YouGov—a large, reputable survey firm—to recruit a sample of Americans to complete a ten-minute online survey between October 10 and 19, 2017. Participants had to (1) identify with either the Republican or Democratic Party, (2) visit Twitter at least three times each week and regularly log on to read messages from other accounts, (3) be willing to share their Twitter handle for research purposes, and (4) be eighteen years or older. YouGov invited 10,634 people, of whom 5,114 accepted the initial invitation—and of those 2,539 were deemed eligible to complete the survey based upon the criteria above. Among those eligible, 285 refused to participate, 500 began but did not complete the survey, and 102 provided responses that were excluded by YouGov's data quality algorithm. That left 1,652 people who provided acceptable responses to our pretreatment survey. Each respondent was told that the survey was designed to "investigate people's experiences on Twitter" and that they would receive $11 for completing the survey and sharing their Twitter handle with the research team. We obtained informed consent from all respondents and told them that they would also be eligible to complete a follow-up study one month later.

The pretreatment survey included a range of questions about respondents' political beliefs, social media behavior, media diet, and frequency of exposure to people from the opposing political party (both online and off-line). The central measure described in chapter 2 consisted of answers to a ten-question index called the Ideological Consistency Scale. This scale has been used in sixteen nationally representative surveys administered by the Pew Research Center over the past two decades. The instrument includes five statements that have a conservative slant—such as "Poor people have it easy because they can get government benefits without doing anything in return"—and five questions that have a liberal slant, such as "Racial discrimination is the main reason why black people can't get ahead these days." The statements covered not only social welfare and racial discrimination but also the environment, immigration, inequality, government regulation of the economy, international relations, and homosexuality. Respondents were asked to agree or disagree with each statement on a seven-point scale, and their responses allowed us to create an index that ranged from extremely liberal to extremely conservative.

Before we randomly assigned respondents to the treatment or control condition, we eliminated some respondents from the study for one of the following reasons. First, we compared demographic information about each respondent's age, gender, race, and geographic location that our survey firm provided to that which could be observed about them on Twitter. We excluded 74 respondents for whom we were able to identify at least two discrepancies between the demographic information described in these two sources and another 4 respondents who provided a famous person's Twitter account instead of their own. We also excluded 44 respondents who did not follow any accounts on Twitter and therefore did not satisfy our requirement that they regularly log in to Twitter to read other peoples' accounts. Finally, our capacity to compare people's Twitter data to our survey data allowed us to identify another important threat to causal inference: causal interference. Imagine that two of the people in our study followed each other on Twitter. If we randomized one of them to our treatment condition and the other one to our control condition, the treated respondent could impact the views of the person in the control condition by retweeting or commenting on one of our bot's messages. For this reason, we excluded an additional 113 people who were either directly connected to each other on Twitter, or part of a cluster of users who might expose each other—directly or indirectly—to the study's bots. We dropped an additional 197 people for providing poor quality data or failing to provide a valid Twitter handle in their survey responses.

The final pretreatment study population consisted of 1,220 respondents (691 Democrats and 529 Republicans). Though our study was not designed to be representative of the U.S. national population, we took additional steps to compare the demographic characteristics of our sample to official U.S. population estimates from the 2016 American Community Survey. Our final sample was older than the U.S. population because of our requirement that study participants be at least eighteen. Our respondents were also less likely to be non-White. Eighty-four percent of our respondents were White, compared to 70 percent in the national population. Though we performed statistical procedures to account for these biases in our analyses, our findings should not be generalized beyond Americans who belong to either the Republican or Democratic Party, visit Twitter regularly, and are willing to share information from their Twitter account with researchers. Readers should also take care in generalizing the findings of this research beyond Twitter, not only since it has distinctive features and characteristics that attract different types of people, but also because it offers a more public form of interaction between its users than other social media platforms, such as Facebook, do.

After excluding respondents from the pretreatment study population for one of the reasons described above, we randomized Republicans and Democrats into treatment or control conditions using a statistical procedure known as block randomization. This technique allows researchers to ensure that there are equal numbers of people in treatment and control conditions who belong to different subpopulations of interest. In our case, we took steps to create balance by respondents' strength of partisanship, frequency of Twitter use, and interest in government and public affairs. On October 21, 2017, we informed respondents in the treatment condition that they could receive $11 for following one of our study's bots for one month and up to $18 in additional incentives for answering questions about the content in the twenty-four messages it would retweet each day. As I mentioned in the main text of this book, our recruitment dialogue employed multiple steps to mitigate both response bias and experimenter effects (or Hawthorne effects). More specifically, we (1) did not disclose in our recruitment dialogue the type of content that the bots would tweet; (2) designed the invitations to complete our surveys and follow the bots so that they would appear unrelated to each other; and (3) made the bots retweet pictures of nature landscapes, instead of political content, for the first few days of the study.

Our bots were designed as follows. We employed a technique developed by the political scientist Pablo Barberá to measure the political ideology of a large group of opinion leaders on Twitter.[1] We began by creating a list of the Twitter handles of all candidates from the 2016 presidential campaign as well as all members of the U.S. House and Senate as of August 5, 2017. We then obtained a list of all accounts that these users followed on Twitter from the company's application programming interface. This yielded a total sample of 636,737 accounts, many of which were not political in nature or did not belong to U.S. opinion leaders. To systematically remove these accounts, we took several steps. First, we eliminated the account of anyone who was not followed by at least fifteen opinion leaders. Second, we removed all accounts for U.S. government agencies, for-profit corporations from anywhere in the world, and users outside the United States. Our final sample included 4,176 accounts created by a range of opinion leaders from the media, nonprofit groups, advocacy organizations, think tanks, and other nongovernment or noncorporate positions within the United States.

To measure the ideological leaning of each person within this network of elected officials and opinion leaders, we used statistical procedures—correspondence analysis and principal component analysis—that group people according to patterns in whom they follow. These techniques allowed us to create a measure of ideological strength that ranged from extreme conservatives to extreme liberals. A weakness of this technique is that it assumes people who follow someone on Twitter tend to share their political views. But many people who follow high-profile accounts such as @realDonaldTrump do so not because they approve of the users but because they want to be informed about the users' messages. If we had not addressed this issue, such accounts would appear more centrist than they actually are. For this reason, we reassigned the small number of opinion leaders in the center of our ideological continuum with more than 100,000 Twitter followers to a score between the first and second quintile associated with their party's side of the liberal-conservative continuum that we created.

Our liberal and conservative Twitter bots were hosted on a virtual machine that ran continuously on Amazon Web Services for several months. Every hour, our bots randomly selected an elected official or opinion leader from the database described in the previous paragraph and queried Twitter's application programming interface to determine whether this user had tweeted within the previous twenty-four hours. If the user had tweeted, the bot retweeted the message. If the user had not tweeted, the bot randomly selected another user from the database until it identified one who had tweeted during the previous day. During the one-month study period, the two bots retweeted 1,293 messages from 1,001 opinion leaders, media organizations, advocacy groups, or nonprofit organizations. Subsequent analyses of these tweets indicate that they represented the full range of views, beliefs, and opinions of both the Republican and Democratic Party and did not retweet more extreme content from one party than the other.[2]

Another key challenge that I discussed in the main text of this book was treatment compliance: even if people said that they would follow the bots, how could we know that they were paying attention to the bots and reading the content they retweeted?

APPENDIX

In chapter 2, I described how we conducted weekly surveys that asked respondents to identify cute animals retweeted by the bots each day but deleted before the administration of the survey. These surveys also included questions about the substance of messages retweeted by the bots. These compliance surveys were fielded on October 27–29, November 3–5, and November 10–13. We defined people as perfectly compliant if they were able to answer all of the questions in each of these three surveys. We defined them as partially compliant if they answered at least one question, but not all questions, correctly. We defined them as minimally compliant if they followed the bot every day during the study period. To increase compliance, we also told respondents that we would monitor whether they muted our account—that is, removed its messages from their timelines without unfollowing it. This is not actually possible, however, and respondents were later debriefed by our survey firm about this deception.

Of the 325 Republicans we invited to follow the liberal bot in our study's treatment condition, 186 agreed to do so. Of these respondents, 119 were able to identify the first cute animal our bot retweeted, and 120 and 113 identified the cute animal tweeted during the second and third week of our study, respectively. Of the Republicans in our treatment condition, 128 were able to correctly answer substantive questions about the content of our bot's tweets during the first week, followed by 134 and 125 in the second and third weekly surveys, respectively. Of the 419 Democrats we invited to participate in our study's treatment condition, 272 agreed. Of these respondents, 170 identified the cute animal during the first week, followed by 175 and 170 in the second and third weeks, respectively. The number of Democrats in our treatment condition who were able to answer substantive questions about our bot's tweets were 226 in the first week, followed by 203 and 176 in the second and third weeks, respectively.

Another threat to causal inference in our study that was not described in the main text of this book is called algorithmic confounding.[3] This confounding occurs when a researcher confuses some form of human behavior with what actually occurs because humans are interacting with algorithms that may be hidden from public view. A classic example of this is Google's Flu Trends, a tool that used search data to monitor the spread of influenza. Though this tool produced very accurate estimates of the seasonal disease for several years, the estimates spiked abruptly in mid-2012. Researchers originally feared that the spike signaled a pandemic, but it was later discovered that the spike in Google searches was driven in part by a shift in the company's algorithm. People who Googled symptoms of the common cold were shown advertisements about the flu. This apparently made many of these people search for terms associated with the flu, which were later mistaken by researchers as evidence that influenza was spreading rapidly.[4]

In our study, we were concerned that Twitter's timeline algorithm—which determines the order in which messages appear in a user's timeline—would create inconsistencies in treatment across subjects. Though Twitter does not make the design of this algorithm public, a publication by data scientists at Twitter indicates that the algorithm learns from user engagement.[5] If users seldom liked or retweeted material from our bot, it might sink to the bottom of their Twitter timelines, possibly giving them a lower dose of our treatment. To discourage this, we asked all respondents to disable Twitter's timeline algorithm in order to make sure they saw our bot's tweets, reminding them that seeing the messages would be necessary to earn the additional $18 described in our recruitment dialogue. We also took steps to assess the possibility of algorithmic confounding related to Twitter's recommender algorithm, which recommends new accounts for a user to follow. We were concerned that this algorithm might recommend more accounts closely related to our bot to users in our study, thereby increasing the amount of treatment they received. Because the literature indicates that this algorithm made recommendations based upon the accounts followed by any particular account, however, we were able to avoid creating such bias by setting up our bots so that they followed no one.[6]

In mid-November 2017, one month after the study's initial survey, we offered all respondents in both the treatment and control conditions $12 to complete a ten-minute follow-up survey that (once again) was designed to appear unrelated to the invitation to follow our bots. This survey included all of the same questions about political beliefs in the first survey, and we used these measures to calculate change in the abovementioned Ideological Consistency Scale over the study period. Of the 1,220 people randomized into the study's treatment or control conditions, 1,069 completed the posttreatment survey. We observed no significant difference in the rate of attrition between those in the treatment and control conditions, which indicated that our treatment did not cause people to leave the study at higher rates compared to those in the control condition—a problem known as posttreatment bias.[7] Fortunately, we also did not observe any evidence of bias in attrition by party affiliation, demographic factors, or geographic location.[8]

In addition to the original survey and bot experiment, we collected a large amount of data about our respondents from Twitter itself. Using the Twitter handles that respondents agreed to share with us, we collected the most recent tweets and likes (or "favorites") of each respondent as well as posts and likes made during the study period and up to one year later. In total, we collected 1,777,280 tweets and 704,951 likes. In addition, we collected all available data from each respondent's public Twitter profile. This included the users' profile descriptions, the number of people they followed and the number of followers they had, and their location (if available). In addition, we wrote code that collected the names of every account that each respondent followed, as well as the names of all Twitter users who followed our respondents. We employed these data to create additional measures to assess the strength of each respondent's echo chamber prior to our experiment, and conduct other robustness checks described elsewhere.[9]

To estimate the effect of following a bot that retweets messages from opinion leaders from the opposing political party for one month, we calculated the amount of change in each respondent's Ideological Consistency Scale score between the first and last survey. By comparing the amount of change among those in the treatment and control conditions, we were able to estimate the effect of following our bots net of people's preexisting beliefs or historical factors that might have shaped them prior to our study, such as the divisive 2016 presidential campaign. This approach, which social scientists often call a difference-in-differences model, cannot rule out the impact of events that occurred during our study period, however. Our models also accounted for how much attention each respondent paid to our bots—that is, the level of compliance with our treatment—using a statistical measure known as the complier average causal effect. Our models also accounted for other confounding factors such as the respondent's age, income, education, gender, race, and geographic region. In addition, our models included a measure of the strength of each respondent's echo chamber that was the average ideological score of the opinion leaders they followed. Finally, our analysis accounted for the amount of off-line exposure people had to members of the opposing political party derived from our pretreatment survey.

The Qualitative Bot Experiment

A major limitation of our quantitative bot experiment is that we were not able to identify the reason why exposure to the other side led people to become more entrenched in their preexisting

142

views. One of the goals of our qualitative bot experiment was to identify the mechanism of this effect by repeating the experiment with a much smaller group of people whom we could interview for at least one hour before and after they followed our bots. These findings are reported in chapter 3, and vignettes about respondents appear at the beginning of chapters 1 and 2. The second, broader, goal of our qualitative bot experiment was to obtain a deeper understanding of how social media shape political polarization more generally. Indeed, a core strength of qualitative research is that it can allow researchers to identify new social processes that are hidden—or those that require lengthier, open-ended observation to discover than large-scale public opinion surveys can provide.[10] These findings informed the discussion in chapters 5 and 6. Because the methodology of this study is not explained elsewhere, I describe it in detail here.

In mid-July 2018, we hired YouGov—the same survey firm that recruited respondents for our quantitative bot study—to recruit a sample of Americans who identified with either the Republican or Democratic Party, were U.S. citizens, visited Twitter at least three times a week, were willing to share their Twitter handle with researchers, and were at least eighteen years old. Our goal was to conduct two open-ended qualitative interviews with sixty Republicans and sixty Democrats during the late summer or early fall of 2018. Using these sampling criteria, YouGov sent the same online survey that we employed in our first bot study to 261 respondents. The sample was stratified to provide comparable numbers of Democrats and Republicans, as well as of those who identified themselves as strong and weak partisans. The sample was also stratified by U.S. states. We used the same data-screening criteria employed in the first survey to identify candidates for qualitative interviews among this population, and once again we obtained informed consent from all respondents to participate in our research. We excluded thirty people who did not provide a valid Twitter handle or provided a handle for a protected Twitter account. We excluded an additional eight people for whom at least two of the demographic features that we observed on their social media accounts conflicted with those reported in the quantitative survey.

From the population of eligible respondents, we randomly sampled 134 candidates for interviews. We sent each of these respondents an email indicating that they could earn a $75 Amazon gift card for participating in a one-hour telephone interview with a member of our research team. If we could not reach respondents via email, we called them using a cell phone number provided by our survey firm. We were unable to reach four people because they had not provided accurate contact information. One person declined to be interviewed. Of the remaining 129 people, 86 agreed to participate, for an effective response rate of 66.7 percent. However, three of those who agreed to participate did not comply, making the real response rate slightly lower. We observed no evidence of response bias by political party or age. Nonetheless, those who participated in our qualitative interviews were slightly less likely to be strong partisans and significantly more likely to be male than those who did not participate.

The mean age of those who participated in the study was forty-four. The youngest respondent was nineteen, and the oldest was seventy-five. Of the respondents, 55 percent were male, and 80 percent were White. Fifty-two percent identified themselves as Democrats, and 48 percent identified themselves as Republicans. Forty-five percent identified themselves as strong partisans, and 55 percent identified themselves as weak partisans. Interviewees were recruited from thirty different states. The largest shares came from New York (eight respondents), Florida (seven), Virginia (seven), North Carolina (six), Texas (five), and California (four). The median annual family income of respondents was $60,000–$70,000, and 52 percent had a four-year college degree. Only one respondent was unemployed, though twelve were retired, five were stay-at-home parents, and ten were college students. Forty-six percent of respondents were married, and 32 percent had children under age eighteen in their homes. The largest groups by religious affiliation were Protestant (thirty-two), agnostic or atheist (twenty-seven), and Catholic (sixteen). Though respondents were recruited from a range of different demographic groups and geographic locations, the sample is not representative of the U.S. population because of its size and because we studied only those who were affiliated with the Republican or Democratic Party and used Twitter regularly. Once again, additional research is needed to confirm that our results can be generalized to other social media platforms—though much of our qualitative analysis analyzed our respondents' behavior outside Twitter. We cannot rule out, however, that Twitter users may have different characteristics than non-Twitter users.

Our first round of interviews was conducted between late July and mid-October 2018. All interviews were conducted via phone and recorded using a mobile app. We hired a team of nine interviewers—all of whom were graduate students in the social sciences or already possessed an advanced degree in a related field. All of the interviewers had completed at least one course in qualitative research methods. Of the nine interviewers, two were male and seven were female. Two had grown up in regions of the United States where Republicans were in the majority, and seven had grown up in predominantly Democratic areas. Wherever possible, interviewers from Republican-majority areas were matched with Republican respondents to reduce interviewer effects associated with the interviewer's accent or other aspects of language style and self-presentation via phone. All interviewers participated in a training session led by me or an advanced graduate student. During these sessions, interviewers practiced conducting interviews on each other before interviewing respondents. Five of the interviewers conducted an additional pilot interview before our fieldwork, which were used to revise our interview questionnaire during in-person and online meetings between members of the research team. We also solicited comments about our interview questionnaire from leading qualitative researchers.

All interviews began with the interviewer asking for permission to record the interview and explaining that the research team would adhere to "strict standards of confidentiality," replacing the respondent's real name with a pseudonym and removing or changing demographic information to increase confidentiality. Next, interviewers paraphrased the following dialogue written by the research team: "Thanks for taking the time to talk with me today. I am a researcher trying to understand how Americans use social media sites such as Twitter and Facebook. I'd like to have a conversation with you today about why you started using social media, how you use social media in your day-to-day life, and what types of things you do and do not like about social media." To encourage respondents to treat the interview as an open-ended conversation and provide detail narratives about their lives, we told them:

> This conversation may be a little bit different than other surveys you have taken on YouGov. Instead of asking you a series of pre-prepared questions and asking you to choose from a list of options, I want to try to understand the world from your point of view. I want to hear what you think is important *in your own words* by letting you tell me about your experience with social media—or by telling me stories about experiences you've had on social media sites or giving me lots of examples from your own life. I'm really hoping we can get to know each other better and have an enjoyable conversation in the short time that we have.

Interviewers then explained the interview would begin with a few broad questions but once again reminded respondents that the interviewer's goal was "to have a conversation where I learn more about you and how social media fits into your life—so please feel free to interrupt me at any point."

Respondents were first asked a series of open-ended questions about why they began using social media. Next, we asked them to tell us what they had done the last two times they logged into a social media site. Third, we asked which types of accounts they followed online. The final open-ended question in the first section of the interview asked respondents, "If I were to look at your social media accounts, but never meet or talk to you in person, would I get a good sense of who you are?" Next, we transitioned to a series of questions about how people got information about news and current events, not only on social media but also through other forms of media such as television and newspapers. First, we asked people how important it was to them to follow news and current events. Second, we asked them to name the sources they used to follow the news (if any) and explain which ones were their favorites, and why. We also asked them whether they used social media to learn about the news. Third, we asked them what topics were important to them in the news—or if they told us they did not follow current events, we asked them to describe the last time they came across a story about politics or government. Finally, we asked people a series of questions about misinformation and media bias.

In the next section of our first interviews with respondents, we began by asking questions about their political views. First, we asked them about their earliest memories of hearing about politics and asked them to describe any people in their lives who influenced their political views. Next, we asked respondents whether they described themselves as Democrats, Republicans, or someone who does not have a political party. We then asked them how well the term "Democrat" or "Republican" described them and why they leaned toward one party or another. We also asked them, "If you could change one thing about each party, what would it be?" We then asked a series of questions about what the respondent thought about people from the opposing political party, and how often they interacted with people who do not share their political views. Then we asked about the outcomes of these interactions.

The next section of our interview covered the social policy issues measured in the Ideological Consistency Scale that we used to assess respondents' political ideology in the quantitative bot study I described earlier in this appendix. First, we asked them whether they thought government regulation of the economy is necessary or if they think it slows down economic progress. Next, we asked them about immigration—specifically, whether the United States should accept more or fewer migrants. We also asked them whether they thought that immigration impacts American jobs and values and whether our country has a responsibility to accept refugees. We then turned to questions about the environment. We asked respondents whether they thought that the government should do anything about climate change and whether they had been personally impacted by the issue. Next, we asked a series of questions about race, inequality, and policing. Specifically, we asked whether respondents thought that racial discrimination is one of the main factors that shape poverty among Blacks, and if police treat Blacks differently from Whites. Last, we asked respondents what they thought of President Trump's job performance— which issues they thought he was doing a "good job on" and "not doing a good job on"—and whether their overall opinion of Trump had improved or declined since the 2016 election.

The final section of our first interview asked respondents a series of open-ended questions about the difference between their online and off-line behavior. First, we asked them whether they had ever seen a social media post that changed the way they thought about an issue or the way they might vote or discuss an issue with others. Next, we asked whether they had ever encountered a social media post that upset them. If so, we asked them how the post had made them feel, whether they commented upon it, and how often they got upset about things they saw on social media. Third, we asked whether they had ever found themselves thinking about someone else's post long after they had read it. Fourth, we asked if they discussed politics off-line with anyone, and whether they discussed things they saw on social media with such people. Fifth, we asked if they engaged in any political behavior off-line such as protesting, boycotting a product, or joining an advocacy group. Finally, we asked whether they would be willing to tell us who they planned to vote for in the midterm elections in November 2018—or, if they were interviewed after the election, for whom they had voted.

We randomized interview participants into treatment and control conditions after stratifying them into groups according to their party affiliation and strength of partisanship. In mid-October 2018, everyone in the treatment condition received an invitation (which was designed to seem unrelated to our interview) to follow one of our study's bots. Once again, we monitored compliance with treatment using weekly surveys that asked respondents whether they could identify cute animal pictures tweeted by our bots and answer substantive questions about the content of their tweets. Overall, 70 percent of the respondents passed at least one of the compliance checks. One week after the one-month treatment period, all respondents in the treatment and control conditions were offered another $75 Amazon gift card for participating in another one-hour interview. Seventy-two of the eight-three respondents who completed the original interview were reinterviewed between late November 2018 and February 2019, for a total of 155 interviews. Of the thirteen people who did not respond to our follow-up invitation, five were Democrats, and eight were Republicans. Eight of the nonresponders had been assigned to the study's treatment condition and five to the control condition.

The posttreatment interview questions differed from those in the pretreatment interview as follows. First, in the second round of interviews, we did not ask respondents about the history of their social media usage or their earliest political memories. Instead, interviewers were instructed to begin by asking a series of questions about respondents' most recent experiences on Twitter. We asked them what they had done the last time they logged onto Twitter. Next, we asked them to give us some examples of things they had seen on Twitter recently. We also asked whether they had followed any new accounts since the last time we interviewed them. Next, we asked what types of issues they had been following recently on social media. The next section of the posttreatment interview repeated questions from the previous interview about political identification and the respondents' attitudes toward both the Democratic and Republican Parties. The posttreatment interview also included the same open-ended questions about five substantive issues—the economy, immigration, the environment, race, and President Trump—covered in the previous interview.

In addition, our follow-up interview included a series of questions designed to probe respondents' attitudes about high-profile events that had occurred during the treatment period. These included the midterm elections of November 2018, the Trump administration's trade deal with Canada and Mexico, and the escalation of a trade war with China. The period also coincided with controversy related to a caravan of migrants headed to the U.S.-Mexico border and the use of tear gas to disperse them by U.S. border agents. Other high-profile events during the month included the Camp Fire—the largest forest fire in California's history at the time—and the shooting of a Black security guard by White police officers in Chicago while he was attempting to apprehend a criminal. During this period, Trump's former campaign manager and lawyer were charged with crimes, and the Mueller investigation of Trump was expanded. Finally, former President George H. W. Bush passed away, and the *Washington Post* journalist Jamal Khashoggi was allegedly assassinated in a

Turkish embassy. We first asked respondents whether they had heard of each of these events. If they had not heard of an event, the interviewer provided a brief explanation of it. In any case, we asked each respondent a series of questions designed to gauge their opinion of each issue.

The posttreatment interview did not include any questions about our bots for two reasons. First, we did not want respondents to connect the invitation they had received to follow a bot to our request to interview them, since this might have increased Hawthorne effects, expressive responding, or other reactions driven by the respondent's opinion of the study instead of how the treatment impacted them. Second, a vast literature indicates that people provide extremely inaccurate explanations of why they change their minds, either because of self-preservation strategies such as motivated reasoning or what social psychologists call the need for certainty—or because of simple errors of memory.[11] Instead, we aimed to assess the impact of following our bots by comparing shifts in the ways people answered questions between our pre- and posttreatment interviews, and by comparing how respondents in the treatment and control condition discussed the high-profile events described in the previous paragraph. Our questions about respondents' recent experiences on Twitter were further designed to encourage respondents to discuss the bot if they chose to do so. Finally, interviewers were not aware of which respondents had been assigned to the treatment and control conditions in the study, and only two members of the research team knew about the experimental component of the study.

All interviews were transcribed and subject to multiple rounds of coding and analysis. In the first round of coding, I wrote code to identify each of the open-ended questions asked by our interviewers in the transcript, as well as the respondents' answers to these questions. In a second round of coding, I read the full text of all 155 interviews and wrote a short memorandum describing the social background of each respondent, including their profession and location and general notes about their political beliefs and behaviors. I also noted any shifts that I observed in the beliefs and behaviors before and after respondents followed our bot. During this coding process, I did not consult a list of which respondents were in the treatment or control conditions to make my analyses as objective as possible. I then read all of the memos and generated a list of new categories to use in coding all of the interviews. Next, I read each of the 155 interviews a second time to apply these codes and assess trends that I had observed across the memos among respondents in the study's treatment and control conditions. Finally, I analyzed the distribution of these codes across all respondents and created lists of respondents that exemplified each process I observed. I then reread the full transcripts of all interviews in each of these groups, taking more detailed notes about each one to craft the narratives presented in this book.

In addition to the interview data collected from respondents in the qualitative bot study, we once again collected all publicly available information that they had produced on Twitter or that Twitter made publicly available about them. As in our quantitative bot study, this information produced a large data set of tweets, likes, profile descriptions, and detailed social network data about each respondent. If respondents provided information about other social media accounts, I also visited these sites and conducted Google searches to perform further research about the daily life of each respondent.

The Simulated Social Media Platform Experiment

The third goal of the research presented throughout this book was to identify how different characteristics of social media platforms contribute to political polarization. This section of the appendix describes an experiment that we conducted to study how anonymity influences political polarization on a social media platform we created for scholarly research. This is the first of several planned studies that will examine other factors such as how social media platforms allocate status to users and how recommendation systems shape the possibility of political compromise. Because the results of this first study using our new platform have not yet been described elsewhere, I provide extensive detail about the research design here.

In mid-January 2020, we hired YouGov—the same survey firm employed in the other field experiments described in this book— to recruit a nonprobability sample of 1,200 people (600 Democrats and 600 Republicans) to complete two online surveys. We planned to offer 900 of the participants additional incentives to use our social media platform. Based upon pilot studies, we learned that recruiting people to complete multiple surveys, install an app, learn how to use it, and successfully employ the app to interact with another user presented considerable logistical challenges. Because we anticipated low response rates and difficulties with treatment compliance, we asked our survey firm to recruit a very large number of respondents to complete our pretreatment survey. In mid-January 2020, 7,074 respondents completed a twenty-minute online survey. Respondents had to (1) be a U.S. citizen, (2) identify with either the Republican or Democratic Party, and (3) report using a smartphone or tablet. All respondents received $12.50 in compensation via our survey firm's points system, which allows panelists to transfer points to Amazon gift cards or other benefits.

The pretreatment survey included an informed consent dialogue and a battery of questions about respondents' political attitudes that we used to create a single index of political polarization. These included a ten-item measure of attitudes about members of the opposing party and a ten-item measure of two social policy issues that we asked users in the study's treatment condition to discuss on our platform: immigration and gun control. In addition, the survey included measures of other issues that might shape how the treatment interacted with the outcome, such as respondents' political knowledge, personality, strength of partisanship, media consumption, and social media usage. In addition, we obtained basic demographic information about all respondents (for example, their age, income, education, and geographic location) from our survey firm.

All study participants were randomized into one of five conditions. In the study's three treatment conditions, respondents were offered the equivalent of $17.50 to use our social media platform. To assess the effect of these treatments, we compared them to two other conditions. In the fourth study condition respondents were asked to write essays about either immigration or gun control, but not discuss these issues with anyone else. Respondents in the fifth study condition did no additional activities. One day after the pretreatment survey, all respondents in the treatment condition received an invitation to help test a new social media platform called DiscussIt that they were told allowed people to "anonymously discuss various topics and issues." The name of the platform and the recruitment dialogue were designed not to focus on politics to mitigate response bias. Users were told that they must engage in a "sincere conversation" in which they made at least fourteen replies to another user on the platform over the course of one week, with each reply defined as a turn in a conversation—that is, a shift from a statement by one person to a statement by another. Respondents were not told that the platform was being developed by academic researchers, since our pilot studies indicated that revealing our identity triggered expressive responding. All study participants were debriefed about this by the survey firm at the conclusion of the study.

Study participants who agreed to use the app were redirected to a screen in the online recruitment dialogue that explained how to install DiscussIt on either an iOS or Android smartphone or tablet. We also gave them an invite code and instructed them to use it when they logged onto the platform. Unbeknown to respondents, our social media platform used this invite code to match them with a member of the opposing political party. The first three onboarding (or introduction) screens in the DiscussIt app reminded the participant that the platform was designed for anonymous conversations and that they would be given a random name while they used the app. These screens also reminded the user that they had to make at least fourteen replies to another user to be compensated for testing the app. This screen encouraged participants to turn on notifications for our app, so they could receive an update when their discussion partner had replied to their messages. On the next screen, users were shown a screen that informed them they had been selected to discuss either immigration or gun control. Next, we asked users how strongly they agreed or disagreed with a statement about the selected topic, to give them the impression that their response would be used to match them with another user. The system then searched for a member of the opposing party who had also completed the onboarding process and been assigned the same discussion topic.

Once respondents were matched, they received a message introducing them to their partner. All participants were given one of the following androgynous pseudonyms: Jamie, Jessie, Taylor, Quinn, or Casey. In addition to the study's main treatment conditions, we also added three subtreatment conditions that included information about the study participant's discussion partner. In one subcondition, participants saw only the name of their partner. In another subcondition, participants were shown the political party of their discussion partner. In a third subcondition, the incorrect political party of their discussion partner was shown. These subconditions were designed to assess the impact of partisan cues' net of anonymity and to determine whether people would be more likely to find common ground across party lines if they thought that they were speaking to a member of the opposing political party or their own party. The findings reported in this book pertain only to people who used the app, regardless of how their partner's party was labeled. My colleagues and I are currently analyzing the three subconditions where party identification of the chat partner was labeled, unlabeled, and mislabeled for a future publication.

Once study participants were matched with their discussion partner, they were redirected to DiscussIt's main chat interface and asked to share their thoughts about one of the following two questions: "Do you think the benefits of immigration outweigh the potential downsides?" or "Do you think the benefits of gun control outweigh the downsides?" After both users completed a reply to each other, they received a pop-up notification informing them that they had to make at least thirteen additional replies to receive compensation for testing the app. The app also included features for notifying delinquent discussion partners and rematching participants whose discussion partners had not replied for more than three days. The app provided conversational prompts in case conversations got stuck, such as "How does this issue affect your life?" and "What's one of the key reasons you have your position?" After users made thirteen replies to each other, they received a pop-up message that informed them they would be redirected to a brief in-app survey after they posted their next message. This in-app survey was designed to measure the immediate effect of the treatment by measuring change in attitudes about immigration or gun control, as well as attitudes toward the opposing political party and their overall experience using the app. A small number of users who completed at least ten replies, but not fourteen, by the end of the one-week testing period were directed to the app's exit survey and considered to have been treated. The exit survey asked them a series of questions about their discussion partner, and several questions about their attitudes toward members of the opposing party.

All respondents were invited to complete a follow-up survey several days after the conclusion of the one-week treatment period. The recruitment dialogue for this survey was designed to appear unrelated to both the previous survey and the invitation to use the app. The follow-up survey included all of the same variables used to measure political polarization in the pretreatment survey, as well as a set of questions about health care and tax reform that were designed to further reduce respondents' ability to connect the survey to the pretreatment survey. In all, 1,306 people used the DiscussIt app, and 525 were assigned to our control condition where they were asked to write an essay about either gun control or immigration; 403 people were assigned to the control condition where they performed no additional activities.

To assess the effect of engaging in anonymous conversations about politics with a member of the opposing party on a new social media platform, we calculated the difference in our polarization index between the pre- and posttreatment surveys. This index was coded so that positive values indicated more polarization (such as a movement away from the policy positions of the opposing party or increasing animosity toward the other party). We ran linear models that compared the change in the polarization index of those in our treatment condition to the change in this index for those in the essay-writing condition, controlling for respondents' political knowledge, personality type, overall interest in politics, strength of partisanship, age, gender, race, and level of education. Overall, these estimates indicate that the effect of using our app resulted in a 0.3 standard deviation decrease in the amount of polarization exhibited by our respondents in the posttreatment survey.

ACKNOWLEDGMENTS

My interest in political polarization is personal. When I was eleven years old, my parents and I moved to a country on the brink of civil war. The French Congo (as it was then known) was run by an oligarchy that stoked conflict between militias called the Cocoye, the Cobras, and the Ninjas. The differences between the Congo's capital city, Brazzaville, where we lived, and the comfortable suburb of Boston that I grew up in were stark. My parents planned to send me to a boarding school in a neighboring country while my father—a doctor turned public health activist—worked for the World Health Organization in Brazzaville. However, we soon learned that the school had closed because that country (then called Zaire) was suffering from even greater ethnic conflict than our new home. On some evenings we could hear bullets—and the occasional grenade—if the water was low enough in the massive river that separated the two countries.

The years that followed changed my life forever. My mother was nearly killed when a knife was thrown near her in a chaotic market where she was trying to find flour to make an American-style pizza for me. My father was incarcerated by one of the militias, whose members were angered by his refusal to pay them to avoid being arrested for a traffic violation. He did not pay the bribe. When my mother left me alone to bail him out, criminals robbed our house, and my parents found me hiding in a closet when they returned. My mother and I took one of the next flights out of the French Congo, and six months later my father became one of the last Americans to leave the country—on a helicopter that was also evacuating Marines from the U.S. embassy.

Whatever routine path might have been available to someone like me before my time in the French Congo was no longer viable. The experience left me with a lifelong desire to understand how people can come to hate each other so deeply. My father, on the other hand, was drawn further into a life of activism: after we returned to the United States, he founded a nonprofit organization to combat poverty and disease in sub-Saharan Africa. While he grew more optimistic in the power of truth and reconciliation, I became deeply pessimistic about human nature and our ability to compromise with each other. I somehow found solace in books I could barely understand by German philosophers whose names I could not pronounce. Whenever my dad brought up his work, I would conjure up the deepest form of skepticism possible—German-style skepticism—about whether his work was anything more than reducing liberal guilt among the Americans he recruited to join him on yearly pilgrimages to Africa.

Before my father passed away last year—from a disease he had acquired in the French Congo—I spent hours interviewing him about his life, trying to understand where his boundless altruism had come from. Around the same time, I began to write this book. All of my previous scholarship was "on brand" with my personality. For example, I had written a book about the seemingly hopeless rise of anti-Muslim extremism in the United States, which warned that social media platforms were only making the problem worse. Somewhere in the process of outlining *Breaking the Social Media Prism*, however, I changed course. I became cautiously optimistic about the fight against political tribalism on social media, even as the United States experienced unprecedented polarization (especially on social media platforms). By the time I was writing the chapters of this book that propose solutions to beat back polarization on our platforms, I realized where this type of stubborn altruism originated inside me. I smiled to myself, shed a few tears, and dedicated this book to my dad. You got me after all, old man.

If it took an unusual childhood to inspire this book, it took truly outstanding partners in the field of book publishing to give me the courage, vision, and stamina to write it. The concept for this book was born through months of conversation, drafting, and redrafting with my incomparable literary agent, Margo Fleming of Brockman, Inc. She not only helped me imagine this book, but she also found the perfect home for it—at Princeton University Press, where Meagan Levinson immediately shared my vision and more importantly challenged me at the end of every draft to make this book so much better than I ever could have made it on my own. She spent many long hours—during a pandemic and with a young child, no less—helping me sharpen my argument, hone my prose, and regretfully informing me that many of my jokes aren't as funny as I think they are. I am also deeply grateful to many other people at the press who made this book possible, especially Maria Whelan, who helped me learn how to communicate my work to a public audience, but also Kathryn Stevens, Colleen Suljic, Laurie Schlesinger, Christie Henry, David Luljak, and copy editor Jeanne Ferris, who almost talked me out of my joke about the Oxford comma.

Of course, this book would not have been possible without the extraordinary interdisciplinary team of researchers with whom I work in the Polarization Lab. I am extraordinarily grateful for my wonderful faculty codirectors Alex Volfovsky and Sunshine Hillygus. I am also deeply indebted to all of the students and research assistants—some of whom are now faculty members, postdocs, or data scientists at social media platforms—who worked on parts of the research presented in this book: Lisa Argyle, Taylor Brown, John Bumpus, Nick Chakraborty, Guanhua Chen, Haohan Chen, Aidan Combs, Juncheng Dong, Brian Guay,

ACKNOWLEDGMENTS

Mary Beth Hunzaker, Neha Karna, Friedolin Merhout, Siqi Mo, Graham Tierney, and Kaicheng Yu. For more than half a year, Marcus Mann led an outstanding team of qualitative researchers who collected a tremendous amount of the data presented within this book: Kirsten Adams, Lara Balian, MaryBeth Grewe, Ashley Hedrick, Mari Kate Mycek, Sarah Mye, Cassandra Rowe, and Jared Wright. I am also very grateful to Amy Binder, Mitchell Stevens, and Jessi Streib, who helped me and my colleagues improve our qualitative research techniques. I am equally indebted to Jonah Berger, Gary King, Skip Lupia, Jim Moody, Brendan Nyhan, Lynn Smith-Lovin, and Duncan Watts, who helped me focus and improve our quantitative field experiments. Jamie Druckman offered more than ten pages of brilliant comments that made this book inestimably better—I cannot thank him enough. I am also very grateful to Mabel Berezin who provided extensive comments on the manuscript as well. Dan Ariely gave me wonderful advice about how to communicate the results of our work to a general audience. Daniel Kreiss and I discussed this book so many times that I did not dare ask him to read it, but his feedback touched many of the chapters nevertheless. Sharique Hasan and Matt Perault offered very useful feedback as well.

This book also would not have been possible without the support of many different organizations. The Carnegie Foundation, Guggenheim Foundation, Russell Sage Foundation, and National Science Foundation provided financial support for our research. The Duke University provost's office provided seed funding that made the Polarization Lab possible. Duke's Social Science Research Institute and Department of Sociology, as well as the Information Initiative at Duke, also supported our lab with office space and other logistical resources that were essential for our research. Venice International University provided me with a most serene escape to write this book—even if La Serenissima occasionally slowed my progress. I am also grateful to my many colleagues and friends who work for social media companies, who helped me develop the message of this book and make sharper recommendations about how to counter polarization on our platforms. Finally, the Summer Institutes in Computational Social Science, which I cofounded with Matt Salganik, remain a remarkable idea incubator where I have the good fortune to meet many of the brightest young minds in computational social science each year—many of whom helped me present the message of this book more effectively.

Finally, I want to thank the thousands of people who participated in the research for this book. Many of them entrusted us with sensitive information about their political beliefs and intimate details about their lives that made this book an honor to write. But my deepest gratitude—in a life currently filled with so many blessings—is to my wonderful friends and family. I write for them, not only because they continually inspire me, laugh with me, and cheer me along, but also because I hope some of what I've written might make the online worlds we inhabit a slightly better place.

NOTES

Chapter One: The Legend of the Echo Chamber

1. The names of all people interviewed for the research in this book have been replaced by pseudonyms to protect their confidentiality. Wherever necessary, details about their demographic characteristics (such as the geographic location, profession, or number of family members) have been modified to further protect their privacy. The vignettes that describe individuals throughout this book were created via multiple in-depth interviews, studying participants' responses to two online surveys, an in-depth analysis of all publicly available information available from their social media accounts and internet searches, and additional information about their demographic characteristics provided by the survey firm used to recruit them. Some direct quotes from publicly available social media accounts have been paraphrased or abbreviated to further protect the privacy of respondents—and in one case, a term from a quote was replaced with a synonym to prevent identification of the respondent via an internet search. For a complete description of the multiple research techniques used to create vignettes about individual social media users such as Dave Kelly, see the appendix.

2. I borrow the title of this section from Guess et al., *Avoiding the Echo Chamber about Echo Chambers.*

3. Throughout this book I use the term "conservative" to describe the set of principles typically associated with the Republican Party in the United States and the term "liberal" to describe those associated with the Democratic Party. In so doing, I recognize that conservative and liberal ideology systems do not always neatly align with the two-party system. I also recognize that these terms become even more vague in an international context, where the term "liberal" is often

used to describe preferences for laissez-faire economic policy. In later chapters of this book, I discuss the mismatch between ideology measures and partisanship in greater detail.

4. The term was originally used to describe an audio-engineering method popular in the 1930s for creating the effect of someone speaking in a large room. As I discuss in more detail in chapter 2, social scientists have been studying how social networks shape political beliefs since the mid-twentieth century, amid heightened interest in propaganda and groupthink after the two world wars. Of particular concern to scholars such as Harold Laswell, Paul Lazarsfeld, Bernard Berelson, Robert Merton, and Elisabeth Noelle-Neumann was how clustering within our social relationships creates repeated exposure to the same types of information. Whereas Laswell and Noelle-Neumann were principally interested in the effect of mass media, Lazarsfeld and Merton probed more specific questions about the intermediary channels that connect the mass media to individual citizens—namely, social networks. In a series of influential qualitative studies, Lazarsfeld traced how mass media messages spread across conversational networks, informing voting choice and public opinion more broadly. Contrary to prevailing understandings of media effects at the time, Lazarsfeld and colleagues showed that newspapers, television programs, and radio broadcasts were not a hypodermic needle through which opinions could be injected into the masses. Instead, the scholars discovered that mass media have indirect effects through the small group of citizens who are politically engaged and pay regular attention to the news. These opinion leaders, the authors showed, are often very critical of mass media messages. Nevertheless, mass media tend to shape the types of topics that opinion leaders discuss. This seminal finding about the indirect effect of mass media influence launched a wide-ranging series of studies about how social networks form, and specifically how individuals tend to seek out like-minded people (a concept known as homophily, which I describe in greater detail in chapter 2). For more details, see Lazarsfeld, Berelson, and Gaudet, *The People's Choice*; Katz and Lazarsfeld, *Personal Influence*. For a historical overview of these studies see Katz, "Communications Research since Lazarsfeld."

5. See Key, *The Responsible Electorate*.

6. Until the 1980s, national news coverage in the United States was dominated by a handful of large media corporations. Many scholars believe that media outlets avoided taking overtly partisan positions during this era because their audiences included large numbers of people from both parties. The 1980s witnessed the segmentation of the market for news, as technological shifts created new opportunities for smaller outlets to compete for audiences on 24/7 cable news

channels and talk radio stations. Unlike their predecessors, these media outlets catered to the preferences of smaller audiences, creating market incentives for corporations to assume increasingly partisan positions to secure new audiences. For a more detailed discussion of the historical forces that shaped the polarization of mass media in the United States, see Starr, *The Creation of the Media*; Prior, *Post-Broadcast Democracy* and "Media and Political Polarization"; Peck, *Fox Populism*; Berry and Sobieraj, *The Outrage Industry*; Sobieraj and Berry, "From Incivility to Outrage"; Arceneaux and Martin Johnson, *Changing Minds or Changing Channels?*

7. See Kull, Ramsay, and Lewis, "Misperceptions, the Media, and the Iraq War." For a broader discussion of how selective exposure to news coverage shapes political views, see Levendusky, "Why Do Partisan Media Polarize Viewers?"

8. See Eady et al., "How Many People Live in Political Bubbles on Social Media?," 18.

9. See Sunstein, *Republic.com*. For a more detailed explanation of how the absence of media gatekeepers online facilitated the spread of uncivil campaigns on social media, see Berry and Sobieraj, *The Outrage Industry*.

10. See Pariser, *The Filter Bubble*.

11. See Bakshy, Messing, and Adamic, "Exposure to Ideologically Diverse News and Opinion on Facebook."

12. See Barberá, "Birds of the Same Feather Tweet Together." One limitation of this study is that it did not consider the valence of messages shared by Twitter users. Therefore, it is possible that some of those who retweeted messages were criticizing them. Also, as I discuss in chapter 7, the most recent evidence indicates that the prevalence of the echo chamber phenomenon on social media has been overstated—at least on Twitter (see Eady et al., "How Many People Live in Political Bubbles on Social Media?," 18; and Barberá, "Social Media, Echo Chambers, and Political Polarization").

13. See Shearer, "Social Media Outpaces Print Newspapers in the U.S. as a News Source."

14. See Watts, *Everything is Obvious*.

15. Studying social media echo chambers creates numerous methodological challenges. First, the echo chamber phenomenon is a group-level process; not an individual-level one. This means that studying echo chambers requires not only data about large groups of people, but also information about how these people are connected to each other. If we use the standard instrument in a social scientist's tool kit—a public opinion survey that samples individuals randomly to make inferences about a large population of people—the social networks that connect

individuals remain invisible. Inattention to how social networks shape individual beliefs is important not only because social networks are key to the study of echo chambers but also because individual opinions that result from peer influence violate core assumptions necessary for statistical inference. For more information about the problem of so-called network autocorrelation, see Dow et al., "Galton's Problem as Network Autocorrelation." For a discussion of how this shapes public opinion dynamics in particular, see Leenders, "Modeling Social Influence through Network Autocorrelation"; Friedkin and Johnsen, *Social Influence Network Theory*; Klar and Shmargad, "The Effect of Network Structure on Preference Formation." Second, echo chambers shape not just individual opinions but also entire worldviews—the beliefs we take for granted when we interpret the world around us and judge what is important, just, or real. These types of belief systems are difficult to measure with conventional public opinion surveys (see Bourdieu, "Public Opinion Does Not Exist"). Finally, evaluating the concept of echo chambers requires us to track how these worldviews become more or less malleable over time, and longitudinal public opinion surveys are not only logistically challenging but also very expensive. To summarize, studying echo chambers is extremely difficult because it requires very detailed information about how a large group of people view the world across multiple points in time.

16. For overviews of the field of computational social science, see Lazer, Pentland, et al., "Computational Social Science"; Golder and Macy, "Digital Footprints"; Bail, "The Cultural Environment"; Salganik, *Bit by Bit*; Edelmann et al., "Computational Social Science and Sociology." For examples of how experiments in computational social science have created positive human behavior, see Bond et al., "A 61-Million-Person Experiment in Social Influence and Political Mobilization"; and Cameron et al., "Social Media and Organ Donor Registration."

17. See Kosinski, Stillwell, and Graepel, "Private Traits and Attributes Are Predictable from Digital Records of Human Behavior."

18. Kosinski and his team recruited 58,366 U.S. Facebook users to install an app called myPersonality to receive information about their personality gleaned from the content or pages that they "liked" on the platform. According to the researchers, these volunteers consented to participate in their study, but their article does not specify precisely what information the volunteers agreed to share. Like many apps created at the time, Kosinski's team's app collected information about each individual via Facebook's Application Programming Interface, which—assuming researchers are given permission via users— could be used to collect data about individual users and, in many

cases, basic information about an individual's friends (e.g., their names, pages liked, birthday, and city of residence, if available). After completing their study—which warned of the danger of microtargeting by corporations or governments—Kosinski and his team publicly released a version of their data. This is a common practice in social science, since allowing other researchers to access data is necessary to ensure their validity or to otherwise expand upon the research findings. However, Facebook banned the app in August 2018 because the researchers did not agree to a request to audit their data and "shared information with researchers as well as companies with only limited protections in place" (see Archibong, "An Update on Our App Investigation"). Though it is currently not known who was provided access to these data, the myPersonality app created widespread concerns that apps created for research in computational social science could be repurposed for nonacademic purposes. The political consulting firm Cambridge Analytica, for example, has been accused of paying workers from the online crowdsourcing site Amazon Mechanical Turk to use an app that was very similar to the one created by Kosinski's research team to generate more data to use for microtargeting purposes (see Weissman, "How Amazon Helped Cambridge Analytica Harvest Americans' Facebook Data"). For a broader discussion of the ethics of research with social media data, see Salganik, *Bit by Bit*.

19. In other work, Kosinski and colleagues report that such microtargeting can increase the number of clicks an ad can receive (see Matz et al., "Psychological Targeting as an Effective Approach to Digital Mass Persuasion"). However, as I discuss in chapter 7, many social scientists are skeptical that the campaign resulted in a large-scale shift in voting behavior (see Eckles, Gordon, and Johnson, "Field Studies of Psychologically Targeted Ads Face Threats to Internal Validity"). This is not only because the effects of microtargeting have not been well established in the domain of politics, but also because a recent meta-analysis indicates that the overall impact of most political campaigns is negligible (see Kalla and Broockman, "The Minimal Persuasive Effects of Campaign Contact in General Elections").

20. For a more detailed discussion of how data from social media sites and other types of digital trace data provide an incomplete record of human behavior, see DiMaggio, Hargittai, et al., "Social Implications of the Internet"; Hargittai, "Whose Space?" and "Potential Biases in Big Data"; boyd and Crawford, "Critical Questions for Big Data"; Bail, "The Cultural Environment"; Tufekci, "Big Data"; Freelon, "On the Interpretation of Digital Trace Data in Communication and Social Computing Research."

Chapter Two: Why Not Break Our Echo Chambers?

1. See Tucker Higgins, "Trump Declares without Evidence That 'Criminals and Unknown Middle Easterners Are Mixed In' with Migrant Caravan Making Its Way from Honduras."

2. See ESPN Internet Ventures, "2016 Election Forecast."

3. See Westwood, Messing, and Lelkes, "Projecting Confidence."

4. See Lazarsfeld, Berelson, and Gaudet, *The People's Choice*; Katz and Lazarsfeld, *Personal Influence*; Merton, Lowenthal, and Curtis, *Mass Persuasion*; and Merton and Lazarsfeld, "Studies in Radio and Film Propaganda." For a more recent review of the large interdisciplinary literature on homophily, see McPherson, Smith-Lovin, and Cook, "Birds of a Feather."

5. See Lazarsfeld and Merton, "Friendship as Social Process," 22.

6. For a comprehensive overview of field experiments in the social sciences, see Gerber and Green, *Field Experiments*.

7. Facebook was heavily criticized for participating in a large-scale study of whether seeing other people display emotions makes someone more likely to become emotional. A team of researchers at Cornell University conducted an experiment involving 689,003 Facebook users. The researchers tweaked the algorithm that determined the order in which half of these users saw their posts so that more positive or negative emotional content would appear earlier. Next, the researchers tracked the frequency of emotional language employed by users in this treatment condition and compared it to the frequency in users whose feeds were unperturbed. The researchers discovered very modest evidence of emotional contagion, but they received widespread criticism for not giving Facebook users the opportunity to opt out of the experiment (see Kramer, Guillory, and Hancock, "Experimental Evidence of Massive-Scale Emotional Contagion through Social Networks"). For additional details about this controversy and others like it, see Salganik, *Bit by Bit*.

8. Though the IRA's social media campaign attracted significant attention from policy makers, pundits, and media outlets, there is relatively little research on its impact on public opinion. In chapter 7, I discuss a study that my colleagues and I conducted that did not find any evidence that exposure to Twitter accounts associated with the IRA influenced six different measures of political attitudes and behaviors (see Bail, Guay, et al., "Assessing the Russian Internet Research Agency's Impact on the Political Attitudes and Behaviors of American Twitter Users in Late 2017").

9. In the past few years, social science research with bots has begun to expand rapidly. Some researchers study the emerging dynamics of human cooperation through studies in which respondents interact with bots while performing collaborative online tasks. For example, see Shirado and Christakis, "Locally Noisy Autonomous Agents Improve Global Human Coordination in Network Experiments"; Traeger et al., "Vulnerable Robots Positively Shape Human Conversational Dynamics in a Human-Robot Team"; Jahani et al., "Exposure to Common Enemies Can Increase Political Polarization." Others have used bots in real-world settings like our study. The political scientist Kevin Munger used bots to study the effects of skin color on censoring racist language on social media and discovered that bot accounts with light-skinned avatars are more influential in convincing people to stop using racist language than those with darker skin tones ("Tweetment Effects on the Tweeted"). For an overview of the new field of bot-based research, see Rahwan et al., "Machine Behaviour."

10. For a more detailed discussion of the limitations of our research design, see Bail, Argyle, et al., "Exposure to Opposing Views on Social Media Can Increase Political Polarization." Because our study examined only self-identified Democrats and Republicans who use Twitter frequently, our results cannot be generalized to the entire U.S. population or even to other social media platforms. For a detailed discussion of how our sample compares to the U.S. population and the statistical procedures we used to assess the impact of age on our study, see the appendix of this book or Bail, Argyle, et al., "Exposure to Opposing Views on Social Media Can Increase Political Polarization."

11. See Barberá, "Birds of the Same Feather Tweet Together."

12. We are unable to list the names of our bots because some of our respondents engaged with the bots. Therefore, naming our bots could compromise the confidentiality of those who participated in our study—particularly as new machine-learning methods become available to link metadata across data sets.

13. An important limitation of our strategy for measuring treatment compliance is that it compromises the external validity of our findings. In other words, the results of our study reveal what happens when people are financially incentivized to pay attention to tweets from the opposing party, instead of simply exposing people to such tweets in general. If our experiment were repeated without financial incentives, it is possible that people would simply ignore messages from the other side.

14. See Landsberger, *Hawthorne Revisited*.

15. Earlier studies that attempted to influence people's views may have triggered "trolling" of researchers—particularly among conservative

students who took part in classic research on the so-called backfire effect (see Wood and Porter, "The Elusive Backfire Effect").

16. This ostensibly unrelated survey design assumes that if respondents are unable to connect the pretreatment survey to the invitation to participate in a treatment condition, they will be less likely to respond to the posttreatment survey in an expressive manner. For further details, see Broockman and Kalla, "Durably Reducing Transphobia."

17. After one month of exposure, Republicans who followed our Democratic bot experienced between a 0.11 and 0.59 standard deviation increase in conservatism on the Ideological Consistency Scale, which indicates a sizable treatment effect compared to those found in many other field experiments in the social sciences.

18. See Q. Yang, Qureshi, and Zaman, "Mitigating the Backfire Effect Using Pacing and Leading."

19. In a 2020 study, mathematicians from Northwestern University provided a formal proof of our findings using agent-based modeling—a technique where researchers create artificial societies and simulate possible outcomes of social interaction (see Sabin-Miller and Abrams, "When Pull Turns to Shove"). Another recent study by Yale economist Ro'ee Levy suggests the story may be slightly more complicated, however (see Levy, "Social Media, News Consumption, and Polarization"). Levy surveyed a large group of Facebook and randomized some of them into a treatment condition where they were asked to subscribe to conservative or liberal news outlets on Facebook. These included eight prominent news organizations such as MSNBC and Fox News, but not the broader spectrum of opinion leaders, advocacy organizations, and pundits that our bots retweeted. Levy found that people who agreed to "like" such organizations— and thus receive messages from them within their news feeds—did not substantially change their political views in either direction. However, people in Levy's treatment condition did exhibit a very small increase in positive sentiment toward the other political party (between .58 and .96 degrees on a 0–100 scale). As Levy warns, this effect should be interpreted cautiously, since people in his control condition were more likely to complete the follow-up survey in his experiment than those who agreed to follow counter-attitudinal news sources. It is therefore possible that the people who remained in his experiment were unusually tolerant to begin with.

20. The notion that intergroup contact reduces tensions between rival groups became popular through the work of Gordon Allport, a social psychologist at Harvard University (see Gordon Willard Allport, *The Nature of Prejudice*). Allport did not argue that all forms of intergroup contact would reduce intergroup prejudice. Instead, he outlined a se-

ries of conditions necessary for contact to have a positive effect. For example, members of rival groups must have similar social status, shared goals, and support from organizations or governing bodies. Absent these conditions, sociologists such as Herbert Blumer predicted that people might experience a group-threat effect, in which members of opposing groups are viewed as either a threat to the status of one's own group or a competitor for scarce social or economic resources (see "Race Prejudice as a Sense of Group Position," 3–7). As others have noted, the contact and group-threat hypotheses are not incompatible with each other, and both stress the importance of the broader social environment in determining the outcome of intergroup contact (see Bobo and Fox, "Race, Racism, and Discrimination").

21. In 2006, the social psychologists Thomas Pettigrew and Linda Tropp conducted a meta-analysis of 515 studies of the relationship between intergroup contact and prejudice ("How Does Intergroup Contact Reduce Prejudice?"). They found that 94 percent of the studies contained evidence of the positive effects of intergroup contact, and the size of this effect grew with the rigor of the study's research design. The authors also reported that the effects of intergroup contacts tended to go beyond individual members of an out-group and spill over onto other members. Finally, they found evidence that intergroup contact reduced prejudice even in studies in which the conditions outlined in Allport's original theory of intergroup contact were not met. Many of the studies in Pettigrew and Tropp's meta-analysis were conducted within laboratories, however. A more recent meta-analysis by Gunnar Lemmer and Ulrich Wagner scrutinized all studies of intergroup contact conducted outside a lab before 2015 ("Can We Really Reduce Ethnic Prejudice outside the Lab?"). They also reported strong positive effects of intergroup contact that persisted over time. Nonetheless, a large literature over the past few decades also found support for the group-threat hypothesis, described above (see Riek, Mania, and Gaertner, "Intergroup Threat and Outgroup Attitudes"). And the political scientist Ryan Enos conducted a field experiment to study group threat in the Boston metropolitan area, where actors were paid to speak Spanish while riding commuter trains in the area over several months ("Causal Effect of Intergroup Contact on Exclusionary Attitudes"). He found that commuters who rode trains with these actors expressed significantly more exclusionary attitudes toward immigrants afterward compared to those in a control condition.

22. Scholars have long argued about how exposure to people with opposing views shapes political attitudes and political participation. The relationship between these factors was first discussed by Paul Lazarsfeld and colleagues (Lazarsfeld, Berelson, and Gaudet, *The People's Choice*),

but it has been analyzed more systematically by the political scientist Diana Mutz (*Hearing the Other Side*). Mutz found that cross-cutting exposure can moderate political views, but this comes at the expense of political participation. A more recent meta-analysis of forty-eight empirical studies involving more than seventy thousand participants found no significant relationship between cross-cutting exposure and political engagement (see Matthes et al., "A Meta-Analysis of the Effects of Cross-Cutting Exposure on Political Participation"). Still another study by Robert Huckfeldt examined the conditions under which disagreement occurs (*Political Disagreement*). This study turned the focus on homophily on its head, showing that cross-partisan contact is correlated with disagreement and that the amount of disagreement grows according to the social distance between people within different network clusters. In more recent years, the importance of cross-party contact for reducing intergroup tension has also been observed in ethnographic studies of polarization in the United States (see Hochschild, *Strangers in Their Own Land*; Klinenberg, *Palaces for the People*).

23. Backfire effects were first reported in the mid-twentieth century (see Lazarsfeld, Berelson, and Gaudet, *The People's Choice*; and Lord and Lepper, "Biased Assimilation and Attitude Polarization: The Effects of Prior Theories on Subsequently Considered Evidence"). Building upon earlier studies, the political scientists Brendan Nyhan and Jason Reifler asked a group of people to read a news article with a misleading statement—for example, that the Iraqi dictator Saddam Hussein possessed nuclear weapons prior to the 2003 U.S. invasion of his country ("When Corrections Fail"). Half of the participants in the study were then shown a corrective statement. Republicans who were exposed to corrective information about this claim were more likely to think that Iraq possessed nuclear weapons than those who did not see the corrective information. This finding was later reproduced in a range of different settings, including corrections of the false claim that autism spectrum disorders are caused by thimerosal in routinely administered childhood vaccines and of the widespread misperception that Barack Obama is a Muslim (see Nyhan et al., "Effective Messages in Vaccine Promotion"; and Berinsky, "Rumors and Health Care Reform"). However, a study by the political scientists Thomas Wood and Ethan Porter ("The Elusive Backfire Effect") that attempted to reproduce these and other backfire effects found very little evidence of their existence in a group of respondents recruited to complete an online survey. Political scientists Andrew Guess and Alexander Coppock also found little evidence of the backfire effect in a similar follow-up study (see Guess and Coppock, "Does Counter-Attitudinal Information Cause Backlash?").

24. Previous studies of the backfire effect have not established precisely why it occurs. One theory draws upon the concept of motivated reasoning: when we are exposed to something that contradicts our beliefs, it makes us angry or scared. This anger leads us to search for information within our environment that validates our feelings or to argue the point with whatever evidence we can find. In either case, we may end up with more reasons to disagree with corrective information than we might have had otherwise. The concept of motivated reasoning was popularized by the late Israeli social psychologist Ziva Kunda, who— in an experiment in which she and a colleague recruited participants to play a history trivia game—first discovered that people will change their definitions of what is accurate to affirm their preexisting views ("The Case for Motivated Reasoning"). The concept was later extended into the realm of politics by the legal scholar Dan Kahan, who demonstrated that Democrats and Republicans will provide false answers to math problems if those answers are in line with their political beliefs ("Ideology, Motivated Reasoning, and Cognitive Reflection"). Interestingly, there is also evidence of this process at a neurological level. The psychologist Drew Westen and his colleagues placed 30 Republicans and Democrats in an fMRI machine during the run up to the 2004 presidential election ("Neural Bases of Motivated Reasoning"). When the authors showed members of each party information that discredited a message from their party's candidate, the regions of the brain responsible for emotions lit up, and those that we think are associated with cold, dispassionate reason shut down. Still another explanation is that the backfire effect is a temporary phenomenon. As people are repeatedly exposed to corrective information, they may gradually let go of their mistaken beliefs through a process that social scientists call Bayesian updating. In a recent article, the political scientist Seth J. Hill found evidence for this process after exposing Republicans and Democrats to a series of corrective statements about presidential candidates from their party ("Learning Together Slowly").

25. Some of the statements retweeted by our bots could be described as misleading, but most were factually accurate. Others created a different type of exposure simply because they raised issues that are more relevant to one party than the other. A conservative following our liberal bot, for example, might have been exposed to more messages about racial discrimination or climate change advocacy. Similarly, a liberal following our conservative bot might have heard more messages about attacks upon police. Exposure to these types of messages might create a very different effect than those that aim to correct people's misperceptions for many different reasons. For instance, the people

in our study were not being told that their views were inaccurate by experts, whom they might have viewed as condescending. Instead, they were being exposed to arguments by a range of public figures in many different formats for a protracted period of time in a real-life setting.

26. For in-depth discussions of this issue, see Gross and Niman, "Attitude-Behavior Consistency"; Haidt, *The Righteous Mind*; Vaisey, "Motivation and Justification"; and Jerolmack and Khan, "Talk Is Cheap."

27. For a more detailed description of the research techniques employed in this study, see the "Qualitative Bot Experiment" section of the appendix.

28. In reporting the findings of qualitative research—where the goal is to identify new social processes inductively rather than to confirm their existence deductively—one always faces a trade-off between breadth and depth (see Tavory and Timmermans, *Abductive Analysis*). One can either give examples of the same thing happening to a large number of people interviewed—which comes at the cost of significant detail—or one can choose a few exemplars and tell more of their story in depth. In chapter 3, I chose the latter path for two reasons. First, the macro-level pattern was established by the previous study. Second, the longitudinal interviews produced a significant amount of data about social processes that unfolded over time. Therefore, describing these processes in detail would require significant space and additional repetition that would come at the expense of detailed exposition of the microlevel mechanisms I describe in greater detail in chapters 4–6.

Chapter Three: What Happens When We Break Them?

1. See Converse, "The Nature of Belief Systems in Mass Publics (1964)." For a more detailed theory of how political apathy shapes public opinion dynamics, see Zaller, *The Nature and Origins of Mass Opinion*.

2. Eliasoph, *Avoiding Politics*.

3. As I discuss in chapter 7, nearly three-quarters of Americans (and nine out of ten of those ages 18–29) use at least one social media site (see Perrin and Anderson, "Share of U.S. Adults Using Social Media, Including Facebook, Is Mostly Unchanged since 2018").

4. Other work has shown that, like Patty, many of the people who voted for Obama in 2012 and for Trump in 2016 were White, did not have a college degree, and had somewhat negative attitudes about immigrants or issues surrounding racial injustice (see Sides, Tesler, and Vavreck, *Identity Crisis*).

5. Patty also expressed more liberal views about the compensation of chief executive officers (CEOs). Though during our first interview she told us she believed that CEOs make too much money, Patty expressed a more elaborate criticism in our second meeting with her: "I think they get too much—*way* too much. I think they should get just about the same as . . . the people that work under them. A lot of them, they get so high up in there that they think they're so much better than everybody else, and they do things that just aren't acceptable. . . . They get paid so much that they think that they're the big leaders of everything. Well, who put them there? They should be thankful and not take everything they can."

6. In addition to showing that most Americans have a low level of engagement with politics, the political scientist John Zaller's influential book on public opinion (*The Nature and Origins of Mass Opinion*) argues that—like Patty—most people have strong views about only a small number of issues. Only a minority of people can articulate detailed opinions about a wide range of issues. Therefore, Zaller argues, in the rare moments when political persuasion is possible, it tends to occur among those who are actively exposed to politics, and it is more likely when the persuasion attempt focuses upon an issue that people care about.

7. An alternative interpretation of our respondents' tendency to express more detailed or sophisticated opinions about politics is that they were simply building more rapport with our research team or felt more comfortable about voicing their views. I think this interpretation is unlikely, however, since whenever possible we intentionally assigned respondents different interviewers in the first and second interview. Also, we did not notice the same scale of shifting among interviewees in our control condition—people who did not follow our bots.

8. For further details about the relationship between social media usage and political activism, see Perrin, "Social Media Usage."

9. A large-scale study of the spread of misinformation and conspiracy theories on Facebook in 2016 revealed that this type of information is mostly shared by people who are stuck inside political echo chambers (see Del Vicario et al., "The Spreading of Misinformation Online"). In a 2019 study of the impact of the IRA on Twitter, my colleagues and I also found that echo chamber strength was one of the strongest predictors of engagement with accounts associated with the IRA (see Bail, Guay, et al., "Assessing the Russian Internet Research Agency's Impact on the Political Attitudes and Behaviors of American Twitter Users in Late 2017").

10. See U.S. Customs and Border Protection, "CBP Use of Force Statistics."

Chapter Four: The Social Media Prism

1. For a more detailed account of Sherif's experiment and his biography, see Perry, *The Lost Boys*.
2. Quoted in ibid., 115.
3. See, for example, Tajfel, *Differentiation between Social Groups*.
4. See Brown, *Human Universals*.
5. For an overview of these studies, see Tajfel, "Experiments in Intergroup Discrimination"; Diehl, "The Minimal Group Paradigm."
6. See Mason, *Uncivil Agreement*.
7. See Goodman, *The Republic of Letters*.
8. See Schudson, "Was There Ever a Public Sphere?"
9. See Habermas, *The Structural Transformation of the Public Sphere*.
10. For example, see Rawls, *A Theory of Justice*.
11. For an overview, see Fishkin and Luskin, "Experimenting with a Democratic Ideal."
12. Other early observers were much more cynical. Even before Cass Sunstein warned that the internet and social media might have a dark side (*Republic.com*), management scholars Marshall van Alstyne and Erik Brynjolfsson worried the internet could create a kind of "cyberbalkanization" ("Electronic Communities: Global Village or Cyberbalkans"). Still others suggested that the primary function of social media was to create appetites for new kinds of political engagement, instead of dampening desire for deliberation altogether (see Papacharissi, *A Private Sphere*).
13. See Levin and Wong, "'He's Learned Nothing.'"
14. See Romm and Dwoskin, "Jack Dorsey Says He's Rethinking the Core of How Twitter Works."
15. Cohen, "Party over Policy."
16. Analyzing two decades of data from the General Social Survey and the American National Election Study, the sociologist Paul DiMaggio and his coauthors concluded that the American public had not grown more polarized between 1974 and 1994, despite widespread belief the country was experiencing a divisive culture war at the time (see DiMaggio, Evans, and Bryson, "Have American's Social Attitudes Become More Polarized?"). In subsequent decades, the political scientists Alan Abramowitz and Morris Fiorina and their coauthors held a lengthy debate about whether polarization has been increasing for more than a decade (see Abramowitz and Saunders, "Is Polarization a Myth?"; Fiorina and Abrams, "Political Polarization in the American Public"; and Campbell, *Polarized*). As I discuss in greater detail in chapters 6 and 8, most scholars now believe that issue-based political polarization has not increased substantially in recent decades. Among

social scientists, the predominant explanation of steady ideological polarization is known as partisan sorting: instead of voters developing increasingly polarized views about substantive issues such as welfare policy, political parties have adopted their platforms to more efficiently encompass voters with different preferences. For detailed analyses of this issue, see Baldassarri and Gelman, "Partisans without Constraint" and Levendusky, *The Partisan Sort*.

17. Almond and Verba, "Civic Culture Study."
18. Iyengar, Sood, and Lelkes, "Affect, Not Ideology."
19. See Boxell, Gentzkow, and Shapiro, "Cross-Country Trends in Affective Polarization."
20. See Hochschild, *Strangers in Their Own Land*.
21. To cite but one of many possible examples, partisan identity is widely considered to be one of the most important factors that drives voting behavior (see Achen and Bartels, *Democracy for Realists*; Sides, Tesler, and Vavreck, *Identity Crisis*). Many social scientists have examined partisanship as the key basis for social identities. For example, see Price, "Social Identification and Public Opinion"; Greene, "Understanding Party Identification"; Haidt, *The Righteous Mind*; Huddy, "Group Identity and Political Cohesion"; Gutmann, *Identity in Democracy*; Mason, *Uncivil Agreement*; Huddy, Mason, and Aarøe, "Expressive Partisanship"; and Klar, "When Common Identities Decrease Trust." But there is growing interest in other collective identities—especially those attached to being White or Caucasian in U.S. politics (see Jardina, *White Identity Politics*). For a broader overview of research on how identity shapes political polarization, see Klein, *Why We're Polarized*.
22. McConnell et al., "The Economic Consequences of Partisanship in a Polarized Era." Another study showed that members of both parties are unwilling to evaluate the factual accuracy of their partisan viewpoints, even when financial incentives are at stake (see Peterson and Iyengar, "Partisan Gaps in Political Information and Information-Seeking Behavior").
23. See Iyengar and Westwood, "Fear and Loathing across Party Lines"; Gift and Gift, "Does Politics Influence Hiring?"
24. See Klar and Krupnikov, *Independent Politics* and Nicholson et al., "The Politics of Beauty." A more recent study suggests that there is not only increasing correspondence in political beliefs between married couples, but also increasing intra-generational transmission of partisanship (see Iyengar, Konitzer, and Tedin, "The Home as a Political Fortress").
25. See DellaPosta, Shi, and Macy, "Why Do Liberals Drink Lattes?"; Shi et al., "Millions of Online Book Co-Purchases Reveal Partisan Differences in the Consumption of Science"; Hetherington and Weiler, *Prius*

or Pickup?; A. Lee, "How the Politicization of Everyday Activities Affects the Public Sphere"; and Klein, *Why We're Polarized.*

26. For example, see Achen and Bartels, *Democracy for Realists*; Mason, *Uncivil Agreement*; Levendusky, *The Partisan Sort.*

27. For examples of studies that detail the fluidity and situational nature of political identities, see Barth, *Ethnic Groups and Boundaries*; Lamont and Molnár, "The Study of Boundaries in the Social Sciences"; Wimmer, "The Making and Unmaking of Ethnic Boundaries"; Douglas, *Purity and Danger*; and Huddy, "Group Identity and Political Cohesion."

28. For example, see Elias, *The Civilizing Process*; Goffman, *The Presentation of Self in Everyday Life*; DiMaggio, "Culture and Cognition"; Baumeister and Leary, "The Need to Belong"; and Cikara and Van Bavel, "The Neuroscience of Intergroup Relations."

29. See Kreiss, Barker, and Zenner, "Trump Gave Them Hope"; Mason, *Uncivil Agreement.*

30. Cultural sociologists and anthropologists have produced a rich literature that describes how people create, maintain, and transcend these so-called symbolic boundaries. For reviews of this literature, see Lamont and Molnár, "The Study of Boundaries in the Social Sciences"; Wimmer, "The Making and Unmaking of Ethnic Boundaries." For exemplars of this scholarly paradigm, see Barth, *Ethnic Groups and Boundaries*; Douglas, *Purity and Danger*; Lamont, *Money, Morals, and Manners.*

31. Cooley, *Human Nature and the Social Order.*

32. The notion that we develop our identities in response to our perceptions of how other people respond to them in social settings is central not only to Cooley's work but also to Erving Goffman's theory of how we present ourselves (*The Presentation of Self in Everyday Life*), Norbert Elias's classic study of shame and social psychology (*The Civilizing Process*), and Leon Festinger's social comparison theory ("A Theory of Social Comparison Processes").

33. See Goffman, *Stigma.*

34. See also Elias and Scotson, *The Established and the Outsiders.*

35. Goffman, *The Presentation of Self in Everyday Life.*

36. See Marwick and boyd, "I Tweet Honestly, I Tweet Passionately." For similar discussions of how social media are changing the presentation of the self, see boyd and Hargittai, "Facebook Privacy Settings"; Murthy, "Towards a Sociological Understanding of Social Media"; Marwick, *Status Update*; Tufekci, "Grooming, Gossip, Facebook and Myspace."

37. See Meshi et al., "The Emerging Neuroscience of Social Media."

38. See Vogel et al., "Who Compares and Despairs?"

39. See Midgley, "When Every Day Is a High School Reunion."

40. Researchers at Facebook reached a similar conclusion in a 2016 study (see Scissors, Burke, and Wengrovitz, "What's in a Like?"), as well as in a 2020 study that analyzed more than 38,000 users (see Burke, Cheng, and de Gant, "Social Comparison and Facebook").
41. See Marwick, *Status Update*.
42. Bazarova et al., "Social Sharing of Emotions on Facebook."
43. See Meshi et al., "The Emerging Neuroscience of Social Media"; Von Der Heide et al., "The Social Network-Network"; and Aral, *The Hype Machine*.
44. Sherman et al., "The Power of the Like in Adolescence," 1027.
45. For a more detailed discussion of how technology firms create addictive products, see Eyal, *Hooked*.
46. Other scholars such as Neil Postman have noted that people often consume news about current events as a form of entertainment, warning that this has dangerous consequences for democracy and our ability to reach rational compromises (see Postman and Postman, *Amusing Ourselves to Death*). My approach is distinct from this argument and recent extensions of it (see, for example, Vaidhyanathan, *Antisocial Media*)—since the mechanism involved in my argument is identity preservation and status seeking, not entertainment.

Chapter Five: How the Prism Drives Extremism

1. Casselman and Tankersley, "Face It."
2. In this chapter, I use the term "extremist" to refer to people who take strong ideological positions and engage in uncivil behavior online, such as making ad hominem comments about people, circulating memes that ridicule others, or spreading misleading or false information to support their political views or discredit their opponents.
3. See Sageman, *Understanding Terror Networks*; Daniels, *Cyber Racism*; Stampnitzky, "Disciplining an Unruly Field"; Bail, *Terrified*. For overviews of the nascent literature on online extremism and trolling, see Marwick and Lewis, "Media Manipulation and Disinformation Online," and Siegal, "Online Hate Speech." For an extended analysis of the history of online extremism, see Phillips, *This Is Why We Can't Have Nice Things*. For a journalistic account of extremism on social media, see Marantz, *Antisocial*.
4. Earlier in my career, for example, I was interested in studying violent radicalization inspired by ISIS. After surveying the literature for some time, I became deeply skeptical of surveys designed to measure support for violent extremism—not only because people tend to hide their

extreme views from others as a result of what social scientists call social desirability bias, but also because online extremists would presumably avoid communicating their views for fear of being discovered by federal authorities or security officials. Several colleagues and I later discovered that Google search data could be used to measure the prevalence of extremist behavior online (see Bail, Merhout, and Ding, "Using Internet Search Data to Examine the Relationship between Anti-Muslim and pro-ISIS Sentiment in U.S. Counties"), though such digital trace data also have a number of limitations. For additional details about the gap between attitudes and behavior among extremists, see Khalil, Horgan, and Zeuthen, "The Attitudes-Behaviors Corrective (ABC) Model of Violent Extremism."

5. For example, see Daniels, *Cyber Racism*; Marwick and Lewis, "Media Manipulation and Disinformation Online"; and other studies reviewed in Siegal, "Online Hate Speech." An important exception is communications scholar Magdalena Wojcieszak's study of neo-Nazi and radical environmentalist groups, though it focuses on the relationship between online and off-line mobilization, and not differences between the presentation of the self in on- and off-line settings, as I do here (see Wojcieszak, "Carrying Online Participation Offline").

6. Though previous studies have not provided a comprehensive analysis of the role of status in online extremism, a growing number of studies in the field of psychology indicate that perceptions of unfairness are a key driver of radicalization in off-line settings (see van den Bos, "Unfairness and Radicalization").

7. For a broader discussion of the polarizing effect in the American West of new wealth from technology entrepreneurs, see Farrell, *Billionaire Wilderness*.

8. Communications scholars Alice Marwick and Rebecca Lewis earlier speculated that status seeking may be a driver of online extremism in their review of the scholarly literature on this topic (see Marwick and Lewis, "Media Manipulation and Disinformation Online," 28).

9. Petersen, Osmundsen, and Arceneaux, "The 'Need for Chaos' and Motivations to Share Hostile Political Rumors."

10. For a more comprehensive discussion of gender-based harassment by online extremists, see Sobieraj, *Credible Threat*.

11. In one of the only studies to trace extremism in both online and off-line settings, communications scholar Magdalena Wojcieszak also discovered that people who are regularly exposed to those who do not share their views in off-line settings may engage in online bonding rituals such as these. Interestingly, her study also showed that exposure to like-minded extremists in off-line settings can also promote collaboration online (see Wojcieszak, "Don't Talk to Me").

12. A recent follow-up to our 2018 bot study provided similar evidence that extremists value status more deeply than they care about their political views (see Yang, Qureshi, and Zaman, "Mitigating the Backfire Effect Using Pacing and Leading"). In this study, the researchers created bots that followed people who expressed anti-immigrant views on Twitter. If the user followed the bot, then the automated account would begin liking the user's tweets and posting tweets about random subjects, tweets that expressed pro-immigrant views, or tweets that expressed anti-immigrant views (along with beginning to tweet pro-immigrant views). Only the Twitter users who were exposed to opposing views about immigration experienced the same reaction that we observed in our 2018 study—that is, they expressed anti-immigrant views even more frequently. In contrast, people who were first exposed to anti-immigrant views and later exposed to pro-immigrant views produced tweets with less anti-immigrant sentiment. One way to interpret these findings is that people will adapt their views to secure status in the form of likes—even if their adapted views conflict with their previous beliefs.

13. Toennies et al., "Max Weber on Church, Sect, and Mysticism."

14. A similar group dynamic was recently observed in a large-scale analysis of the diffusion of moral language on Twitter, though the authors of this research were not studying political extremists exclusively (see Brady et al., "Emotion Shapes the Diffusion of Moralized Content in Social Networks").

15. See Festinger, Riecken, and Schachter, *When Prophecy Fails*. See also Martin, "Power, Authority, and the Constraint of Belief Systems"; Christakis, *Blueprint*; Rawlings, "Cognitive Authority and the Constraint of Attitude Change in Group."

16. Following the work of Merton, a series of subsequent studies came to describe this type of cognitive bias using the better-known phrase "the false consensus effect" (see Robert K. Merton, *Sociological Ambivalence and Other Essays*; Ross, Greene, and House, "The 'False Consensus Effect'"; and Goel et al., "Real and Perceived Attitude Agreement in Social Networks"). The same dynamic—in which homophilous social networks shape perceptions of the size of minority groups relative to that of the majority group—was demonstrated in a recent large-scale study of six other real-world networks and the political scientist Jaime Settle's large-scale study of political polarization among Facebook users (see E. Lee et al., "Homophily and Minority Size Explain Perception Biases in Social Networks"; Settle, *Frenemies*). Another survey of neo-Nazi and radical environmental groups discovered significant evidence that the false consensus effect is particularly strong in online settings (see Wojcieszak, "False Consensus Goes Online").

17. Settle, *Frenemies*. A similar dynamic was also observed in a recent study by a group of political scientists who were testing the effect of exposing Democrats and Republicans to uncivil criticism from the opposing political party on social media. Across two experiments, this team observed that such exposure creates marked increases in intergroup prejudice, or affective polarization—particularly among people with strong partisan views (see Suhay, Bello-Pardo, and Maurer, "The Polarizing Effects of Online Partisan Criticism").

Chapter Six: How the Prism Mutes Moderates

1. Though political ideology is often described as if it exists on a unidimensional scale that ranges from extremely liberal to extremely conservative, there is growing consensus among social scientists that Americans' political views are much more multidimensional. As the political scientists Shawn Treier and D. Sunshine Hillygus have shown, many Americans hold liberal preferences on one issue but conservative preferences on another ("The Nature of Political Ideology in the Contemporary Electorate"). These cross-pressured people usually identify themselves as moderate on conventional ideology measures or answer "don't know" when asked about their ideology. In addition, measures that ask people about their party affiliation have measurement errors. For example, many people who identify themselves as political independents actually hold very strong views that make them, in effect, too conservative or too liberal to support established parties (see Broockman, "Approaches to Studying Policy Representation").
2. See American National Election Study, "2016 Time Series Study."
3. See DiMaggio, Evans, and Bryson, "Have American's Social Attitudes Become More Polarized?"; Baldassarri and Gelman, "Partisans without Constraint"; Levendusky, *The Partisan Sort*; Lelkes, "Mass Polarization."
4. See survey questionnaire from American National Election Study, "2018 Pilot Study."
5. See Duggan, "Online Harassment 2017."
6. Threats against women on social media also very frequently result in the type of self-censorship conducted by Sara Rendon (see Sobieraj, *Credible Threat*).
7. I discuss the concept of false polarization in greater detail in chapter 8. For a more detailed discussion of the concept, see Pronin, Lin, and Ross, "The Bias Blind Spot." The University of Pennsylvania political scientist Yphtach Lelkes has further linked this concept to political polarization, though he uses the term "perceived polarization" in lieu of false polarization ("Mass Polarization," 392).

8. See Levendusky and Malhotra, "(Mis)perceptions of Partisan Polarization in the American Public."

9. See Pew Research Center, "Republicans, Democrats See Opposing Party as More Ideological Than Their Own."

10. See also Banks et al., "#PolarizedFeeds." I discuss the relationship between social media and false polarization in more detail in chapter 8.

11. See Pew Research Center, "National Politics on Twitter." In a more systematic analysis of the spread of hyperpartisan news content on Twitter during the 2012 presidential campaign, two political scientists confirmed that most of it was spread by a small fraction of social media users (see Barberá and Rivero, "Understanding the Political Representativeness of Twitter Users").

12. See Hughes, "A Small Group of Prolific Users Account for a Majority of Political Tweets Sent by U.S. Adults." Reviews of the literature about online extremism also indicate most extreme content is produced by relatively small groups of people (see Marwick and Lewis, "Media Manipulation and Disinformation Online"; and Siegal, "Online Hate Speech").

13. See Barnidge, "Exposure to Political Disagreement in Social Media versus Face-to-Face and Anonymous Online Settings."

14. See Settle, *Frenemies*.

15. See Duggan and Smith, "Political Content on Social Media."

16. See Anderson and Quinn, "46% of U.S. Social Media Users Say They Are 'Worn Out' by Political Posts and Discussions."

17. See Hughes, "A Small Group of Prolific Users Account for a Majority of Political Tweets Sent by U.S. Adults."

18. See Pew Research Center, "National Politics on Twitter."

19. The data set is available via Duggan and Smith, "Political Content on Social Media."

Chapter Seven: Should I Delete My Account?

1. See Lanier, *Ten Arguments for Deleting Your Social Media Accounts Right Now*.

2. See Perrin, "Americans Are Changing Their Relationship with Facebook."

3. Social scientists also conducted a variety of studies of the effect of internet use on sociability before social media became so pervasive. For example, a time-diary study by Norman Nie and colleagues showed that internet use was associated with people spending less time with family members and friends—even though it led to increased social contacts at work (see Nie, Hillygus, and Erbring, "Internet Use, Interpersonal Relations, and Sociability").

4. See Allcott et al., "The Welfare Effects of Social Media."
5. At the same time, the people who deactivated their accounts also had less knowledge about politics, so the depolarizing effect may have come at the cost of civic engagement more broadly (see ibid.).
6. See Perrin and Anderson, "Share of U.S. Adults Using Social Media, Including Facebook, Is Mostly Unchanged since 2018."
7. See Allcott et al., "The Welfare Effects of Social Media."
8. See Lanier, "Jaron Lanier Fixes the Internet."
9. See Perrin and Anderson, "Share of U.S. Adults Using Social Media, Including Facebook, Is Mostly Unchanged since 2018."
10. See Anderson and Jiang, "Teens, Social Media & Technology 2018."
11. See ibid.
12. And even though there are clearly sizeable groups of people who view social media platforms as a net negative, it is also clear that many others believe they are a net positive. According to a survey by Pew, less than a quarter of U.S. teens believe social media has a "mostly negative" impact on people their age. In contrast, nearly one-third of U.S. teens believe social media has a "mostly positive" impact, and 45 percent believe its impacts are "neither positive nor negative" (see Anderson and Jiang, "Teens, Social Media & Technology 2018").
13. See Shepherd and Lane, "In the Mix."
14. See Shearer and Grieco, "Americans Are Wary of the Role Social Media Sites Play in Delivering the News."
15. See Shearer, "Social Media Outpaces Print Newspapers in the U.S. as a News Source."
16. See ibid.
17. See Lalancette and Raynauld, "The Power of Political Image"; Parmelee and Roman, "Insta-Politicos."
18. See Serrano, Papakyriakopoulos, and Hegelich, "Dancing to the Partisan Beat."
19. See McPherson, Smith-Lovin, and Brashears, "Social Isolation in America"; Klinenberg, *Heat Wave*, *Going Solo*, and *Palaces for the People*; Parigi and Henson, "Social Isolation in America."
20. See B. Lee and Bearman, "Political Isolation in America."
21. See Bishop, *The Big Sort*.
22. See Abrams and Fiorina, "'The Big Sort' That Wasn't."
23. See Huber and Malhotra, "Political Homophily in Social Relationships."
24. There is also experimental evidence that Democrats and Republicans consider membership in the party to be a more important consideration in romantic relationships than physical attractiveness (see Klar and Krupnikov, *Independent Politics*; and Nicholson et al., "The Politics of Beauty").

25. See Chen and Rohla, "The Effect of Partisanship and Political Advertising on Close Family Ties."
26. See Eyal, *Indistractable*; McNamee, *Zucked*.
27. See Bosker, "The Binge Breaker." Social media companies have also been sharply criticized for creating political polarization in recent academic work. For example, see Vaidhyanathan, *Antisocial Media*.
28. Such accusations are compelling because they contradict the mottos of technology companies. Google's motto "don't be evil" masks its participation in a sinister new form of capitalism where data is the most important commodity, according to the technology critic Shoshana Zuboff (*The Age of Surveillance Capitalism*). Others lament Facebook's mantra to "move fast and break things"—a process that, they believe, broke a few too many of our democratic institutions along the way. And while technology giants state that their work is inspired by goodwill, Silicon Valley apostates warn that this is all window dressing by executives who are seeking to maintain their wealth and status (for example, see McNamee, *Zucked*).
29. For a concise overview of the need for academic research to address political problems related to social media, see Persily and Tucker, "Conclusion: The Challenges and Opportunities for Social Media Research." See also Aral, *The Hype Machine*.
30. See Tufekci, "YouTube, the Great Radicalizer"; and Roose, "The Making of a YouTube Radical." See also Lewis, "'Fiction Is Outperforming Reality.'"
31. See Ribeiro et al., "Auditing Radicalization Pathways on YouTube." A more recent study used a web-crawling technique created by Guillaume Chaslot, a former Google engineer, to identify the recommendations YouTube made from a VPN account set up to simulate the search behavior of a user in St. Louis, Missouri (see Alfano et al., "Technologically Scaffolded Atypical Cognition"). The authors searched for video content in six areas—ranging from material by far-right pundits to information about martial arts and natural foods—and then hand-coded the content recommended to the web crawler to determine whether it contained conspiratorial content, which they defined as claims that "powerful forces" were trying to influence something. Notwithstanding this capacious definition of conspiratorial content, the authors discovered that the YouTube algorithm recommended a significant amount of such content only to those who searched for far-right pundits. What is more, the researchers did not actually study whether people actually clicked on such content, only whether it was recommended to them. Finally, no studies have yet examined whether YouTube continued to recommend a significant amount of radical or conspiratorial content to users after early 2018, when it was originally accused of so doing.

32. See Bakshy, Messing, and Adamic, "Exposure to Ideologically Diverse News and Opinion on Facebook."

33. See Munger and Phillips, "A Supply and Demand Framework for You-Tube Politics."

34. On the other hand, the *Wall Street Journal* reports Facebook employees uncovered evidence that recommender algorithms were promoting extremist content in Germany (see Horwitz and Seetharaman, "Facebook Executives Shut Down Efforts to Make the Site Less Divisive"). According to this report, Facebook employees discovered extreme political content "in more than one-third of large German political groups on the platform." Yet this content was reportedly created by a "subset of hyperactive users," which is in line with previous studies of fake news and misinformation campaigns by social scientists (e.g., Guess, Nagler, and Tucker, "Less than You Think"; and Bail, Guay, et al. "Assessing the Russian Internet Research Agency's Impact on the Political Attitudes and Behaviors of American Twitter Users in Late 2017"). The same report also cited an internal Facebook presentation that reportedly claimed "64% of all extremist group joins" were due to Facebook's recommendation tools. It is unclear, however, whether the recommendation algorithm actually influenced people's views, or provided a more efficient means for those who already had extreme views to connect with each other.

35. See Grinberg et al., "Fake News on Twitter during the 2016 U.S. Presidential Election."

36. See Allcott and Gentzkow, "Social Media and Fake News in the 2016 Election."

37. See Guess, Nagler, and Tucker, "Less than You Think." See also Watts and Rothschild, "Don't Blame the Election on Fake News," and Allen et al., "Evaluating the Fake News Problem at the Scale of the Information Ecosystem."

38. See Aral and Eckles, "Protecting Elections from Social Media Manipulation."

39. See Bail, Guay, et al., "Assessing the Russian Internet Research Agency's Impact on the Political Attitudes and Behaviors of American Twitter Users in Late 2017."

40. See Bennett and Iyengar, "A New Era of Minimal Effects?"

41. See Kalla and Broockman, "The Minimal Persuasive Effects of Campaign Contact in General Elections." On the other hand, the study of social media advertising in shaping political campaigns is still in its infancy (see Fowler, Franz, and Ridout, "Online Political Advertising in the United States"). One of the first studies of this subject found such advertising has a small impact on primary elections but no impact on general elections (see Shaw, Blunt, and Seaborn, "Testing Overall and

Synergistic Campaign Effects in a Partisan Statewide Election"). This indicates online advertising may be more effective at generating awareness about candidates or issues than exerting direct influence on the opinions and behaviors of voters (see Berger, *The Catalyst*).

42. See Hersh and Schaffner, "Targeted Campaign Appeals and the Value of Ambiguity"; Bailey, Hopkins, and Rogers, "Unresponsive and Unpersuaded"; Vogel et al., "Who Compares and Despairs?"

43. See Gordon et al., "A Comparison of Approaches to Advertising Measurement."

44. See Eady et al., "How Many People Live in Political Bubbles on Social Media?"

45. A similar study of Google News found no evidence that personalized searches trapped people within filter bubbles (see Haim, Graefe, and Brosius, "Burst of the Filter Bubble?").

46. See Flaxman, Goel, and Rao, "Filter Bubbles, Echo Chambers, and Online News Consumption." See also Guess, "(Almost) Everything in Moderation." The finding that echo chamber effects are most influential among strong partisans has also been identified by previous research (see Levendusky, "Why do Partisan Media Polarize Viewers?").

47. See Salganik et al., "Measuring the Predictability of Life Outcomes with a Scientific Mass Collaboration."

48. An earlier study that attempted to predict the viral spread of Twitter messages using the latest advances in machine learning provided similarly underwhelming results (see Martin et al., "Exploring Limits to Prediction in Complex Social Systems"). The scholars were not even able to explain half of the variance in how many times tweets are shared using these state of the art methods. For a broader discussion of the problem of prediction in social science, see Risi et al., "Predicting History." Still others argue that applying machine learning to social science problems exacerbates social inequalities related to race, gender, and other social chasms (see Noble, *Algorithms of Oppression*; Obermeyer et al., "Dissecting Racial Bias in an Algorithm Used to Manage the Health of Populations"; Kleinberg et al., "Algorithmic Fairness"; and Athey, "Beyond Prediction: Using Big Data for Policy Problems").

49. See Smith, "Public Attitudes toward Technology Companies."

50. See Smith, "Public Attitudes towards Computer Algorithms."

Chapter Eight: Hacking the Prism

1. See Prior, *Post-Broadcast Democracy*.

2. See DiMaggio, Evans, and Bryson, "Have American's Social Attitudes Become More Polarized?"

3. See Robinson et al., "Actual versus Assumed Differences in Construal." For an overview of the synergy between cultural sociology and social psychology, see DiMaggio, "Culture and Cognition"; Dimaggio and Markus, "Culture and Social Psychology."
4. See Levendusky and Malhotra, "(Mis)perceptions of Partisan Polarization in the American Public."
5. See Enders and Armaly, "The Differential Effects of Actual and Perceived Polarization."
6. See Moore-Berg et al., "Exaggerated Meta-Perceptions Predict Intergroup Hostility between American Political Partisans"; Lees and Cikara, "Inaccurate Group Meta-Perceptions Drive Negative Out-Group Attributions in Competitive Contexts."
7. For example, see Schudson, "How Culture Works"; Gamson and Modigliani, "Media Discourse and Public Opinion on Nuclear Power"; Dimaggio et al., "The Role of Religious Actors and Religious Arguments in Public Conflicts over the Arts"; Snow, "Framing Processes, Ideology, and Discursive Fields." For a more detailed report on the perception gap between Republicans and Democrats in recent years, see Yudkin, Hawkins, and Dixon, *The Perception Gap*.
8. See Bail, *Terrified*.
9. See Berry and Sobieraj, *The Outrage Industry*.
10. See Levendusky and Malhotra, "Does Media Coverage of Partisan Polarization Affect Political Attitudes?"
11. See J. Yang et al., "Why Are 'Others' So Polarized?"
12. See ibid. See also Banks et al., "#PolarizedFeeds."
13. See McGregor, "Social Media as Public Opinion."
14. See Ahler and Sood, "The Parties in Our Heads."
15. In an earlier study, social psychologists showed these types of large misperceptions extend into the domain of moral judgments as well. Democrats and Republicans both exaggerated the extent to which people from the other party hold different beliefs about human values such as compassion, fairness, loyalty, and respect (see Graham, Nosek, and Haidt, "The Moral Stereotypes of Liberals and Conservatives").
16. See Lees and Cikara, "Inaccurate Group Meta-Perceptions Drive Negative Out-Group Attributions in Competitive Contexts."
17. See Robinson et al., "Actual versus Assumed Differences in Construal."
18. See Bialik, "14% of Americans Have Changed Their Mind about an Issue Because of Something They Saw on Social Media."
19. See Van Boven, Judd, and Sherman, "Political Polarization Projection."
20. See Chang, Cheng, and Danescu-Niculescu-Mizil, "Don't Let Me Be Misunderstood."
21. See Sherif, "Social Categorization as a Function of Latitude of Acceptance and Series Range." See also Berger, *The Catalyst*, which de-

scribes two related concepts: the zone of acceptance and the zone of rejection.

22. See Sherif, "Social Categorization." For a more recent argument that parallels the concept of the latitude of acceptance, see Levendusky, "When Efforts to Depolarize the Electorate Fail."

23. See Dorison, Minson, and Rogers, "Selective Exposure Partly Relies on Faulty Affective Forecasts." Similarly, communications scholars Magdalena Wojcieszak and Benjamin R. Warner found that imagined or vicarious contact between Republicans and Democrats in the United States can decrease animosity between members of the two groups as well (see Wojcieszak and Warner, "Can Interparty Contact Reduce Affective Polarization?").

24. See Wolak, *Compromise in an Age of Party Polarization*.

25. See Feinberg and Willer, "From Gulf to Bridge."

26. See Feinberg and Willer, "Moral Reframing."

27. See B. Lee and Bearman, "Political Isolation in America"; Parigi and Bergemann, "Strange Bedfellows"; McPherson, Smith-Lovin, and Brashears, "Social Isolation in America."

28. See Van Boven, Judd, and Sherman, "Political Polarization Projection."

29. See Dorison and Minson, "You Can't Handle the Truth!"

30. See Minson, "Just Listen." This phenomenon has also been observed in online settings as well (see Wojcieszak and Price, "Perceived versus Actual Disagreement"; and Wojcieszak and Price, "Facts versus Perceptions"). Finally, a team of researchers at Northeastern University who studied how political conversations occur using longitudinal data about an entire social network of college students also discovered that stimulating cross-party conversations about politics is not as difficult as previous studies suggest—and can be generated via incidental contact, not just purposive action (see Minozzi et al., "The Incidental Pundit").

31. See Klar, Krupnikov, and Ryan, "Affective Polarization or Partisan Disdain?"

32. See ibid., 382.

33. See Bail, "Want to Bridge Divides?"

34. See Rainie, Keeter, and Perrin, *Trust and Distrust in America*, 67.

Chapter Nine: A Better Social Media

1. See Sewell, "Historical Events as Transformations of Structures"; Wagner-Pacifici, "Theorizing the Restlessness of Events"; Berezin, "Events as Templates of Possibility"; Bail, *Terrified*.

2. Walt, "The Case against Peace"; Skrentny, "The Effect of the Cold War on African-American Civil Rights."

3. See Safegraph, "U.S. Geographic Responses to Shelter in Place Orders".
4. See Bartik et al., "How Are Small Businesses Adjusting to COVID-19?"
5. See Safegraph, "Foot Traffic Patterns by State and Industry" Some of the figures reported in this paragraph are from my analysis of Safegraph data.
6. See Koeze and Popper, "The Virus Changed the Way We Internet."
7. See Green et al., "Elusive Consensus."
8. See Van Green and Tyson, "5 Facts about Partisan Reactions to COVID-19 in the U.S."
9. See Vavreck, "COVID-19: Tracking American Responses."
10. See Baum, Ognyanova, and Lazer, "These Three Governors Are Reopening Their States Faster than Their Voters Want."
11. See More in Common, "COVID-19."
12. See Pew Research Center, "Republicans, Democrats Move Even Further Apart in Coronavirus Concern."
13. See Rivlin, "Wallflower at the Web Party."
14. See Arrington, "It's Official(ish)."
15. See Constine, "Instagram's Growth Speeds up as It Hits 700 Million Users."
16. See Shontell, "The Truth about Snapchat's Active Users"; D'Onfro, "Snapchat Now Has Nearly 100 Million Daily Active Users."
17. See Leskin, "Inside the Rise of TikTok."
18. See Perrin and Anderson, "Share of U.S. Adults Using Social Media, Including Facebook, Is Mostly Unchanged since 2018."
19. See Lazarsfeld, Berelson, and Gaudet, *The People's Choice*; Katz and Lazarsfeld, *Personal Influence*; Zaller, *The Nature and Origins of Mass Opinion*; Burt, "The Social Capital of Opinion Leaders"; Watts and Dodds, "Influentials, networks, and public opinion formation."
20. A recent assessment of this shift indicates that the expansion of character limits increased the amount of polite discourse on Twitter (see Jaidka, Zhou, and Lelkes, "Brevity Is the Soul of Twitter").
21. See Phillips, *This Is Why We Can't Have Nice Things.*
22. See Safronova, "The Rise and Fall of Yik Yak, the Anonymous Messaging App."
23. See Papacharissi, "Democracy Online."
24. See Tan et al., "Winning Arguments."
25. For a more detailed description of this experiment, see the "Simulated Social Media Platform Experiment" section of the appendix.
26. After the conclusion of the study, all respondents were debriefed about its true purpose by the survey firm.
27. Even more encouraging is that another study of anonymous conversation produced a very similar finding. Political scientist Erin Rossiter recruited Republicans and Democrats from Amazon's Mechanical Turk

website to engage in conversations about gun control on a website she created. Like us, she found brief conversations create significant decreases in interparty animosity. Interestingly, her study also examined whether the depolarizing effect of anonymous conversations was stronger for nonpolitical conversations. Surprisingly, she found cross-party conversations created significant decreases in animosity regardless of whether respondents were cued to discuss a political topic (see Rossiter, "The Consequences of Interparty Conversation on Outparty Affect and Stereotypes"). The depolarizing effect of anonymity was further demonstrated by a recent study that asked groups of Republicans and Democrats to participate in an online game where they guessed the answer to a complicated question about climate change. When the players of this game were anonymous to each other, they tended to produce more accurate predictions—a phenomenon commonly referred to as the "wisdom of crowds." When the researchers labeled the political background of the people playing the game, they found that people produced less accurate answers (see Guilbeault, Becker, and Centola, "Social Learning and Partisan Bias in the Interpretation of Climate Trends").

28. See Zuckerberg, "Bringing the World Closer Together."
29. See Carlson, "The Real History of Twitter."
30. See Garber, "Instagram Was First Called 'Burbn.'"
31. Previous studies indicate the norms established by online platforms and discussion groups exert significant influence upon the behavior of the people who use them. For example, a group of computational social scientists conducted an experiment where people were asked to comment upon a news article about politics. In one of the study's experimental conditions, participants were shown a comment below the article with uncivil content. Research participants in this treatment condition were significantly more likely to engage in uncivil behavior than those who were not shown the extreme comment (see Cheng et al., "Anyone Can Become a Troll"). Conversely, psychologist J. Nathan Matias conducted a large-scale experiment on an online discussion about science where participants were randomized into a treatment condition where they were shown an announcement about community rules. Study participants in this treatment condition not only complied with these community rules more often than those who were not shown the announcement but were also more likely to participate in the discussions in general (see Matias, "Preventing Harassment and Increasing Group Participation through Social Norms in 2,190 Online Science Discussions").
32. For a detailed discussion of the importance of transparency in the moderation and regulation of political advertising on social media, see Kreiss and Mcgregor, "The 'Arbiters of What Our Voters See.'"

33. See Barabas, Narula, and Zuckerman, "Decentralized Social Networks Sound Great."
34. See Zuckerman, "The Case for Digital Public Infrastructure."

Appendix: Research Methods

1. See Barberá, "Birds of the Same Feather Tweet Together."
2. For further information about the content retweeted by our study's bots, see Bail, Argyle, et al., "Exposure to Opposing Views on Social Media Can Increase Political Polarization."
3. See Salganik, *Bit by Bit.*
4. See Lazer et al., "The Parable of Google Flu."
5. See Gupta et al., "WTF."
6. See ibid.
7. See Montgomery, Nyhan, and Torres, "How Conditioning on Post-treatment Variables Can Ruin Your Experiment and What to Do about It."
8. For more information about how we analyzed attrition bias, see Bail, Argyle, et al., "Exposure to Opposing Views on Social Media Can Increase Political Polarization."
9. See ibid.
10. See Tavory and Timmermans, *Abductive Analysis*; Deterding and Waters, "Flexible Coding of In-Depth Interviews."
11. See Jerolmack and Khan, "Talk Is Cheap"; Vaisey, "Motivation and Justification" and "Is Interviewing Compatible with the Dual-Process Model of Culture?"

BIBLIOGRAPHY

Abramowitz, Alan I., and Kyle L. Saunders. "Is Polarization a Myth?" *Journal of Politics* 70, no. 2 (April 1, 2008): 542–55. https://doi.org/10.1017/S0022381608080493.

Abrams, Samuel J., and Morris P. Fiorina. "'The Big Sort' That Wasn't: A Skeptical Reexamination." *PS: Political Science and Politics* 45, no. 2 (April 2012): 203–10. https://doi.org/10.1017/S1049096512000017.

Achen, Christopher, and Larry Bartels. *Democracy for Realists: Why Elections Do Not Produce Responsive Government.* Princeton, NJ: Princeton University Press, 2017.

Ahler, Douglas J., and Gaurav Sood. "The Parties in Our Heads: Misperceptions about Party Composition and Their Consequences." *Journal of Politics* 80, no. 3 (April 27, 2018): 964–81. https://doi.org/10.1086/697253.

Alfano, Mark, Amir Ebrahimi Fard, J. Adam Carter, Peter Clutton, and Colin Klein. "Technologically Scaffolded Atypical Cognition: The Case of YouTube's Recommender System." *Synthese*, June 9, 2020. https://doi.org/10.1007/s11229-020-02724-x.

Allcott, Hunt, Luca Braghieri, Sarah Eichmeyer, and Matthew Gentzkow. "The Welfare Effects of Social Media." *American Economic Review* 110, no. 3 (March 2020): 629–76. https://doi.org/10.1257/aer.20190658.

Allcott, Hunt, and Matthew Gentzkow. "Social Media and Fake News in the 2016 Election." *Journal of Economic Perspectives* 31, no. 2 (2017): 211–36. https://www.aeaweb.org/articles?id=10.1257/jep.31.2.211.

Allen, Jennifer, Baird Howland, Markus Mobius, David Rothschild, and Duncan J. Watts. "Evaluating the fake news problem at the scale of the information ecosystem." *Science Advances*, 6, no. 14 (2020): 1–6. https://advances.sciencemag.org/content/6/14/eaay3539.

Allport, Gordon Willard. *The Nature of Prejudice.* Cambridge, MA: Addison-Wesley, 1954.

Almond, Gabriel, and Sydney Verba. "Civic Culture Study, 1959–1960" [data set]. ICPSR07201-v2. Inter-University Consortium for Political and Social Research, 1960. https://www.icpsr.umich.edu/web/ICPSR/studies /7201/versions/V2/variables.

American National Election Study. "2016 Time Series Study" [data set]. Ann Arbor: University of Michigan, 2016.

———. "2018 Pilot Study" [data set]. Ann Arbor: University of Michigan, 2018.

Anderson, Monica, and Jingjing Jiang. "Teens, Social Media & Technology 2018." Pew Research Center, May 31, 2018. https://www.pewresearch.org/internet/2018/05/31/teens-social-media-technology -2018/.

Anderson, Monica, and Dennis Quinn. "46% of U.S. Social Media Users Say They Are 'Worn Out' by Political Posts and Discussions." *Fact Tank* (blog). Pew Research Center, August 8, 2019. https://www.pewresearch .org/fact-tank/2019/08/08/46-of-u-s-social-media-users-say-they-are -worn-out-by-political-posts-and-discussions/.

Aral, Sinan. *The Hype Machine: How Social Media Disrupts Our Elections, Our Economy, and Our Health—and How We Must Adapt.* New York: Currency, 2020.

Aral, Sinan, and Dean Eckles. "Protecting Elections from Social Media Manipulation." *Science* 365, no. 6456 (August 30, 2019): 858–61. https:// doi.org/10.1126/science.aaw8243.

Arceneaux, Kevin, and Martin Johnson. *Changing Minds or Changing Channels? Partisan News in an Age of Choice.* Chicago: University of Chicago Press, 2013.

Archibong, Ime. "An Update on Our App Investigation." Facebook.com (newsroom blog), August 22, 2018. https://about.fb.com/news/2018/08 /update-on-app-investigation/.

Arrington, Michael. "It's Official(ish): MySpace Is Biggest Site on Internet." *TechCrunch*, December 12, 2006. https://techcrunch.com/2006/12/12 /its-officialish-myspace-is-biggest-site-on-internet/.

Athey, Susan. "Beyond Prediction: Using Big Data for Policy Problems." *Science* 355, no. 6324: 483–85. https://science.sciencemag.org/content/355 /6324/483.

Bail, Christopher. "The Cultural Environment: Measuring Culture with Big Data." *Theory and Society* 43, nos. 3–4 (2014): 465–82. http://dx.doi.org /10.1007/s11186-014-9216-5.

———. *Terrified: How Anti-Muslim Fringe Organizations Became Mainstream.* Princeton, NJ: Princeton University Press, 2015.

———. "Want to Bridge Divides? Clean Your Twitter House First." CNN, November 22, 2019. https://www.cnn.com/2019/11/22/opinions/twitter -political-divide-bridge-bail/index.html.

BIBLIOGRAPHY

Bail, Christopher, Lisa P. Argyle, Taylor W. Brown, John P. Bumpus, Haohan Chen, M. B. Fallin Hunzaker, Jaemin Lee, Marcus Mann, Friedolin Merhout, and Alexander Volfovsky. "Exposure to Opposing Views on Social Media Can Increase Political Polarization." *Proceedings of the National Academy of Sciences of the United States of America* 115, no. 37 (September 11, 2018): 9216–21. https://doi.org/10.1073/pnas.1804840115.

Bail, Christopher, Brian Guay, Emily Maloney, Aidan Combs, D. Sunshine Hillygus, Friedolin Merhout, Deen Freelon, and Alexander Volfovsky. "Assessing the Russian Internet Research Agency's Impact on the Political Attitudes and Behaviors of American Twitter Users in Late 2017." *Proceedings of the National Academy of Sciences of the United States of America* 117, no. 1 (January 7, 2020): 243–50. https://doi.org/10.1073/pnas.1906420116.

Bail, Christopher, Friedolin Merhout, and Peng Ding. "Using Internet Search Data to Examine the Relationship between Anti-Muslim and pro-ISIS Sentiment in U.S. Counties." *Science Advances* 4, no. 6 (June 1, 2018): eaao5948. https://doi.org/10.1126/sciadv.aao5948.

Bailey, Michael A., Daniel J. Hopkins, and Todd Rogers. "Unresponsive and Unpersuaded: The Unintended Consequences of a Voter Persuasion Effort." *Political Behavior* 38, no. 3 (September 1, 2016): 713–46. https://doi.org/10.1007/s11109-016-9338-8.

Bakshy, Eytan, Solomon Messing, and Lada A. Adamic. "Exposure to Ideologically Diverse News and Opinion on Facebook." *Science* 348, no. 6239 (June 5, 2015): 1130–32. https://doi.org/10.1126/science.aaa1160.

Baldassarri, Delia, and Andrew Gelman. "Partisans without Constraint: Political Polarization and Trends in American Public Opinion." *American Journal of Sociology* 114, no. 2 (January 28, 2008): 408–46. https://doi.org/10.2139/ssrn.1010098.

Banks, Antoine, Ernesto Calvo, David Karol, and Shibley Telhami. "#PolarizedFeeds: Three Experiments on Polarization, Framing, and Social Media." *International Journal of Press/Politics*, July 23, 2020, 1940161220940964. https://doi.org/10.1177/1940161220940964.

Barabas, Chelsea, Neha Narula, and Ethan Zuckerman. "Decentralized Social Networks Sound Great. Too Bad They'll Never Work." *Wired*, September 8, 2017. https://www.wired.com/story/decentralized-social-networks-sound-great-too-bad-theyll-never-work/.

Barberá, Pablo. "Birds of the Same Feather Tweet Together: Bayesian Ideal Point Estimation Using Twitter Data." *Political Analysis* 23, no. 1 (January 1, 2015): 76–91. https://doi.org/10.1093/pan/mpu011.

———. "Social Media, Echo Chambers, and Political Polarization." In *Social Media and Democracy: The State of the Field, Prospects for Reform*, edited by Nathaniel Persily and Joshua A. Tucker, 34–54. Cambridge: Cambridge University Press, 2020.

BIBLIOGRAPHY

Barberá, Pablo, and Gonzalo Rivero. "Understanding the Political Representativeness of Twitter Users." *Social Science Computer Review* 33, no. 6 (December 1, 2015): 712–29. https://doi.org/10.1177/0894439314558836.

Barnidge, Matthew. "Exposure to Political Disagreement in Social Media versus Face-to-Face and Anonymous Online Settings." *Political Communication* 34, no. 2 (April 3, 2017): 302–21. https://doi.org/10.1080 /10584609.2016.1235639.

Barth, Frederick. *Ethnic Groups and Boundaries: The Social Organization of Cultural Difference.* Boston: Little, Brown, 1969.

Bartik, Alexander W., Marianne Bertrand, Zoë B. Cullen, Edward L. Glaeser, Michael Luca, and Christopher T. Stanton. "How Are Small Businesses Adjusting to COVID-19? Early Evidence from a Survey." NBER Working Paper 26989, National Bureau of Economic Research, Cambridge, MA, April 2020. https://doi.org/10.3386/w26989.

Baum, Matthew, Katherine Ognyanova, and David Lazer. "These Three Governors Are Reopening Their States Faster than Their Voters Want." *Monkey Cage* (blog). *Washington Post*, April 29, 2020. https://www .washingtonpost.com/politics/2020/04/29/these-three-governors-are -reopening-their-states-faster-than-their-voters-want/.

Baumeister, Roy F., and Mark R. Leary. "The Need to Belong: Desire for Interpersonal Attachments as a Fundamental Human Motivation." *Psychological Bulletin* 117, no. 3 (1995): 497–529.

Bazarova, Natalya (Natalie), Yoon Choi, Victoria Schwanda Sosik, Dan Cosley, and Janis Whitlock. "Social Sharing of Emotions on Facebook." In *Proceedings of the 18th ACM Conference on Computer Supported Cooperative Work and Social Computing*, 154–64. New York: Association for Computing Machinery, 2015. https://doi.org/10.1145/2675133.2675297.

Bennett, W. Lance, and Shanto Iyengar. "A New Era of Minimal Effects? The Changing Foundations of Political Communication." *Journal of Communication* 58, no. 4 (December 1, 2008): 707–31. https://doi.org/10 .1111/j.1460-2466.2008.00410.x.

Berezin, Mabel. "Events as Templates of Possibility: An Analytic Typology of Political Facts." In *The Oxford Handbook of Cultural Sociology*, edited by Jeffrey C. Alexander, Ronald N. Jacobs, and Philip Smith, 613–35. New York: Oxford University Press, 2012.

Berger, Jonah. *The Catalyst: How to Change Anyone's Mind.* New York: Simon and Schuster, 2020.

Berinsky, Adam J. "Rumors and Health Care Reform: Experiments in Political Misinformation." *British Journal of Political Science* 47, no. 2 (April 2017): 241–62. https://doi.org/10.1017/S0007123415000186.

Berry, Jeffrey M., and Sarah Sobieraj. *The Outrage Industry: Political Opinion Media and the New Incivility.* Oxford: Oxford University Press, 2013.

BIBLIOGRAPHY

Bialik, Kristen. "14% of Americans Have Changed Their Mind about an Issue Because of Something They Saw on Social Media." *Fact Tank* (blog). Pew Research Center, August 15, 2018. https://www.pewresearch .org/fact-tank/2018/08/15/14-of-americans-have-changed-their-mind -about-an-issue-because-of-something-they-saw-on-social-media/.

Bishop, Bill. *The Big Sort: Why the Clustering of Like-Minded America Is Tearing Us Apart.* Boston: Mariner Books, 2009.

Blumer, Herbert. "Race Prejudice as a Sense of Group Position." *Pacific Sociological Review* 1, no. 1 (Spring 1958): 3–7. https://doi.org/10.2307/1388607.

Bobo, Lawrence, and Cybelle Fox. "Race, Racism, and Discrimination: Bridging Problems, Methods, and Theory in Social Psychological Research." *Social Psychology Quarterly* 66, no. 4 (December 2003): 319–32. https://psycnet.apa.org/doi/10.2307/1519832.

Bond, Robert M., Christopher J. Fariss, Jason J. Jones, Adam D. I. Kramer, Cameron Marlow, Jaime E. Settle, and James H. Fowler. "A 61-Million-Person Experiment in Social Influence and Political Mobilization." *Nature* 489, no. 7415 (September 13, 2012): 295–98. https://doi.org/10.1038 /nature11421.

Bosker, Bianca. "The Binge Breaker." *The Atlantic*, November 2016. https:// www.theatlantic.com/magazine/archive/2016/11/the-binge-breaker /501122/.

Bourdieu, Pierre. "Public Opinion Does Not Exist." In *Communication and Class Struggle*, vol. 1: *Capitalism, Imperialism*, edited by Armand Mattelart and Seth Siegelaub, 124–30. New York: International General, 1979.

Boxell, Levi, Matthew Gentzkow, and Jesse M. Shapiro. "Cross-Country Trends in Affective Polarization." NBER Working Paper 26669, National Bureau of Economic Research, Cambridge, MA, April 2020. https:// www.nber.org/papers/w26669.

boyd, danah, and Kate Crawford. "Critical Questions for Big Data: Provocations for a Cultural, Technological, and Scholarly Phenomenon." *Information, Communication and Society* 15, no. 5 (2012): 662–79. https:// doi.org/10.1080/1369118X.2012.678878.

boyd, danah, and Eszter Hargittai. "Facebook Privacy Settings: Who Cares?" *First Monday* 15, no. 8 (July 27, 2010). https://firstmonday.org /article/view/3086/2589.

Brady, William J., Julian A. Wills, John T. Jost, Joshua A. Tucker, and Jay J. Van Bavel. "Emotion Shapes the Diffusion of Moralized Content in Social Networks." *Proceedings of the National Academy of Sciences of the United States of America* 114, no. 28 (July 11, 2017): 7313–18. https://doi .org/10.1073/pnas.1618923114.

Broockman, David E. "Approaches to Studying Policy Representation." *Legislative Studies Quarterly* 41, no. 1 (2016): 181–215. https://doi.org/10 .1111/lsq.12110.

Broockman, David, and Joshua Kalla. "Durably Reducing Transphobia: A Field Experiment on Door-to-Door Canvassing." *Science* 352, no. 6282 (2016): 220–24.

Brown, Donald. *Human Universals*. New York: McGraw-Hill, 1991.

Burke, Moira, Justin Cheng, and Bethany de Gant. "Social Comparison and Facebook: Feedback, Positivity, and Opportunities for Comparison." In *CHI '20: Proceedings of the 2020 CHI Conference on Human Factors in Computing Systems*, 1–13. New York: Association for Computing Machinery, 2020. https://doi.org/10.1145/3313831.3376482.

Burt, Ronald S. "The Social Capital of Opinion Leaders." *ANNALS of the American Academy of Political and Social Science* 566, no. 1 (November 1, 1999): 37–54. https://doi.org/10.1177/000271629956600104.

Cameron, A. M., A. B. Massie, C. E. Alexander, B. Stewart, R. A. Montgomery, N. R. Benavides, G. D. Fleming, and D. L. Segev. "Social Media and Organ Donor Registration: The Facebook Effect." *American Journal of Transplantation* 13, no. 8 (August 1, 2013): 2059–65.

Campbell, James E. *Polarized: Making Sense of a Divided America*. Princeton, NJ: Princeton University Press, 2016.

Carlson, Nicholas. "The Real History of Twitter." *Businessinsider.com*, April 13, 2011. https://www.businessinsider.com/how-twitter-was -founded-2011-4.

Casselman, Ben, and Jim Tankersley. "Face It: You (Probably) Got a Tax Cut." *New York Times*, November 19, 2019. https://www.nytimes.com /2019/04/14/business/economy/income-tax-cut.html.

Chang, Jonathan P., Justin Cheng, and Cristian Danescu-Niculescu-Mizil. "Don't Let Me Be Misunderstood: Comparing Intentions and Perceptions in Online Discussions." In *WWW '20: Proceedings of The Web Conference 2020*, 2066–77. New York: Association for Computing Machinery, 2020. https://doi.org/10.1145/3366423.3380273.

Chen, M. Keith, and Ryne Rohla. "The Effect of Partisanship and Political Advertising on Close Family Ties." *Science* 360, no. 6392 (June 1, 2018): 1020–24. https://doi.org/10.1126/science.aaq1433.

Cheng, Justin, Michael Bernstein, Cristian Danescu-Niculescu-Mizil, and Jure Leskovec. "Anyone Can Become a Troll: Causes of Trolling Behavior in Online Discussions." In *CSCW '17: Proceedings of the 2017 ACM Conference on Computer Supported Cooperative Work and Social Computing*, 1217–30. New York: Association for Computing Machinery, 2017. https://doi.org/10.1145/2998181.2998213.

Christakis, Nicholas A. *Blueprint: The Evolutionary Origins of a Good Society*. New York: Little, Brown Spark, 2019.

Cikara, Mina, and Jay Van Bavel. "The Neuroscience of Intergroup Relations: An Integrative Review." *Perspectives on Psychological Science* 9, no. 3 (2014): 245–74. https://doi.org/10.1177/1745691614527464.

Cohen, Geoffrey L. "Party over Policy: The Dominating Impact of Group Influence on Political Beliefs." *Journal of Personality and Social Psychology* 85, no. 5 (2003): 808–22. https://doi.org/10.1037/0022-3514.85.5.808.

Constine, Josh. "Instagram's Growth Speeds up as It Hits 700 Million Users." *TechCrunch*, April 26, 2017. https://techcrunch.com/2017/04/26/instagram-700-million-users/.

Converse, Philip E. "The Nature of Belief Systems in Mass Publics (1964)." *Critical Review* 18, nos. 1–3 (2006): 1–74. https://doi.org/10.1080/08913810608443650.

Cooley, Charles Horton. *Human Nature and the Social Order.* New York: Charles Scribner's Sons, 1902.

Daniels, Jessie. *Cyber Racism: White Supremacy Online and the New Attack on Civil Rights.* Lanham, MD: Rowman and Littlefield, 2009.

DellaPosta, Daniel, Yongren Shi, and Michael Macy. "Why Do Liberals Drink Lattes?" *American Journal of Sociology* 120, no. 5 (March 1, 2015): 1473–511. https://doi.org/10.1086/681254.

Del Vicario, Michela, Alessandro Bessi, Fabiana Zollo, Fabio Petroni, Antonio Scala, Guido Caldarelli, H. Eugene Stanley, and Walter Quattrociocchi. "The Spreading of Misinformation Online." *Proceedings of the National Academy of Sciences of the United States of America* 113, no. 3 (January 19, 2016): 554–59. https://doi.org/10.1073/pnas.1517441113.

Deterding, Nicole M., and Mary C. Waters. "Flexible Coding of In-Depth Interviews: A Twenty-First-Century Approach." *Sociological Methods and Research*, October 1, 2018, 004912411879937. https://doi.org/10.1177/004912411879937.

Diehl, Michael. "The Minimal Group Paradigm: Theoretical Explanations and Empirical Findings." *European Review of Social Psychology* 1, no. 1 (1990): 263–92. https://doi.org/10.1080/14792779108401864.

DiMaggio, Paul. "Culture and Cognition." *Annual Review of Sociology* 23 (1997): 263–87. https://doi.org/10.1146/annurev.soc.23.1.263.

Dimaggio, Paul, Wendy Cadge, Lynn Robinson, and Brian Steensland. "The Role of Religious Actors and Religious Arguments in Public Conflicts over the Arts: A Case Study of the Philadelphia Area, 1965–1997." Working paper, Princeton University Woodrow Wilson School of Public and International Affairs, Center for Arts and Cultural Policy Studies.

DiMaggio, Paul, John Evans, and Bethany Bryson. "Have American's Social Attitudes Become More Polarized?" *American Journal of Sociology* 102, no. 3 (1996): 690–755. https://doi.org/10.1086/230995.

DiMaggio, Paul, Eszter Hargittai, W. Russell Neuman, and John P. Robinson. "Social Implications of the Internet." *Annual Review of Sociology* 27 (January 1, 2001): 307–36. https://doi.org/10.1146/annurev.soc.27.1.307.

BIBLIOGRAPHY

Dimaggio, Paul, and Hazel Rose Markus. "Culture and Social Psychology: Converging Perspectives." *Social Psychology Quarterly* 73, no. 4 (December 1, 2010): 347–52. https://doi.org/10.1177/0190272510389010.

D'Onfro, Jillian. "Snapchat Now Has Nearly 100 Million Daily Active Users." *Businessinsider.com*, May 26, 2015. https://www.businessinsider.com/snapchat-daily-active-users-2015-5.

Dorison, Charles A., and Julia Minson. "You Can't Handle the Truth! Errors in Affective Perspective-Taking during Disagreement." Working paper, Harvard Kennedy School, Cambridge, MA, accessed August 30, 2020. http://www.charlesdorison.com/uploads/1/2/4/4/124452321/dorisonminson.2019.pdf.

Dorison, Charles A., Julia A. Minson, and Todd Rogers. "Selective Exposure Partly Relies on Faulty Affective Forecasts." *Cognition* 188 (July 1, 2019): 98–107. https://doi.org/10.1016/j.cognition.2019.02.010.

Douglas, Mary. *Purity and Danger: An Analysis of Concepts of Pollution and Taboo.* New York: Praeger, 1966.

Dow, Malcolm M., Michael L. Burton, Douglas R. White, and Karl P. Reitz. "Galton's Problem as Network Autocorrelation." *American Ethnologist* 11, no. 4 (1984): 754–70. https://doi.org/10.1525/ae.1984.11.4.02a00080.

Duggan, Maeve. "Online Harassment 2017." Pew Research Center, July 11, 2017. https://www.pewresearch.org/internet/2017/07/11/online-harassment-2017/.

Duggan, Maeve, and Aaron Smith. "Political Content on Social Media." Pew Research Center, October 25, 2016. https://www.pewresearch.org/internet/2016/10/25/political-content-on-social-media/.

Eady, Gregory, Jonathan Nagler, Andy Guess, Jan Zalinsky, and Joshua A. Tucker. "How Many People Live in Political Bubbles on Social Media? Evidence from Linked Survey and Twitter Data." *SAGE Open*, 2019, 1–21. https://doi.org/10.1177%2F2158244019832705.

Eckles, Dean, Brett R. Gordon, and Garrett A. Johnson. "Field Studies of Psychologically Targeted Ads Face Threats to Internal Validity." *Proceedings of the National Academy of Sciences of the United States of America* 115, no. 23 (June 5, 2018): E5254–55. https://doi.org/10.1073/pnas.1805363115.

Edelmann, Achim, Tom Wolff, Danielle Montagne, and Christopher A. Bail. "Computational Social Science and Sociology." *Annual Review of Sociology* 46 (2020): 61–81. https://doi.org/10.1146/annurev-soc-121919-054621.

Elias, Norbert. *The Civilizing Process: Sociogenetic and Psychogenetic Investigations.* Rev. ed. Oxford: Blackwell Publishers, 1969.

Elias, Norbert, and John L Scotson. *The Established and the Outsiders: A Sociological Enquiry into Community Problems.* 2nd ed. London: Sage, 1994.

Eliasoph, Nina. *Avoiding Politics: How Americans Produce Apathy in Everyday Life.* Cambridge: Cambridge University Press, 1998.

Enders, Adam M., and Miles T. Armaly. "The Differential Effects of Actual and Perceived Polarization." *Political Behavior* 41, no. 3 (September 1, 2019): 815–39. https://doi.org/10.1007/s11109-018-9476-2.

Enos, Ryan. "Causal Effect of Intergroup Contact on Exclusionary Attitudes." *Proceedings of the National Academy of Sciences of the United States of America* 111, no. 10 (2014): 3699–3704. https://doi.org/10.1073/pnas.1317670111.

ESPN Internet Ventures. "2016 Election Forecast." fivethirtyeight.com, accessed September 2020. https://projects.fivethirtyeight.com/2016-election-forecast/.

Eyal, Nir. *Hooked: How to Build Habit-Forming Products.* Edited by Ryan Hoover. New York: Portfolio, 2014.

———. *Indistractable: How to Control Your Attention and Choose Your Life.* Dallas, TX: BenBella Books, 2019.

Farrell, Justin. *Billionaire Wilderness: The Ultra-Wealthy and the Remaking of the American West.* Princeton, NJ: Princeton University Press, 2020.

Feinberg, Matthew, and Robb Willer. "From Gulf to Bridge: When Do Moral Arguments Facilitate Political Influence?" *Personality and Social Psychology Bulletin* 41, no. 12 (December 1, 2015): 1665–81. https://doi.org/10.1177/0146167215607842.

———. "Moral Reframing: A Technique for Effective and Persuasive Communication across Political Divides." *Social and Personality Psychology Compass* 13, no. 12 (December 2019): 2. https://doi.org/10.1111/spc3.12501.

Festinger, Leon. "A Theory of Social Comparison Processes." *Human Relations* 7, no. 2 (May 1, 1954): 117–40. https://doi.org/10.1177/001872675400700202.

Festinger, Leon, Henry Riecken, and Stanley Schachter. *When Prophecy Fails.* Eastford, CT: Martino Fine Books, 2009.

Fiorina, Morris P., and Samuel J. Abrams. "Political Polarization in the American Public." *Annual Review of Political Science* 11, no. 1 (2008): 563–88. https://doi.org/10.1146/annurev.polisci.11.053106.153836.

Fishkin, James S., and Robert C. Luskin. "Experimenting with a Democratic Ideal: Deliberative Polling and Public Opinion." *Acta Politica* 40, no. 3 (2005): 284–98. https://doi.org/10.1057/palgrave.ap.5500121.

Flaxman, Seth, Sharad Goel, and Justin M. Rao. "Filter Bubbles, Echo Chambers, and Online News Consumption." *Public Opinion Quarterly* 80, no. S1 (January 1, 2016): 298–320. https://doi.org/10.1093/poq/nfw006.

Fowler, Erika Franklin, Michael M. Franz, and Travis N. Ridout. "Online Political Advertising in the United States." In *Social Media and Democracy: The State of the Field, Prospects for Reform*, edited by Nathaniel Persily and Joshua A. Tucker, 111–38. Cambridge: Cambridge University Press, 2020.

Freelon, Deen. "On the Interpretation of Digital Trace Data in Communication and Social Computing Research." *Journal of Broadcasting and Electronic Media* 58, no. 1 (January 2, 2014): 59–75. https://doi.org/10.1080/08838151.2013.875018.

Friedkin, Noah E., and Eugene C. Johnsen. *Social Influence Network Theory: A Sociological Examination of Small Group Dynamics.* New York: Cambridge University Press, 2014.

Gamson, William, and Andre Modigliani. "Media Discourse and Public Opinion on Nuclear Power: A Constructionist Approach." *American Journal of Sociology* 95, no. 1 (1989): 1–37. https://doi.org/10.1086/229213.

Garber, Megan. "Instagram Was First Called 'Burbn.'" *The Atlantic*, July 2, 2014. https://www.theatlantic.com/technology/archive/2014/07/instagram-used-to-be-called-brbn/373815/.

Gerber, Alan S., and Donald P. Green. *Field Experiments: Design, Analysis, and Interpretation.* New York: W. W. Norton, 2012.

Gift, Karen, and Thomas Gift. "Does Politics Influence Hiring? Evidence from a Randomized Experiment." *Political Behavior* 37, no. 3 (September 1, 2015): 653–75. https://doi.org/10.1007/s11109-014-9286-0.

Goel, Sharad, Winter Mason, and Duncan J. Watts. "Real and Perceived Attitude Agreement in Social Networks." *Journal of Personality and Social Psychology* 99, no. 4 (2010): 611–21. https://psycnet.apa.org/doiLanding?doi=10.1037%2Fa0020697.

Goffman, Erving. *The Presentation of Self in Everyday Life.* New York: Doubleday and Company, 1959.

———. *Stigma: Notes on the Management of Spoiled Identity.* New York: Touchstone, 1963.

Golder, Scott, and Michael Macy. "Digital Footprints: Opportunities and Challenges for Social Research." *Annual Review of Sociology* 40 (2014). https://doi.org/10.1146/annurev-soc-071913-043145.

Goodman, Dena. *The Republic of Letters: A Cultural History of the French Enlightenment.* Ithaca, NY: Cornell University Press, 1996.

Gordon, Brett R., Florian Zettelmeyer, Neha Bhargava, and Dan Chapsky. "A Comparison of Approaches to Advertising Measurement: Evidence from Big Field Experiments at Facebook." *Marketing Science* 38, no. 2 (2019): 193–364.

Graham, Jesse, Brian A. Nosek, and Jonathan Haidt. "The Moral Stereotypes of Liberals and Conservatives: Exaggeration of Differences across the Political Spectrum." *PLOS One* (2012). https://doi.org/10.1371/journal.pone.0050092.

Green, Jon, Jared Edgerton, Daniel Naftel, Kelsey Shoub, and Skyler J. Cranmer. "Elusive Consensus: Polarization in Elite Communication on the COVID-19 Pandemic." *Science Advances* 6, no. 28 (July 1, 2020): eabc2717. https://doi.org/10.1126/sciadv.abc2717.

Greene, Steven. "Understanding Party Identification: A Social Identity Approach." *Political Psychology* 20, no. 2 (1999): 393–403. https://doi.org /10.1111/0162-895X.00150.

Grinberg, Nir, Kenneth Joseph, Lisa Friedland, Briony Swire-Thompson, and David Lazer. "Fake News on Twitter during the 2016 U.S. Presidential Election." *Science* 363, no. 6425 (January 25, 2019): 374–78. https:// doi.org/10.1126/science.aau2706.

Gross, Steven Jay, and C. Michael Niman. "Attitude-Behavior Consistency: A Review." *Public Opinion Quarterly* 39, no. 3 (January 1, 1975): 358–68. https://doi.org/10.1086/268234.

Guess, Andrew. "(Almost) Everything in Moderation: New Evidence on Americans' Online Media Diets." *American Journal of Political Science* 64, no. 4 (2020; forthcoming).

Guess, Andrew, and Alexander Coppock. "Does Counter-Attitudinal Information Cause Backlash? Results from Three Large Survey Experiments." *British Journal of Political Science* 50, no. 4 (2018): 1497–1515. https://doi .org/10.1017/S0007123418000327.

Guess, Andrew, and Benjamin A. Lyons. "Misinformation, Disinformation, and Online Propaganda." In *Social Media and Democracy: The State of the Field, Prospects for Reform*, edited by Nathaniel Persily and Joshua A. Tucker, 10–33. Cambridge: Cambridge University Press, 2020.

Guess, Andrew, Benjamin Lyons, Brendan Nyhan, and Jason Reifler. *Avoiding the Echo Chamber about Echo Chambers: Why Selective Exposure to Like-Minded Political News Is Less Prevalent Than You Think*. The Knight Foundation, 2018. https://kf-site-production.s3.amazonaws.com/media _elements/files/000/000/133/original/Topos_KF_White-Paper_Nyhan _V1.pdf.

Guess, Andrew, Jonathan Nagler, and Joshua Tucker. "Less than You Think: Prevalence and Predictors of Fake News Dissemination on Facebook." *Science Advances* 5, no. 1 (January 1, 2019): eaau4586. https://doi.org/10 .1126/sciadv.aau4586.

Guilbeault, Douglas, Joshua Becker, and Damon Centola. "Social Learning and Partisan Bias in the Interpretation of Climate Trends." *Proceedings of the National Academy of Sciences of the United States of America* 115, no. 39 (2018): 9714–19. https://www.pnas.org/content/115/39/9714.

Gupta, Pankaj, Ashish Goel, Jimmy Lin, Aneesh Sharma, Dong Wang, and Reza Zadeh. "WTF: The Who to Follow Service at Twitter." In *Proceedings of the 22nd International Conference on World Wide Web*, edited by Daniel Scwabe, Virgilio Almeida, and Hartmut Glaser, 505–14. New York: Association for Computing Machinery, 2013. https://doi.org/10 .1145/2488388.2488433.

Gutmann, Amy. *Identity in Democracy*. Princeton, NJ: Princeton University Press, 2003.

BIBLIOGRAPHY

Habermas, Jürgen. *The Structural Transformation of the Public Sphere: An Inquiry into a Category of Bourgeois Society.* 6th ed. Translated by Thomas Burger. Cambridge, MA: MIT Press, 1991.

Haidt, Jonathan. *The Righteous Mind: Why Good People Are Divided by Politics and Religion.* New York: Vintage Books, 2012.

Haim, Mario, Andreas Graefe, and Hans-Bernd Brosius. "Burst of the Filter Bubble?" *Digital Journalism* 6, no. 3 (March 16, 2018): 330–43. https://doi.org/10.1080/21670811.2017.1338145.

Hargittai, Eszter. "Potential Biases in Big Data: Omitted Voices on Social Media." *Social Science Computer Review* 38, no. 1 (February 1, 2020): 10–24. https://doi.org/10.1177/0894439318788322.

———. "Whose Space? Differences among Users and Non-Users of Social Network Sites." *Journal of Computer-Mediated Communication* 13, no. 1 (October 1, 2007): 276–97. https://doi.org/10.1111/j.1083-6101.2007 .00396.x.

Hersh, Eitan D., and Brian F. Schaffner. "Targeted Campaign Appeals and the Value of Ambiguity." *Journal of Politics* 75, no. 2 (April 1, 2013): 520–34.https://doi.org/10.1017/S0022381613000182.

Hetherington, Marc, and Jonathan Weiler. *Prius or Pickup? How the Answers to Four Simple Questions Explain America's Great Divide.* Boston: Houghton Mifflin Harcourt, 2018.

Higgins, Tucker. "Trump Declares Without Evidence That 'Criminals and Unknown Middle Easterners Are Mixed In' with Migrant Caravan Making Its Way from Honduras." CNBC.com, October 22, 2018. https:// www.cnbc.com/2018/10/22/trump-says-unknown-middle-easterners -are-mixed-in-migrant-caravan.html.

Hill, Seth J. "Learning Together Slowly: Bayesian Learning about Political Facts." *Journal of Politics* 79, no. 4 (October 1, 2017): 1403–18. https://doi .org/10.1086/692739.

Hochschild, Arlie. *Strangers in Their Own Land: Anger and Mourning on the American Right.* New York: New Press, 2018.

Horwitz, Jeff, and Deepa Seetharaman. "Facebook Executives Shut Down Efforts to Make the Site Less Divisive." *Wall Street Journal*, May 26, 2020. https://www.wsj.com/articles/facebook-knows-it-encourages-division -top-executives-nixed-solutions-11590507499.

Huber, Gregory A., and Neil Malhotra. "Political Homophily in Social Relationships: Evidence from Online Dating Behavior." *Journal of Politics* 79, no. 1 (January 1, 2017): 269–83. https://doi.org/10.1086 /687533.

Huckfeldt, Robert. *Political Disagreement: The Survival of Diverse Opinions within Communication Networks.* Cambridge: Cambridge University Press, 2004.

Huddy, Leonie. "Group Identity and Political Cohesion." In *Emerging Trends in the Social and Behavioral Sciences*, edited by Robert Scott and Stephen Kosslyn, 1–14. New York: John Wiley and Sons, 2015.

Huddy, Leonie, Lilliana Mason, and Lene Aarøe. "Expressive Partisanship: Campaign Involvement, Political Emotion, and Partisan Identity." *American Political Science Review* 109, no. 1 (February 2015): 1–17. https://doi.org/10.1017/S0003055414000604.

Hughes, Adam. "A Small Group of Prolific Users Account for a Majority of Political Tweets Sent by U.S. Adults." *Fact Tank* (blog). Pew Research Center, October 23, 2019. https://www.pewresearch.org/fact-tank/2019/10/23/a-small-group-of-prolific-users-account-for-a-majority-of-political-tweets-sent-by-u-s-adults/.

Iyengar, Shanto, Tobias Konitzer, and Kent Tedin. "The Home as a Political Fortress: Family Agreement in an Era of Polarization." *Journal of Politics* 80, no. 4 (October 1, 2018): 1326–38. https://doi.org/10.1086/698929.

Iyengar, Shanto, Guarav Sood, and Yphtach Lelkes. "Affect, Not Ideology: A Social Identity Perspective on Polarization." *Public Opinion Quarterly* 76, no. 3 (2012): 405–31.

Iyengar, Shanto, and Sean J. Westwood. "Fear and Loathing across Party Lines: New Evidence on Group Polarization." *American Journal of Political Science* 59, no. 3 (2015): 690–707. https://doi.org/10.1111/ajps.12152.

Jahani, Eaman, Natalie Gallagher, Friedolin Merhout, Nicolo Cavalli, Douglas Guibeault, and Yan Leng. "Exposure to Common Enemies Can Increase Political Polarization: Evidence from a Cooperation Experiment with Automated Partisans." Working paper, Polarization Lab, Duke University, 2020.

Jaidka, Kokil, Alvin Zhou, and Yphtach Lelkes. "Brevity Is the Soul of Twitter: The Constraint Affordance and Political Discussion." *Journal of Communication* 69, no. 4 (August 1, 2019): 345–72. https://doi.org/10.1093/joc/jqz023.

Jardina, Ashley. *White Identity Politics*. Cambridge: Cambridge University Press, 2019.

Jerolmack, Colin, and Shamus Khan. "Talk Is Cheap: Ethnography and the Attitudinal Fallacy." *Sociological Methods and Research* 43, no. 2 (March 9, 2014): 178–209. https://doi.org/10.1177/0049124114523396.

Kahan, Dan. "Ideology, Motivated Reasoning, and Cognitive Reflection." *Judgment and Decision Making* 8, no. 4 (2013): 407–24. https://doi.org/10.2139/SSRN.2182588.

Kalla, Joshua L., and David E. Broockman. "The Minimal Persuasive Effects of Campaign Contact in General Elections: Evidence from 49 Field Experiments." *American Political Science Review* 112, no. 1 (February 2018): 148–66. https://doi.org/10.1017/S0003055417000363.

Katz, Elihu. "Communications Research since Lazarsfeld." *Public Opinion Quarterly* 51, no. 4 (1987): S25–45.

Katz, Elihu, and Paul Lazarsfeld. *Personal Influence: The Part Played by People in the Flow of Mass Communications.* 2nd ed. New Brunswick, NJ: Transaction Publishers, 1955.

Key, V. O. *The Responsible Electorate.* Cambridge, MA: Harvard University Press, 1966.

Khalil, James, John Horgan, and Martine Zeuthen. "The Attitudes-Behaviors Corrective (ABC) Model of Violent Extremism." *Terrorism and Political Violence.* Accessed June 1, 2020. https://doi.org/10.1080/09546553.2019.1699793.

Klar, Samara. "When Common Identities Decrease Trust: An Experimental Study of Partisan Women." *American Journal of Political Science* 62, no. 3 (2018): 610–22. https://doi.org/10.1111/ajps.12366.

Klar, Samara, and Yanna Krupnikov. *Independent Politics: How American Disdain for Parties Leads to Political Inaction.* New York: Cambridge University Press, 2016.

Klar, Samara, Yanna Krupnikov, and John Barry Ryan. "Affective Polarization or Partisan Disdain? Untangling a Dislike for the Opposing Party from a Dislike of Partisanship." *Public Opinion Quarterly* 82, no. 2 (June 26, 2018): 379–90. https://doi.org/10.1093/poq/nfy014.

Klar, Samara, and Yotam Shmargad. "The Effect of Network Structure on Preference Formation." *Journal of Politics* 79, no. 2 (April 1, 2017): 717–21. https://doi.org/10.1086/689972.

Klein, Ezra. *Why We're Polarized.* New York: Avid Reader Press, 2020.

Kleinberg, Jon, Jens Ludwig, Sendhil Mullainathan, and Ashesh Rambachan. "Algorithmic Fairness." *AEA Papers and Proceedings* 108 (May 2018): 22–27. https://www.aeaweb.org/articles?id=10.1257/pandp.20181018.

Klinenberg, Eric. *Going Solo: The Extraordinary Rise and Surprising Appeal of Living Alone.* New York: Penguin Books, 2013.

———. *Heat Wave: A Social Autopsy of Disaster in Chicago.* Chicago: University of Chicago Press, 2002.

———. *Palaces for the People: How Social Infrastructure Can Help Fight Inequality, Polarization, and the Decline of Civic Life.* New York: Crown, 2018.

Koeze, Ella, and Nathaniel Popper. "The Virus Changed the Way We Internet." *New York Times*, April 7, 2020. https://www.nytimes.com/interactive/2020/04/07/technology/coronavirus-internet-use.html.

Kosinski, Michal, David Stillwell, and Thore Graepel. "Private Traits and Attributes Are Predictable from Digital Records of Human Behavior." *Proceedings of the National Academy of Sciences of the United States of*

America 110, no. 15 (April 9, 2013): 5802–5. https://doi.org/10.1073/pnas.1218772110.

Kramer, Adam D. I., Jamie E. Guillory, and Jeffrey T. Hancock. "Experimental Evidence of Massive-Scale Emotional Contagion through Social Networks." *Proceedings of the National Academy of Sciences of the United States of America* 111, no. 24 (June 17, 2014): 8788–90.

Kreiss, Daniel, Joshua O. Barker, and Shannon Zenner. "Trump Gave Them Hope: Studying the Strangers in Their Own Land." *Political Communication* 34, no. 3 (July 3, 2017): 470–78. https://doi.org/10.1080/10584609.2017.1330076.

Kreiss, Daniel, and Shannon C. Mcgregor. "The 'Arbiters of What Our Voters See': Facebook and Google's Struggle with Policy, Process, and Enforcement around Political Advertising." *Political Communication* 36, no. 4 (October 2, 2019): 499–522. https://doi.org/10.1080/10584609.2019.1619639.

Kull, Steven, Clay Ramsay, and Evan Lewis. "Misperceptions, the Media, and the Iraq War." *Political Science Quarterly* 118, no. 4 (2003): 569–98. https://doi.org/10.1002/j.1538-165X.2003.tb00406.x.

Kunda, Ziva. "The Case for Motivated Reasoning." *Psychological Bulletin* 108, no. 3 (1990): 480–98.

Lalancette, Mireille, and Vincent Raynauld. "The Power of Political Image: Justin Trudeau, Instagram, and Celebrity Politics." *American Behavioral Scientist* 63, no. 7 (June 2019): 888–924. https://doi.org/10.1177/0002764217744838.

Lamont, Michèle. *Money, Morals, and Manners: The Culture of the French and American Upper-Middle Class.* Chicago: University of Chicago Press, 1992.

Lamont, Michèle, and Virág Molnár. "The Study of Boundaries in the Social Sciences." *Annual Review of Sociology* 28 (2002): 167–95. https://doi.org/10.1146/annurev.soc.28.110601.141107.

Landsberger, Henry A. *Hawthorne Revisited: Management and the Worker: Its Critics, and Developments in Human Relations in Industry.* Ithaca, NY: Cornell University Press, 1958.

Lanier, Jaron. "Jaron Lanier Fixes the Internet." Produced by Adam Westbrook. *New York Times*, September 23, 2019. Video. https://www.nytimes.com/interactive/2019/09/23/opinion/data-privacy-jaron-lanier.html.

———. *Ten Arguments for Deleting Your Social Media Accounts Right Now.* New York: Henry Holt, 2018.

Lazarsfeld, Paul, Bernard Berelson, and Hazel Gaudet. *The People's Choice: How the Voter Makes Up His Mind in a Presidential Campaign.* New York: Columbia University Press, 1948.

Lazarsfeld, Paul F., and Robert K. Merton. "Friendship as Social Process: A Substantive and Methodological Analysis." In *Freedom and Control in*

Modern Society, edited by Morroe Berger, Theodore Abel, and Charles H. Page, 18–66. New York: Van Nostrand, 1954.

Lazer, David, Ryan Kennedy, Gary King, and Alessandro Vespignani. "The Parable of Google Flu: Traps in Big Data Analysis." *Science* 343, no. 6176 (March 14, 2014): 1203–5.

Lazer, David, Alex Pentland, Lada Adamic, Sinan Aral, Albert-László Barabási, Devon Brewer, Nicholas Christakis, Noshir Contractor, James Fowler, Myron Gutmann, et al. "Computational Social Science." *Science* 323, no. 5915 (February 6, 2009): 721–23. https://doi.org/10.1126 /science.1167742.

Lee, Amber Hye-Yon. "How the Politicization of Everyday Activities Affects the Public Sphere: The Effects of Partisan Stereotypes on Cross-Cutting Interactions." *Journal of Communication* (2020; forthcoming). https://doi .org/10.1080/10584609.2020.1799124.

Lee, Byungkyu, and Peter Bearman. "Political Isolation in America." *Network Science* 8, no. 3 (September 2020): 333–55. https://doi.org/10.1017 /nws.2020.9.

Lee, Eun, Fariba Karimi, Claudia Wagner, Hang-Hyun Jo, Markus Strohmaier, and Mirta Galesic. "Homophily and Minority Size Explain Perception Biases in Social Networks." *Nature Human Behaviour* 3 (2019): 1078–87. https://doi.org/10.1038/s41562-019-0677-4.

Leenders, Roger Th. A. J. "Modeling Social Influence through Network Autocorrelation: Constructing the Weight Matrix." *Social Networks* 24, no. 1 (January 1, 2002): 21–47. https://doi.org/10.1016/S0378-8733(01) 00049-1.

Lees, Jeffrey, and Mina Cikara. "Inaccurate Group Meta-Perceptions Drive Negative Out-Group Attributions in Competitive Contexts." *Nature Human Behaviour* 4, no. 3 (March 2020): 279–86. https://doi.org/10.1038 /s41562-019-0766-4.

Lelkes, Yphtach. "Mass Polarization: Manifestations and Measurements." *Public Opinion Quarterly* 80, no. S1 (January 1, 2016): 392–410. https:// doi.org/10.1093/poq/nfw005.

Lemmer, Gunnar, and Ulrich Wagner. "Can We Really Reduce Ethnic Prejudice outside the Lab? A Meta-Analysis of Direct and Indirect Contact Interventions." *European Journal of Social Psychology* 45, no. 2 (2015): 152–68. https://doi.org/10.1002/ejsp.2079.

Leskin, Paige. "Inside the Rise of TikTok, the Viral Video-Sharing App Wildly Popular with Teens and Loathed by the Trump Administration." *Businessinsider.com*, August 7, 2020. https://www.businessinsider.com /tiktok-app-online-website-video-sharing-2019-7.

Levendusky, Matthew. *The Partisan Sort: How Liberals Became Democrats and Conservatives Became Republicans*. Chicago: University of Chicago Press, 2009.

———. "When Efforts to Depolarize the Electorate Fail." *Public Opinion Quarterly* 82, no. 3 (October 18, 2018): 583–92. https://doi.org/10.1093/poq/nfy036.

———. "Why Do Partisan Media Polarize Viewers?" *American Journal of Political Science* 57, no. 3 (February 26, 2013): 611–23. https://www.jstor.org/stable/23496642.

Levendusky, Matthew, and Neil Malhotra. "Does Media Coverage of Partisan Polarization Affect Political Attitudes?" *Political Communication* 33, no. 2 (April 2, 2016): 283–301. https://doi.org/10.1080/10584609.2015.1038455.

Levendusky, Matthew S., and Neil Malhotra. "(Mis)perceptions of Partisan Polarization in the American Public." *Public Opinion Quarterly* 80, no. S1 (January 1, 2016): 378–91. https://doi.org/10.1093/poq/nfv045.

Levin, Sam, and Julia Carrie Wong. "'He's Learned Nothing': Zuckerberg Floats Crowdsourcing Facebook Fact-Checks." *The Guardian*, February 20, 2019. https://www.theguardian.com/technology/2019/feb/20/facebook-fact-checking-crowdsourced-mark-zuckerberg.

Levy, Ro'ee. "Social Media, News Consumption, and Polarization: Evidence from a Field Experiment." Social Science Research Network, August 19, 2020. https://papers.ssrn.com/sol3/papers.cfm?abstract_id=3653388.

Lewis, Paul. "'Fiction Is Outperforming Reality': How YouTube's Algorithm Distorts Truth." *The Guardian*, February 2, 2018. https://www.theguardian.com/technology/2018/feb/02/how-youtubes-algorithm-distorts-truth.

Lord, Charles G., Ross Lee, and Mark R. Lepper. "Biased Assimilation and Attitude Polarization: The Effects of Prior Theories on Subsequently Considered Evidence." *Journal of Personality and Social Psychology* 37, no. 11 (1979): 2098–109.

Marantz, Andrew. *Antisocial: Online Extremists, Techno-Utopians, and the Hijacking of the American Conversation*. New York: Viking, 2019.

Martin, John Levi. "Power, Authority, and the Constraint of Belief Systems." *American Journal of Sociology* 107, no. 4 (2002): 861–904. https://doi.org/10.1086/343192.

Martin, Travis, Jake M. Hofman, Amit Sharma, Ashton Anderson, and Duncan Watts. "Exploring Limits to Prediction in Complex Social Systems." *Proceedings of the 25th International Conference on World Wide Web,* (April 2016): 683–94. https://dl.acm.org/doi/abs/10.1145/2872427.2883001.

Marwick, Alice E. *Status Update: Celebrity, Publicity, and Branding in the Social Media Age*. New Haven, CT: Yale University Press, 2013.

Marwick, Alice E., and danah boyd. "I Tweet Honestly, I Tweet Passionately: Twitter Users, Context Collapse, and the Imagined Audience." *New Media and Society* 13, no. 1 (2011): 114–33. https://journals.sagepub.com/doi/10.1177/1461444810365313.

BIBLIOGRAPHY

Marwick, Alice, and Rebecca Lewis. "Media Manipulation and Disinformation Online." New York: Data & Society Research Institute.

Mason, Lilliana. *Uncivil Agreement: How Politics Became Our Identity.* Chicago: University of Chicago Press, 2018.

Matias, J. Nathan. "Preventing Harassment and Increasing Group Participation through Social Norms in 2,190 Online Science Discussions." *Proceedings of the National Academy of Sciences of the United States of America* 116, no. 20 (2019): 9785–89.

Matthes, Jörg, Johannes Knoll, Sebastián Valenzuela, David Nicolas Hopmann, and Christian Von Sikorski. "A Meta-Analysis of the Effects of Cross-Cutting Exposure on Political Participation." *Political Communication* 36, no. 4 (October 2, 2019): 523–42. https://doi.org/10.1080/10584609.2019.1619638.

Matz, S. C., M. Kosinski, G. Nave, and D. J. Stillwell. "Psychological Targeting as an Effective Approach to Digital Mass Persuasion." *Proceedings of the National Academy of Sciences of the United States of America* 114, no. 48 (November 28, 2017): 12714–19. https://doi.org/10.1073/pnas.1710966114.

McConnell, Christopher, Yotam Margalit, Neil Malhotra, and Matthew Levendusky. "The Economic Consequences of Partisanship in a Polarized Era." *American Journal of Political Science* 62, no. 1 (2018): 5–18. https://doi.org/10.1111/ajps.12330.

McGregor, Shannon C. "Social Media as Public Opinion: How Journalists Use Social Media to Represent Public Opinion." *Journalism* 20, no. 8 (August 1, 2019): 1070–86. https://doi.org/10.1177/1464884919845458.

McNamee, Roger. *Zucked: Waking Up to the Facebook Catastrophe.* New York: Penguin Press, 2019.

McPherson, Miller, Lynn Smith-Lovin, and Matthew E. Brashears. "Social Isolation in America: Changes in Core Discussion Networks over Two Decades." *American Sociological Review* 71, no. 3 (June 1, 2006): 353–75. https://doi.org/10.1177/000312240607100301.

McPherson, Miller, Lynn Smith-Lovin, and James M. Cook. "Birds of a Feather: Homophily in Social Networks." *Annual Review of Sociology* 27, no. 1 (2001): 415–44. https://doi.org/10.1146/annurev.soc.27.1.415.

Merton, Robert K. *Mass Persuasion: The Social Psychology of a War Bond Drive.* New York: Harper and Brothers, 1947.

Merton, Robert K. *Sociological Ambivalence and Other Essays.* New York: Free Press, 1976.

Merton, Robert, and Paul Lazarsfeld. "Studies in Radio and Film Propaganda." In *Social Theory and Social Structure*, edited by Robert Merton, 553–70. New York: Free Press, 1949.

Merton, Robert, Marjorie Lowenthal, and Alberta Curtis. *Mass Persuasion: The Social Psychology of a War Bond Drive.* New York: Harper, 1946.

Meshi, Dar, Diana I. Tamir, and Hauke R. Heekeren. "The Emerging Neuroscience of Social Media." *Trends in Cognitive Sciences* 19, no. 12 (December 2015): 771–82. https://www.sciencedirect.com/science/article/abs/pii/S1364661315002284.

Midgley, Claire. "When Every Day Is a High School Reunion: Social Media Comparisons and Self-Esteem." PhD diss., University of Toronto, 2019. https://tspace.library.utoronto.ca/handle/1807/95911.

Minozzi, William, Hyunjin Song, David M. J. Lazer, Michael A. Neblo, and Katherine Ognyanova. "The Incidental Pundit: Who Talks Politics with Whom, and Why?" *American Journal of Political Science* 64, no. 1 (2020): 135–51. https://onlinelibrary.wiley.com/doi/full/10.1111/ajps.12469.

Minson, Julia. "Just Listen: How Do Emotions Shape Our Willingness to Engage with Others." Harvard Kennedy School, Winter 2020. https://www.hks.harvard.edu/faculty-research/policy-topics/democracy-governance/julia-minson-just-listen.

Montgomery, Jacob M., Brendan Nyhan, and Michelle Torres. "How Conditioning on Posttreatment Variables Can Ruin Your Experiment and What to Do about It." *American Journal of Political Science* 62, no. 3 (July 2018): 760–75. https://doi.org/10.1111/ajps.12357.

Moore-Berg, Samantha, Lee-Or Ankori-Karlinsky, Boaz Hameiri, and Emile Bruneau. "Exaggerated Meta-Perceptions Predict Intergroup Hostility between American Political Partisans." *Proceedings of the National Academy of Sciences* 117, no. 26 (January 9, 2020): 14864–72. https://doi.org/10.1073/pnas.2001263117.

More in Common. "COVID-19: Polarization and the Pandemic." Working paper, More in Common Foundation, April 3, 2020. https://www.moreincommon.com/media/z4fdmdpa/hidden-tribes_covid-19-polarization-and-the-pandemic-4-3-20.pdf.

Munger, Kevin. "Tweetment Effects on the Tweeted: Experimentally Reducing Racist Harassment." *Political Behavior* 39, no. 3 (September 1, 2017): 629–49. https://doi.org/10.1007/s11109-016-9373-5.

Munger, Kevin, and Joseph Phillips. "A Supply and Demand Framework for YouTube Politics." Working paper, Department of Political Science, Penn State University, 2020. https://osf.io/73jys/download.

Murthy, Dhiraj. "Towards a Sociological Understanding of Social Media: Theorizing Twitter." *Sociology* 46, no. 6 (December 1, 2012): 1059–73. https://doi.org/10.1177/0038038511422553.

Mutz, Diana C. *Hearing the Other Side: Deliberative versus Participatory Democracy.* Cambridge: Cambridge University Press, 2006.

Nicholson, Stephen P., Chelsea M. Coe, Jason Emory, and Anna V. Song. "The Politics of Beauty: The Effects of Partisan Bias on Physical Attractiveness." *Political Behavior* 38, no. 4 (December 1, 2016): 883–98. https://doi.org/10.1007/s11109-016-9339-7.

Nie, Norman H., D. Sunshine Hillygus, and Lutz Erbring. "Internet Use, Interpersonal Relations, and Sociability: A Time Diary Study." In *The Internet in Everyday Life*, edited by Barry Wellman and Caroline Haythornthwaite, 213–43. John Wiley and Sons, 2002.

Noble, Safiya Umoja. *Algorithms of Oppression: How Search Engines Reinforce Racism*. New York: NYU Press, 2018.

Nyhan, Brendan, and Jason Reifler. "When Corrections Fail: The Persistence of Political Misperceptions." *Political Behavior* 32, no. 2 (March 2010): 303–30. https://doi.org/10.1007/s11109-010-9112-2.

Nyhan, Brendan, Jason Reifler, Sean Richey, and Gary L. Freed. "Effective Messages in Vaccine Promotion: A Randomized Trial." *Pediatrics* 146, no. 3 (February 1, 2014): 2013–365. https://doi.org/10.1542/peds.2013 -2365.

Obermeyer, Ziad, Brian Powers, Christine Vogeli, and Sendhil Mullainathan. "Dissecting Racial Bias in an Algorithm Used to Manage the Health of Populations." *Science* 366, no. 6464 (2019): 447–53. https:// science.sciencemag.org/content/366/6464/447.

Papacharissi, Zizi. "Democracy Online: Civility, Politeness, and the Democratic Potential of Online Political Discussion Groups." *New Media and Society* 6, no. 2 (2004): 259–83. http://journals.sagepub.com/doi/10.1177 /1461444804041444.

Papacharissi, Zizi A. *A Private Sphere: Democracy in a Digital Age*. Cambridge: Polity, 2010.

Parigi, Paolo, and Patrick Bergemann. "Strange Bedfellows: Informal Relationships and Political Preference Formation within Boardinghouses, 1825–1841." *American Journal of Sociology* 122, no. 2 (September 1, 2016): 501–31. https://doi.org/10.1086/688606.

Parigi, Paolo, and Warner Henson. "Social Isolation in America." *Annual Review of Sociology* 40 (2014): 153–71.

Pariser, Eli. *The Filter Bubble: How the New Personalized Web Is Changing What We Read and How We Think*. New York: Penguin Books, 2012.

Parmelee, John H., and Nataliya Roman. "Insta-Politicos: Motivations for Following Political Leaders on Instagram." *Social Media + Society* 5, no. 2 (April 1, 2019). https://doi.org/10.1177/2056305119837662.

Peck, Reece. *Fox Populism: Branding Conservatism as Working Class*. Cambridge: Cambridge University Press, 2019.

Perrin, Andrew. "Americans Are Changing Their Relationship with Facebook." *Fact Tank* (blog). Pew Research Center, September 5, 2018. https://www.pewresearch.org/fact-tank/2018/09/05/americans-are -changing-their-relationship-with-facebook/.

———. "Social Media Usage: 2005–2015." Pew Research Center, October 8, 2015. http://www.pewinternet.org/2015/10/08/social-networking-usage -2005-2015/.

Perrin, Andrew, and Monica Anderson. "Share of U.S. Adults Using Social Media, Including Facebook, Is Mostly Unchanged since 2018." *Fact Tank* (blog). Pew Research Center, April 10, 2019. https://www.pewresearch .org/fact-tank/2019/04/10/share-of-u-s-adults-using-social-media -including-facebook-is-mostly-unchanged-since-2018/.

Perry, Gina. *The Lost Boys: Inside Muzafer Sherif's Robbers Cave Experiment.* Melbourne, Australia: Scribe, 2018.

Persily, Nathaniel, and Joshua Tucker. "Conclusion: The Challenges and Opportunities for Social Media Research." In *Social Media and Democracy: The State of the Field, Prospects for Reform*, edited by Nathaniel Persily and Joshua A. Tucker, 313–331. Cambridge: Cambridge University Press, 2020.

Petersen, Michael Bang, Mathias Osmundsen, and Kevin Arceneaux. "The 'Need for Chaos' and Motivations to Share Hostile Political Rumors." PsyArXiv, May 2020. https://doi.org/10.31234/osf.io/6m4ts.

Peterson, Erik, and Shanto Iyengar. "Partisan Gaps in Political Information and Information-Seeking Behavior: Motivated Reasoning or Cheerleading?" *American Journal of Political Science.* Published ahead of print, June 17, 2020. https://doi.org/10.1111/ajps.12535.

Pettigrew, Thomas F., and Linda R. Tropp. "How Does Intergroup Contact Reduce Prejudice? Meta-Analytic Tests of Three Mediators." *European Journal of Social Psychology* 38, no. 6 (September 1, 2008): 922–34. https://doi.org/10.1002/ejsp.504.

Pew Research Center. "National Politics on Twitter: Small Share of U.S. Adults Produce Majority of Tweets." Pew Research Center, October 2019. https://www.pewresearch.org/politics/wp-content/uploads/sites/4 /2019/10/PDL_10.23.19_politics.twitter_FULLREPORT.pdf.

———. "Republicans, Democrats Move Even Further Apart in Coronavirus Concern." Pew Research Center, June 25, 2020. https://www.pew research.org/politics/2020/06/25/republicans-democrats-move-even -further-apart-in-coronavirus-concerns/.

———. "Republicans, Democrats See Opposing Party as More Ideological Than Their Own." Pew Research Center, September 13, 2018. https://www .people-press.org/2018/09/13/republicans-democrats-see-opposing-party -as-more-ideological-than-their-own/.

Phillips, Whitney. *This Is Why We Can't Have Nice Things: Mapping the Relationship between Online Trolling and Mainstream Culture.* Cambridge, MA: MIT Press, 2015.

Postman, Neil, and Andrew Postman. *Amusing Ourselves to Death: Public Discourse in the Age of Show Business.* Anniversary ed. New York: Penguin Books, 1985.

Price, Vincent. "Social Identification and Public Opinion: Effects of Communicating Group Conflict." *Public Opinion Quarterly* 53 (1989): 197–224.

Prior, Markus. "Media and Political Polarization." *Annual Review of Political Science* 16 (2013): 101–27. https://doi.org/10.1146/annurev-polisci -100711-135242.

———. *Post-Broadcast Democracy: How Media Choice Increases Inequality in Political Involvement and Polarizes Elections.* New York: Cambridge University Press, 2007.

Pronin, Emily, Daniel Y. Lin, and Lee Ross. "The Bias Blind Spot: Perceptions of Bias in Self versus Others." *Personality and Social Psychology Bulletin* 28, no. 3 (2002): 369–81. https://doi.org/10.1177/014616720228 6008.

Rahwan, Iyad, Manuel Cebrian, Nick Obradovich, Josh Bongard, Jean-François Bonnefon, Cynthia Breazeal, Jacob W. Crandall, Nicholas A. Christakis, Iain D. Couzin, Matthew O. Jackson, et al. "Machine Behaviour." *Nature* 568, no. 7753 (April 2019): 477–86. https://doi.org/10 .1038/s41586-019-1138-y.

Rainie, Lee, Scott Keeter, and Andrew Perrin. *Trust and Distrust in America.* Pew Research Center, July 22, 2019. https://www.pewresearch .org/politics/wp-content/uploads/sites/4/2019/07/PEW-RESEARCH -CENTER_TRUST-DISTRUST-IN-AMERICA-REPORT_2019-07-22-1.pdf.

Rawlings, Craig. "Cognitive Authority and the Constraint of Attitude Change in Group." Working paper, Department of Sociology, Duke University, 2020.

Rawls, John. *A Theory of Justice.* Cambridge, MA: Harvard University Press, 1971.

Ribeiro, Manoel Horta, Raphael Ottoni, Robert West, Virgílio A. F. Almeida, and Wagner Meira. "Auditing Radicalization Pathways on YouTube." ArXiv 1908.08313 [Cs], December 4, 2019. http://arxiv.org/abs/1908 .08313.

Riek, Blake M., Eric W. Mania, and Samuel L. Gaertner. "Intergroup Threat and Outgroup Attitudes: A Meta-Analytic Review." *Personality and Social Psychology Review* 10, no. 4 (November 1, 2006): 336–53. https:// doi.org/10.1207/s15327957pspr1004_4.

Risi, Joseph, Amit Sharma, Rohan Shah, Matthew Connelly, and Duncan J. Watts. "Predicting History." *Nature Human Behavior* 3 (2019): 906–12. https://www.nature.com/articles/s41562-019-0620-8.

Rivlin, Gary. "Wallflower at the Web Party." *New York Times,* October 15, 2006. https://www.nytimes.com/2006/10/15/business/yourmoney/15 friend.html.

Robinson, Robert J., Dacher Keltner, Andrew Ward, and Lee Ross. "Actual versus Assumed Differences in Construal: 'Naive Realism' in Intergroup Perception and Conflict." *Journal of Personality and Social Psychology* 68, no. 3 (1995): 404–17. https://doi.org/10.1037/0022-3514.68.3.404.

Romm, Tony, and Elizabeth Dwoskin. "Jack Dorsey Says He's Rethinking the Core of How Twitter Works." *Washington Post,* August 15, 2018.

https://www.washingtonpost.com/technology/2018/08/15/jack
-dorsey-says-hes-rethinking-core-how-twitter-works/.

Roose, Kevin. "The Making of a YouTube Radical." *New York Times*, June 8,
2019.

Ross, Lee, David Greene, and Pamela House. "The 'False Consensus Effect':
An Egocentric Bias in Social Perception and Attribution Processes."
Journal of Experimental Social Psychology 13, no. 3 (May 1, 1977): 279–301.
https://doi.org/10.1016/0022-1031(77)90049-X.

Rossiter, Erin. "The Consequences of Interparty Conversation on Outparty
Affect and Stereotypes." Working paper, Department of Political Science, Washington University, St. Louis, MO, 2020. https://erossiter.com
/files/conversations.pdf.

Sabin-Miller, David, and Daniel M. Abrams. "When Pull Turns to Shove: A
Continuous-Time Model for Opinion Dynamics." *Physical Review Research* 2 (October 2020). https://journals.aps.org/prresearch/abstract
/10.1103/PhysRevResearch.2.043001.

Safegraph. "Foot Traffic Patterns by State and Industry." Safegraph.com,
May 24, 2020. https://www.safegraph.com/dashboard/reopening-the
-economy-foot-traffic?s=US&d=05-24-2020&i=all.

———. "U.S. Geographic Responses to Shelter in Place Orders." Safegraph
.com, May 22, 2020. https://www.safegraph.com/dashboard/covid19
-shelter-in-place?s=US&d=05-22-2020&t=counties&m=index.

Safronova, Valeriya. "The Rise and Fall of Yik Yak, the Anonymous Messaging App." *New York Times*, May 27, 2017. https://www.nytimes.com
/2017/05/27/style/yik-yak-bullying-mary-washington.html.

Sageman, Marc. *Understanding Terror Networks*. Philadelphia: University of
Pennsylvania Press, 2004.

Salganik, Matthew. *Bit by Bit: Social Research in the Digital Age*. Princeton,
NJ: Princeton University Press, 2018.

Salganik, Matthew J., Ian Lundberg, Alexander T. Kindel, Caitlin E. Ahearn,
Khaled Al-Ghoneim, Abdullah Almaatouq, Drew M. Altschul, Jennie E.
Brand, Nicole Bohme Carnegie, Ryan James Compton, et al. "Measuring the Predictability of Life Outcomes with a Scientific Mass Collaboration." *Proceedings of the National Academy of Sciences of the United States
of America* 117, no. 15 (April 14, 2020): 8398–8403. https://doi.org/10
.1073/pnas.1915006117.

Schudson, Michael. "How Culture Works: Perspectives from Media Studies on the Efficacy of Symbols." *Theory and Society* 18, no. 2 (1989): 153–
80. https://doi.org/10.1007/BF00160753.

———. "Was There Ever a Public Sphere? If So, When? Reflections on the
American Case." In *Habermas and the Public Sphere*, edited by Craig Cal-
houn, 143–63. Cambridge, MA: MIT Press, 1992.

Scissors, Lauren E., Moira Burke, and Steven M. Wengrovitz. "What's in
a Like? Attitudes and Behaviors around Receiving Likes on Facebook."

In *CSCW '16: Proceedings of the Computer-Supported Cooperative Work and Social Computing Conference*, 1501–10. New York: Association for Computing Machinery, 2016. https://doi.org/10.1145/2818048.2820066.

Serrano, Juan Carlos Medina, Orestis Papakyriakopoulos, and Simon Hegelich. "Dancing to the Partisan Beat: A First Analysis of Political Communication on TikTok." ArXiv 2004.05478 [Cs], May 11, 2020. http://arxiv.org/abs/2004.05478.

Settle, Jaime E. *Frenemies: How Social Media Polarizes America*. Cambridge: Cambridge University Press, 2018.

Sewell, William. "Historical Events as Transformations of Structures: Inventing Revolution at the Bastille." *Theory and Society* 25, no. 6 (December 1, 1996): 841–81. https://doi.org/10.1007/BF00159818.

Shaw, Daron, Christopher Blunt, and Brent Seaborn. "Testing Overall and Synergistic Campaign Effects in a Partisan Statewide Election." *Political Research Quarterly* 71, no. 2 (2017): 361–79. https://journals.sagepub.com/doi/abs/10.1177/1065912917738577.

Shearer, Elisa. "Social Media Outpaces Print Newspapers in the U.S. as a News Source." *Fact Tank* (blog). Pew Research Center, December 10, 2018. https://www.pewresearch.org/fact-tank/2018/12/10/social-media-outpaces-print-newspapers-in-the-u-s-as-a-news-source/.

Shearer, Elisa, and Elizabeth Grieco. "Americans Are Wary of the Role Social Media Sites Play in Delivering the News." Pew Research Center, October 2, 2019. https://www.journalism.org/2019/10/02/americans-are-wary-of-the-role-social-media-sites-play-in-delivering-the-news/.

Shepherd, Hana, and Jeffrey Lane. "In the Mix: Social Integration and Social Media Adoption." *Social Science Research* 82 (August 1, 2019): 1–17. https://doi.org/10.1016/j.ssresearch.2019.02.004.

Sherif, Carolyn W. "Social Categorization as a Function of Latitude of Acceptance and Series Range." *Journal of Abnormal and Social Psychology* 67, no. 2 (1963): 148–56. https://doi.org/10.1037/h0043022.

Sherman, Lauren, Ashley Payton, Leanna Hernandez, Patricia Greenfield, and Mirella Dapretto. "The Power of the Like in Adolescence: Effects of Peer Influence on Neural and Behavioral Responses to Social Media." *Psychological Science* 27, no. 7 (May 31, 2016): 1027–35. https://doi.org/10.1177/0956797616645673.

Shi, Feng, Yongren Shi, Fedor A. Dokshin, James A. Evans, and Michael W. Macy. "Millions of Online Book Co-Purchases Reveal Partisan Differences in the Consumption of Science." *Nature Human Behaviour* 1, article no. 0079, April 3, 2017. https://doi.org/10.1038/s41562-017-0079.

Shirado, Hirokazu, and Nicholas A. Christakis. "Locally Noisy Autonomous Agents Improve Global Human Coordination in Network Experiments." *Nature* 545, no. 7654 (May 2017): 370–74. https://doi.org/10.1038/nature22332.

Shontell, Alyson. "The Truth about Snapchat's Active Users (the Numbers the Company Doesn't Want You to See)." *Businessinsider.com*, December 9, 2013. https://www.businessinsider.com/snapchat-active-users -exceed-30-million-2013-12.

Sides, John, Michael Tesler, and Lynn Vavreck. *Identity Crisis: The 2016 Presidential Campaign and the Battle for the Meaning of America*. Princeton, NJ: Princeton University Press, 2018.

Siegal, Alexandra A. "Online Hate Speech." In *Social Media and Democracy: The State of the Field, Prospects for Reform*, edited by Nathaniel Persily and Joshua A. Tucker, 56–88. Cambridge: Cambridge University Press, 2020.

Skrentny, John. "The Effect of the Cold War on African-American Civil Rights: America and the World Audience, 1945–1968." *Theory and Society* 27, no. 2 (April 1998): 237–85.

Smith, Aaron. "Public Attitudes towards Computer Algorithms." Pew Research Center, November 16, 2018. https://www.pewresearch.org /internet/2018/11/16/public-attitudes-toward-computer-algorithms/.

———. "Public Attitudes toward Technology Companies." Pew Research Center, June 28, 2018. https://www.pewresearch.org/internet/2018/06 /28/public-attitudes-toward-technology-companies/.

Snow, David. "Framing Processes, Ideology, and Discursive Fields." In *The Blackwell Companion to Social Movements*, edited by David A. Snow, Sarah A. Soule, and Hanspeter Kriesi, 380–412. Hoboken, NJ: Wiley-Blackwell, 2004.

Sobieraj, Sarah. *Credible Threat: Attacks against Women Online and the Future of Democracy*. Oxford: Oxford University Press, 2020.

Sobieraj, Sarah, and Jeffrey Berry. "From Incivility to Outrage: Political Discourse in Blogs, Talk Radio, and Cable News." *Political Communication* 28, no. 1 (2011): 19–41. https://doi.org/10.1080/10584609.2010 .542360.

Stampnitzky, Lisa. "Disciplining an Unruly Field: Terrorism Experts and Theories of Scientific/Intellectual Production." *Qualitative Sociology* 34, no. 1 (March 1, 2011): 1–19. https://doi.org/10.1007/s11133-010-9187-4.

Starr, Paul. *The Creation of the Media: Political Origins of Modern Communications*. New York: Basic Books, 2005.

Suhay, Elizabeth, Emily Bello-Pardo, and Brianna Maurer. "The Polarizing Effects of Online Partisan Criticism: Evidence from Two Experiments." *International Journal of Press/Politics* 23, no. 1 (January 1, 2018): 95–115. https://doi.org/10.1177/1940161217740697.

Sunstein, Cass R. *Republic.com*. Princeton, NJ: Princeton University Press, 2001.

Tajfel, Henri. *Differentiation between Social Groups: Studies in the Social Psychology of Intergroup Relations*. London: Academic Press, 1979.

———. "Experiments in Intergroup Discrimination." *Scientific American* 223, no. 5 (1970): 96–103.

Tan, Chenhao, Vlad Niculae, Cristian Danescu-Niculescu-Mizil, and Lillian Lee. "Winning Arguments: Interaction Dynamics and Persuasion Strategies in Good-Faith Online Discussions." In *Proceedings of the 25th International Conference on World Wide Web*, edited by Jacqueline Bourdeau, 613–24. Montreal: International World Wide Web Conferences Steering Committee, 2016. https://doi.org/10.1145/2872427.2883081.

Tavory, Iddo, and Stefan Timmermans. *Abductive Analysis*. Chicago: University of Chicago Press, 2014. https://press.uchicago.edu/ucp/books/book/chicago/A/bo18785947.html.

Toennies, Ferdinand, Georg Simmel, Ernst Troeltsch, and Max Weber. "Max Weber on Church, Sect, and Mysticism." *Sociological Analysis* 34, no. 2 (1973): 140–49. https://doi.org/10.2307/3709720.

Traeger, Margaret L., Sarah Strohkorb Sebo, Malte Jung, Brian Scassellati, and Nicholas Christakis. "Vulnerable Robots Positively Shape Human Conversational Dynamics in a Human-Robot Team." *Proceedings of the National Academy of Sciences of the United States of America* 117, no. 12 (2020): 6370–75. https://doi.org/10.1073/pnas.1910402117.

Treier, Shawn, and D. Sunshine Hillygus. "The Nature of Political Ideology in the Contemporary Electorate." *Public Opinion Quarterly* 73, no. 4 (January 1, 2009): 679–703. https://doi.org/10.1093/poq/nfp067.

Tufekci, Zeynep. "Big Data: Pitfalls, Methods and Concepts for an Emergent Field." Social Science Research Network, March 7, 2013. http://papers.ssrn.com/abstract=2229952.

———. "Grooming, Gossip, Facebook and Myspace." *Information, Communication and Society* 11, no. 4 (June 1, 2008): 544–64. https://doi.org/10.1080/13691180801999050.

———. "YouTube, the Great Radicalizer." *New York Times*, March 10, 2018. https://www.nytimes.com/2018/03/10/opinion/sunday/youtube-politics-radical.html.

U.S. Customs and Border Protection. "CBP Use of Force Statistics." U.S. Customs and Border Protection, 2018. https://www.cbp.gov/newsroom/stats/cbp-use-force.

Vaidhyanathan, Siva. *Antisocial Media: How Facebook Disconnects Us and Undermines Democracy*. New York: Oxford University Press, 2018.

Vaisey, Stephen. "Is Interviewing Compatible with the Dual-Process Model of Culture?" *American Journal of Cultural Sociology* 2, no. 1 (February 1, 2014): 150–58. https://doi.org/10.1057/ajcs.2013.8.

———. "Motivation and Justification: Toward a Dual-Process Theory of Culture in Action." *American Journal of Sociology* 114, no. 6 (2009): 1675–715. https://doi.org/10.1086/597179.

Van Alstyne, Marshall, and Erik Brynjolfsson. "Electronic Communities: Global Village or Cyberbalkans." In *Proceedings of the 17th International Conference on Information Systems*, edited by Simane Hammoudi, Leszek Maciaszek, and Ernest Teniente. New York: Wiley, 1996.

Van Boven, Leaf, Charles M. Judd, and David K. Sherman. "Political Polarization Projection: Social Projection of Partisan Attitude Extremity and Attitudinal Processes." *Journal of Personality and Social Psychology* 103, no. 1 (July 2012): 84–100. https://doi.org/10.1037/a0028145.

Van den Bos, Kees. "Unfairness and Radicalization." *Annual Review of Psychology* 71, no. 1 (2020): 563–88. https://doi.org/10.1146/annurev-psych-010419-050953.

Van Green, Ted, and Alec Tyson. "5 Facts about Partisan Reactions to COVID-19 in the U.S." *Fact Tank* (blog). Pew Research Center, April 2, 2020. https://www.pewresearch.org/fact-tank/2020/04/02/5-facts-about-partisan-reactions-to-covid-19-in-the-u-s/.

Vavreck, Lynn. "COVID-19: Tracking American Responses." Democracy Fund Voter Study Group, August 5, 2020. https://www.voterstudygroup.org/covid-19-updates.

Vogel, Erin, Jason Rose, Bradley Okdie, Katheryn Eckles, and Brittany Franz. "Who Compares and Despairs? The Effect of Social Comparison Orientation on Social Media Use and Its Outcomes." *Personality and Individual Differences* 86 (November 30, 2015): 249–56. https://doi.org/10.1016/j.paid.2015.06.026.

Von Der Heide, Rebecca, Govinda Vyas, and Ingrid R. Olson. "The Social Network-Network: Size Is Predicted by Brain Structure and Function in the Amygdala and Paralimbic Regions." *Social Cognitive and Affective Neuroscience* 9, no. 12 (December 2014): 1962–72. https://www.ncbi.nlm.nih.gov/pmc/articles/PMC4249478/.

Wagner-Pacifici, Robin. "Theorizing the Restlessness of Events." *American Journal of Sociology* 115, no. 5 (March 1, 2010): 1351–86. https://doi.org/10.1086/651462.

Walt, Stephen. "The Case against Peace." *Foreign Policy*, June 17, 2016. https://foreignpolicy.com/2016/06/17/the-case-against-peace-syria-europe-brexit-donald-trump/.

Watts, Duncan. *Everything is Obvious*. New York: Penguin Random House, 2012.

Watts, Duncan, and Peter S. Dodds. "Influentials, Networks, and Public Opinion." *Journal of Consumer Research* 34 no. 4 (2017): 441–58.

Watts, Duncan, and David M. Rothschild. "Don't Blame the Election on Fake News: Blame it on the Media." *Columbia Journalism Review*, December 5, 2017. https://www.cjr.org/analysis/fake-news-media-election-trump.php.

Weissman, Cale Guthrie. "How Amazon Helped Cambridge Analytica Harvest Americans' Facebook Data." *Fast Company,* March 27, 2018. https://www.fastcompany.com/40548348/how-amazon-helped -cambridge-analytica-harvest-americans-facebook-data.

Westen, Drew, Pavel S. Blagov, Keith Harenski, Clint Kilts, and Stephan Hamann. "Neural Bases of Motivated Reasoning: An FMRI Study of Emotional Constraints on Partisan Political Judgment in the 2004 U.S. Presidential Election." *Journal of Cognitive Neuroscience* 18, no. 11 (November 2006): 1947–58. https://doi.org/10.1162/jocn.2006.18.11.1947.

Westwood, Sean Jeremy, Solomon Messing, and Yphtach Lelkes. "Projecting Confidence: How the Probabilistic Horse Race Confuses and Demobilizes the Public." *Journal of Politics* 82, no. 4. Published ahead of print, February 25, 2020. https://doi.org/10.1086/708682.

Wimmer, Andreas. "The Making and Unmaking of Ethnic Boundaries: A Multilevel Process Theory." *American Journal of Sociology* 113, no. 4 (2008): 970–1022. https://doi.org/10.1086/522803.

Wojcieszak, Magdalena. "Carrying Online Participation Offline— Mobilization by Radical Online Groups and Politically Dissimilar Offline Ties." *Journal of Communication* 59, no. 3 (2009): 564–86. https://onlinelibrary.wiley.com/doi/abs/10.1111/j.1460-2466.2009.01436.x.

———. "'Don't Talk to Me': Effects of Ideologically Homogeneous Online Groups and Politically Dissimilar Offline Ties on Extremism." *New Media and Society* 12, no. 4 (2010): 637–55. https://journals.sagepub.com /doi/abs/10.1177/1461444809342775.

———. "False Consensus Goes Online: Impact of Ideologically Homogeneous Groups on False Consensus." *Public Opinion Quarterly* 72, no. 4 (2008): 781–91.

Wojcieszak, Magdalena, and Vincent Price. "Facts versus Perceptions: Who Reports Disagreement during Deliberation and Are the Reports Accurate?" *Political Communication* 29, no. 3 (2012): 299–318. https:// www.tandfonline.com/doi/abs/10.1080/10584609.2012.694984.

———. "Perceived versus Actual Disagreement: Which Influences Deliberative Experiences?" *Journal of Communication* 62, no. 3 (2012): 418–36. https://academic.oup.com/joc/article-abstract/62/3/418/4085789.

Wojcieszak, Magdalena, and Benjamin R. Warner. "Can Interparty Contact Reduce Affective Polarization? A Systematic Test of Different Forms of Intergroup Contact." *Political Communication.* Published ahead of print, June 4, 2020. https://doi.org/10.1080/10584609.2020.1760406.

Wolak, Jennifer. *Compromise in an Age of Party Polarization.* New York: Oxford University Press, 2020.

Wood, Thomas, and Ethan Porter. "The Elusive Backfire Effect: Mass Attitudes' Steadfast Factual Adherence." *Political Behavior* 41, no. 1 (March 1, 2019): 135–63. https://doi.org/10.1007/s11109-018-9443-y.

Yang, JungHwan, Hernando Rojas, Magdalena Wojcieszak, Toril Aalberg, Sharon Coen, James Curran, Kaori Hayashi, Shanto Iyengar, Paul K. Jones, Gianpietro Mazzoleni, et al. "Why Are 'Others' So Polarized? Perceived Political Polarization and Media Use in 10 Countries." *Journal of Computer-Mediated Communication* 21, no. 5 (2016): 349–67. https://doi.org/10.1111/jcc4.12166.

Yang, Qi, Khizar Qureshi, and Tauhid Zaman. "Mitigating the Backfire Effect Using Pacing and Leading." ArXiv 2008.00049v1, July 31, 2020. https://arxiv.org/pdf/2008.00049.pdf.

Yudkin, Daniel, Stephen Hawkins, and Tim Dixon. *The Perception Gap: How False Impressions Are Pulling Americans Apart.* New York: More in Common, 2019. https://perceptiongap.us/media/zaslaroc/perception-gap-report-1-0-3.pdf.

Zaller, John R. *The Nature and Origins of Mass Opinion.* Cambridge: Cambridge University Press, 1992.

Zuboff, Shoshana. *The Age of Surveillance Capitalism: The Fight for a Human Future at the New Frontier of Power.* New York: PublicAffairs, 2019.

Zuckerberg, Mark. "Bringing the World Closer Together." Facebook.com, June 22, 2017. https://www.facebook.com/notes/mark-zuckerberg/bringing-the-world-closer-together/10154944663901634/.

Zuckerman, Ethan. "The Case for Digital Public Infrastructure." Knight First Amendment Institute, Columbia University, January 17, 2020. https://knightcolumbia.org/content/the-case-for-digital-public-infrastructure.

INDEX

Abramowitz, Alan, 178n16
addiction, to social media, 9, 10, 52, 88–89
Ahler, Douglas, 103
Alcott, Hunt, 94
algorithms, 5, 92–94, 131, 188n34
Allport, Gordon, 173n20
Al Qaeda, 4
Amash, Justin, 65
Amazon Mechanical Turk, 169n18, 192n27
American National Election Study, 46, 72, 73
anonymity, in online exchanges, 123–27, 129–31, 193n27
argument, attitudes toward, 2, 9, 39, 47, 62–64, 69, 71, 81, 108–15
Armaly, Miles, 100

backfire effects, 174n23, 175n24
Bannon, Steve, 54
Barnidge, Matthew, 76
Bearman, Peter, 90
behavior: individuals' explanations of their, 23; partial record of, captured by social media, 7–8. *See also* political attitudes and behaviors; social media users
Berelson, Bernard, 166n4
Berry, Jeffrey, 101

Bishop, Bill, *The Big Sort*, 90
Blumer, Herbert, 173n20
bots, 16–20, 24–25, 171n9
boyd, danah, 50
Breitbart, 34
Brooks, David, 39
Brown, Michael, Jr., 64
Brynjolfsson, Erik, 178n12
Bullock, Steve, 39
Bush, George H. W., 25
Bush, George W., 37

Cambridge Analytica, 7, 16, 85, 169n18
campaigns, influence of, 95–96, 169n19, 188n41
Camp Fire (California), 13, 24
Carlson, Tucker, 3
Ceasefire, 123
Change My View, 123–24
Chen, Keith, 90–91
Cher, 85
Cikara, Mina, 104
Clinton, Bill, 1, 58, 99
Clinton, Hillary, 13–14, 58, 59, 64, 78
Clinton Foundation, 58
CNN, 13, 27–28
Cohen, Ellen, 65
Cohen, Geoffrey, 45–46
Comey, James, 14

225

political attitudes and behaviors
(*continued*)
media linked to, 89–91, 122–27,
170n8; strengthening of views
after exposure to alternatives,
13, 20–23, 21f, 25, 29–31,
38–40, 107–8, 174n22. *See also*
behavior; extremists; moderates; partisanship
political-ideological exposure: in
anonymous settings, 123–27,
129–31, 193n27; backfire effects
from, 174n23, 175n24; bots
trained for, 16–20; individuals'
experience of, 22–25, 31–32;
moderation of views after,
22, 38–39, 108–15, 125, 129,
172–73n20, 173–74n22;
scholarship on, 173–74n22;
social media experiments on,
16–21, 123–27; strengthening of
views after, 13, 20–23, 21f, 25,
29–31, 38–40, 107–8, 173–
74n22. *See also* worldviews
political isolation, 89–91, 117
political tribalism. *See* polarization
Porter, Ethan, 174n23
Postman, Neil, 181n46
psychology. *See* identity; personal
psychology
public sphere, 44–45, 89–91

qualitative research, methodological
considerations in, 176n28

racial discrimination, 80–81
radicalization, 92–94
rationality, 44–47
Reagan, Ronald, 1, 57
Reddit, 123–24
Reifler, Jason, 174n23
Republicans: attitudes of, about
Democrats, 46–47, 100–103,

110–13, 120, 124–27, 190n15,
193n27; attitudes of, toward
social media platforms, 98;
consequences of exposure to
opposing views, 20, 21f, 172n17;
COVID-19 response of, 118–20;
echo chambers' influence on,
4; geographic isolation from
Democrats, 90; immigration
views held by, 28, 73; and
polarization, 99; self-criticism
of, 113
Robinson, Robert, 99–100
Rockefeller Foundation, 41
Rogers, Todd, 109
Rohla, Ryne, 90–91
Romney, Mitt, 60
Roose, Kevin, 93
Rossiter, Erin, 192n27
Ryan, John, 112

Safegraph, 117
Salganik, Matthew, 97
salons, 44
Sanders, Bernie, 12, 65
Schumer, Chuck, 37
Scott, Keith Lamont, 81
self. *See* identity; personal
psychology
self-fulfilling prophecies, 50, 56
self-worth, 49, 66–67, 107
Settle, Jaime, 67, 76–77
Sherif, Carolyn, 108
Sherif, Muzafer, 41–43, 116
Silicon Valley, 9–10, 52, 89, 91–92,
96, 187n28
smartphones, 87
Snapchat, 86, 121
snopes.com, 35, 37
Sobieraj, Sarah, 74, 101
social isolation, 89–91, 117
social media: addiction to, 9, 10, 52,
88–89; anonymity on, 123–27,

MAY 11 2021

Riverhead Free Library
330 Court Street
Riverhead NY 11901